D0945036

Zoot Suit Riots

Zoot Suit Riots

Roger Bruns

Landmarks of the American Mosaic

AN IMPRINT OF ABC-CLIO, LLC
Santa Barbara, California • Denver, Colorado • Oxford, England

Copyright 2014 by ABC-CLIO, LLC

All rights reserved. No part of this publication may be reproduced, stored
in a retrieval system, or transmitted, in any form or by any means, electronic,
mechanical, photocopying, recording, or otherwise, except for the inclusion
of brief quotations in a review, without prior permission in writing from the
publisher.

Library of Congress Cataloging-in-Publication Data

Bruns, Roger A., 1941–
   Zoot suit riots / Roger Bruns.
      pages cm. — (Landmarks of the American mosaic)
   Includes bibliographical references and index.
   ISBN 978-0-313-39878-0 (hardcopy : acid-free paper) —
ISBN 978-0-313-39879-7 (ebook)   1. Zoot Suit Riots, Los Angeles,
Calif., 1943.   2. Mexican Americans—California—Los Angeles—Social
conditions—20th century.   3. Violence—California—Los Angeles—
History—20th century.   4. Los Angeles (Calif.)—Race relations.
5. Los Angeles (Calif.)—Social conditions—20th century.   I. Title.
   F869.L89M4223   2014
   306.09794'94053—dc23   2013033288

ISBN: 978-0-313-39878-0
EISBN: 978-0-313-39879-7

18   17   16   15   14   2   3   4   5

This book is also available on the World Wide Web as an eBook.
Visit www.abc-clio.com for details.

Greenwood
An Imprint of ABC-CLIO, LLC

ABC-CLIO, LLC
130 Cremona Drive, P.O. Box 1911
Santa Barbara, California 93116-1911

This book is printed on acid-free paper ∞

Manufactured in the United States of America

Contents

Series Foreword

THE LANDMARKS OF THE AMERICAN MOSAIC series comprises individual volumes devoted to exploring an event or development central to this country's multicultural heritage. The topics illuminate the struggles and triumphs of American Indians, African Americans, Latinos, and Asian Americans, from European contact through the turbulent last half of the 20th century. The series covers landmark court cases, laws, government programs, civil rights infringements, riots, battles, movements, and more. Written by historians especially for high school students, undergraduates, and general readers, these content-rich references satisfy thorough research needs and provide a deeper understanding of material that students might only be exposed to in a short section of a textbook or a superficial explanation online.

Each book on a particular topic is a one-stop reference source. The series format includes

- Introduction
- Chronology
- Narrative chapters that trace the evolution of the event or topic chronologically
- Biographical profiles of key figures
- Selection of crucial primary documents
- Glossary
- Bibliography
- Index

This landmark series promotes respect for cultural diversity and supports the social studies curriculum by helping students understand multicultural American history.

Introduction

IN THE SPRING OF 1943, people in Los Angeles had many wartime concerns. Sailors, soldiers, and marines were in the city in large numbers returning from or preparing to head for battle in the Pacific. The administration of Franklin Roosevelt had already issued orders to remove Japanese Americans from their homes and place them in relocation camps. Fears mounted about Japanese submarines off the coast of California. On February 24, a rumored enemy attack on Los Angeles by the Japanese air force and subsequent anti-aircraft fire by the U.S. military plunged the city into near hysteria. Military officials soon reassured the jittery public that the incident was not a Japanese attack but a false alarm triggered by, among other things, meteorological balloons. And now, in early June, citizens of Los Angeles could read about another war that had broken out, one in their own city, on their own streets. In describing the sudden violence in their midst, local newspapers and tabloids, in heated language, talked about "battles" and "blitzes" and perhaps the need for martial law. They talked about anti-Americans in their city, about escalating attacks. But what was this new or other war gripping the city? It had to do with "Zoot suits."

By the 1940s, Mexican-American youths in large numbers were now wearing their own type of uniform—the Zoot suit—and they were carrying on their own kind of rebellion, one rooted in a cultural clash nourished through generations. Although it had earlier been something of a black youth fashion identified with the jazz culture, the Zoot suit had been adopted by a generation of Mexican-American teenagers. Along with an oversize coat, with its wide, padded shoulders, most of the boys sported the signature "ducktail" hair style, long, especially on the sides, and swept back in waves. They also wore a broad-brimmed hat and carried a long watch chain dangling down the side of their pants. Most of them also embraced jazz and other "hip" music and adopted signature language expressions, derived from Caló, an argot traced to Spanish gypsies.

Some referred to themselves as "pachucos" and many hung out in groups defined by the neighborhoods in which they lived. Over the years, scholars have traced the roots of the pachuco phenomenon to various sources—to Spanish gypsies, to lower-class settlers of the Borderlands during the late 18th and 19th centuries, and even to the common soldiers who made up the army of Pancho Villa during the Mexican Revolution of 1910. Other scholars have simply pointed to the pressures of urbanization, ethnic prejudice, and the wracking poverty of the time as the logical, bitter reasons for development of the pachuco culture. To these young people, the Zoot look was both a statement of defiance and an assertion of identity. To most of the general public, however, the Zoot suit represented the decline of the city.

Tensions between the pachuco youngsters and Los Angeles authorities had escalated since the summer of 1942 when the death of a man named José Díaz sparked a roundup of Zoot suiters as possible suspects. A young Mexican national, Díaz was found dead near a reservoir nicknamed "Sleepy Lagoon." Los Angeles police herded over 600 Latinos through police stations on the nights of August 10 and 11. Over 20 members of the "38th Street Gang," as described by a local tabloid, were charged with the murder of Díaz.

For several weeks before the trial and during it, the racial and cultural divide between the two sides—the Anglo authorities and the Mexican-American defendants—became increasingly clear. A member of the sheriff's department issued a supposedly scientific report to the grand jury considering the case that Mexican Americans were something akin to wild cats, with a predisposition to violence.

During the so-called Sleepy Lagoon Trial, the Mexican-American co-defendants were tried en masse. They were not allowed to change their clothes—their Zoot suits—or to cut their hair. The judge reasoned that the jury must be allowed to see the pachucos in their authentic attire—the long, dark, menacing coats and oversize pants. Throughout the proceedings, witnesses talked about the blood lust of Zoot suiters and the ruthlessness that defined their cultural identity.

For five months, the trial mesmerized readers of the Los Angeles tabloids, and with each new story about the ferocity of the gangs, the fears and racial tensions in the city ominously escalated. The menace was no longer the Japanese, who had by order of the federal government already been removed to the internment camps, but the Mexicans. Across the city, citizens feared that if strong measures were not undertaken a crime wave would rip apart any semblance of law and order.

On January 12, 1943, the jury convicted three of the defendants of first-degree murder and sentenced them to life in prison; nine were convicted of second-degree murder and sentenced to five years to life, and five were convicted of assault and released for time served. The 12 convicted of first- or second-degree murder began serving their sentences in January 1943 at San Quentin Prison.

Throughout the spring, in the wake of the trial, there were a number of scrapes between U.S. servicemen, who often went looking for excitement in Mexican-American areas of the city, and Zoot suiters, who resented their intrusions. Tensions rose to combustible levels. And in mid-June, service- men went on the prowl in large numbers to wage their own urban warfare. Armed with clubs and bats, they charged into Mexican-American areas of Los Angeles attacking anyone wearing a Zoot suit, mostly teenagers or young men in their early 20s. The military men carried out "raids" on bars, movie houses, and stores—anywhere they could find groups or single indi- viduals wearing Zoot suits.

For several nights the violence continued, with hundreds of sailors and soldiers moving through East Los Angeles. Marching abreast, they broke into stores, bars, and theaters, assaulting any individual sporting a Zoot suit or anything close to it. On successive nights, they invaded the areas in taxicabs. Not only did the police stand by and watch the grisly sport, but also the local newspapers portrayed the invading soldiers as heroes fight- ing off the Latino crime wave.

Zoot suiters by the hundreds were beaten, stripped, and humiliated. In the end, the violence would be called "The Zoot Suit Riots." The week would live in the memories of those in the Mexican-American communities affected and in the cultural expression of generations of Mexican Ameri- cans in their quest for individual rights, justice, acceptance, and citizenship.

So outrageous was the spectacle that First Lady Eleanor Roosevelt la- mented in a press conference that racial hatred against the Mexicans was at the root of the military riots in the Latino sections of Los Angeles. The wearing of Zoot suits, she said, was only an excuse and pretext for the vio- lence. The largest newspaper in the city, the *Los Angeles Times*, along with the other papers and tabloids that had cheered on the rioting servicemen, responded to Mrs. Roosevelt's remarks with a gratuitous charge. Not only was she wrong and misguided, they charged, but she may have been also influenced by communists.

The impact of the Sleepy Lagoon murder case and the subsequent Zoot Suit Riots was a glaring testament to the climate of racial tension and mis- understanding that pervaded Los Angeles. For two years after the bizarre trial and the week of riots, a group of volunteers led by progressive writer Carey McWilliams and an activist named Alice Greenfield worked with groups and organizations to overturn the convictions on the basis of insufficient evidence. Finally, the Second District Court of Appeals released the defendants.

But in the minds of Mexican Americans, the Zoot Suit Riots represented a defining moment. In the years following, as Latinos steadily gained political and economic power, as they asserted rights previously denied and fought against prejudice and racial hurdles, those wartime memories, especially those days in early June 1943, burrowed deeply in their culture—in a major play that reached Broadway, a motion picture, in poetry and song, in sociological studies, in tales and recollections handed down through several generations. This is the story of those times.

Chronology

1941 December 7: Japanese forces attack Pearl Harbor on the Hawaiian island of Oahu. On the following day, President Franklin Roosevelt asks Congress for a declaration of war.

1942 February 19: President Roosevelt signs an executive order granting U.S. military forces authority to relocate Japanese Americans and place them in camps. During the next 18 months, over 100,000 people of Japanese descent in the states of California, Washington, Oregon, and Arizona are moved from their homes to several camps across the West, including Manzanar relocation camp in northeastern California where many Japanese residents from Los Angeles are sent.

February 24: A rumored enemy attack on Los Angeles by the Japanese and subsequent anti-aircraft fire plunge the city of Los Angeles into near hysteria. The U.S. military soon reassures the public that the incident was a false alarm triggered by, among other things, meteorological balloons. The events are later called by some "The Battle of Los Angeles."

Spring 1942: Amid the tensions and uncertainties in wartime Los Angeles, many Mexican-American juveniles, who had adopted a cultural style recognizable by wearing so-called Zoot suits—oversized pants and jackets, broad-brimmed hats, and hanging watch chains—become the object of intense press reporting. Although crimes among Mexican-American youths had declined in 1942 according to statistics released by Los Angeles police, the press begins to focus much attention on Mexican crime and youth gangs.

June 12: A young Mexican American named Frank Clanton is shot at a high school track meet at the Los Angeles Memorial Coliseum. The incident, provoking a near riot, further inflames news coverage of Mexican boy gangs.

Summer: A series of fights involving navy personnel and Mexican-American youths in downtown Los Angeles increase growing tensions and antagonisms between the groups.

August 1–2: At a birthday party near a reservoir nicknamed "Sleepy Lagoon," a fight between youngsters from separate neighborhoods ends with the death of a Mexican-American young man named José Díaz.

August 3: Press coverage of the event focuses on the violence between separate Mexican gangs and the murder gains traction as a leading cover story.

August 4: The Los Angeles Police Department begins a dragnet of Mexican-American young men and women who may have seen something at the murder site. Over 600 people are brought in for questioning in the days following.

August: Lieutenant Edward Duran Ayres of the Los Angeles County Sheriff's Department submits to a grand jury considering the Sleepy Lagoon murder case a document purporting to contain scientific evidence that individuals of Mexican descent, like wild cats, were biologically inclined toward violence and criminal behavior.

October 16: Twenty-two indicted young men face murder charges in Los Angeles for the killing of José Díaz. *People v. Zammora* becomes the largest mass trial in California history.

Late October: Labor organizer LaRue McCormick, aided by other activists, forms the Citizens' Committee for the Defense of Mexican American Youth (CCDMAY), a group dedicated to fighting the racism and institutional forces arrayed against the defendants in the trial as well as other Mexican-American youngsters.

November: Alan Cranston, an official in the Office of War Information in Washington, travels to Los Angeles and encourages the press to moderate the inflammatory attacks against Mexican Americans in relation to the Sleepy Lagoon case.

December: *Sensation* magazine, a pulp tabloid feeds the yellow journalism smear of the Sleepy Lagoon defendants with an article written by Clem Peoples, chief of the Criminal Division of the Sheriff's Office, who labels them "Baby Gangsters" and compares them to wolf packs.

1943 January 12: The verdicts in *People v. Zammora* are read. Three defendants are convicted of first-degree murder, nine of second-degree murder, and five of lesser charges.

Spring: Under the leadership of Carey McWilliams and others, the CCDMAY is renamed the Sleepy Lagoon Defense Committee. Its goal is to push for an appellate case to free those jailed in *People v. Zammora*.

May 9: Several hundred soldiers, sailors, and local teenagers drag Mexican Americans out of the Aragon Ballroom on the Lick Pier after rumors circulate that a serviceman had been knifed. Clashes ensue along Ocean Front Walk at Navy Street and Speedway in front of a crowd of over 2,000 spectators. Thirteen Mexican-American youths are arrested and cleared at trial a week later.

May 31: A dozen sailors and soldiers walking on Main Street clash with a group of Mexican-American youths near Chinatown. One of the sailors suffers a broken jaw.

June 3: What will later be called the Zoot Suit Riots begins when groups of sailors leave the Naval Reserve Armory at Chavez Ravine and, armed with clubs, belts, bats, and other instruments, begin beating up and disrobing Mexican-American youths on the street, in clubs, theaters, and stores. The Los Angeles police largely ignore the attacks.

June 4: Emboldened by beatings administered on Zoot suiters the previous night and the lack of police intervention, an increased number of servicemen, this time using taxicabs to invade East Los Angeles, escalate the attacks on Mexican Americans.

June 5: With local newspapers lauding the attacks on the Mexican Americans and police arrests mostly confined to Zoot suiters, the melees continue for the third night with numerous humiliating beatings administered by the sailors and soldiers.

June 6: As the rioting escalates, California attorney general Robert Kenney and Carey McWilliams persuade Governor Earl Warren to appoint a committee to investigate the causes of the civil unrest. Joseph T. McGucken, auxiliary bishop of Los Angeles, agrees to chair the committee.

June 7: With a new surge of violence, Los Angeles Chief of Police C. B. Horrall declares a general riot and orders the police to attempt to clear the streets of thousands of servicemen and civilians.

June 8: Rear Admiral David W. Bagley, commandant of the 11th Naval District, issues an order declaring the city of Los Angeles "out of bounds" for all enlisted sailors, marines, and members of the Coast Guard. The Los Angeles City Council passes a resolution banning the wearing of Zoot suits in public. Some Los Angeles newspapers begin to link the riots to the influence of agents of German leader Adolph Hitler.

June 9: After Mexican government officials express deep concern about the possible attacks on Mexican nationals in Los Angeles, Mayor

Fletcher Bowron delivers a statement saying that he had assured the State Department that no violence has been directed at Mexican citizens.

June 10: Representatives for Nelson Rockefeller, coordinator of Inter-American Affairs, begin an investigation to determine the possible diplomatic fallout from the Zoot Suit Riots.

June 12: McGucken Committee issues eight-page report declaring that the streets of Los Angeles must be made safe for all citizens, regardless of ethnic origins. Emphasizing that race prejudice cannot be ignored in causing the riots, the report calls for educational and recreational programs directed toward minority youth in the city.

June 16: First Lady Eleanor Roosevelt declares in a press conference that she believes the Los Angeles disturbances could be traced to long-standing racial discrimination against Mexican immigrants.

June 18: The *Los Angeles Times* attacks Mrs. Roosevelt for her remarks, even comparing her arguments to those made by Communists and others attempting to divide the United States and its ally, Mexico.

Summer: Screenwriter Guy Endore publishes a pamphlet titled *The Sleepy Lagoon Mystery*, a scathing attack against yellow journalism as practiced by William Randolph Hearst and other Los Angeles publishers that accuses them of unwittingly fomenting racial strife that benefits the Axis powers in the war.

October: Attorney Ben Margolis Jr., representing the Sleepy Lagoon defendants, delivers a 508-page appeal brief to the Second District Court of Appeals.

1944 May 15: Attorney Ben Margolis delivers oral arguments as the appellate trial in the Sleepy Lagoon case begins in the Second District Court of Appeals.

October 4: The Second District Court of Appeals, in a decision written by Associate Justice Thomas P. White, reverses the Sleepy Lagoon verdicts on the ground of insufficient evidence.

October 23: In Los Angeles Superior Court, packed with members of the friends and families of the Sleepy Lagoon defendants, Judge Clement D. Nye dismisses the case, based on the decision of the Second District Court of Appeals. The defendants are released and their records cleared.

1978 The play *Zoot Suit*, written and directed by Luis Valdez, head of El Teatro Campesino, is produced with the Center Theatre Group of Los Angeles and opens at the Mark Taper Forum. Because of sold-out performances it is later moved to the larger Aquarius Theater.

1979 *Zoot Suit* opens at the Winter Garden in New York, the first play written and produced by a Mexican American ever to reach Broadway.

1981 *Zoot Suit* is made into a film starring Edward James Olmos.

2010 *Zoot Suit* opens in Mexico City to enthusiastic audiences. The play has particular interest because of a new restrictive, controversial illegal immigration law recently enacted in Arizona. Nearly 60 years after the riots, the issues of race, ethnicity, and discrimination that played out in the streets and courts of Los Angeles still resonate.

ONE

The Setting

FACING CRISIS WAS NOT NEW to the Mexican-American immigrant community in Los Angeles. After all, as the United States entered World War II, it had only been a decade since the so-called Mexican Repatriation. At that time, during the early years of the Great Depression, the country's leaders decided that one of the solutions to the economic disaster plaguing the nation was to send as many individuals in the Mexican communities in the United States back to Mexico.

The argument was simple. If Mexicans were sent out of the country, the job market would not only be better for Anglos but there would also be less government benefits to pay out because of the exodus. Thus, using power granted under formal legislation enacted by the U.S. government, law enforcement agencies began to round up individuals of Mexican ancestry, many of them U.S. citizens, and forced them to head to Mexico. The towering irony in all of this was that prior to the Great Depression, those same Mexican Americans had been vigorously recruited to work in the United States by businesses because they offered a source of cheap labor in railroad construction, ranching, mining, and, especially in California, farm labor.

The entire repatriation enterprise—unjust, demeaning, and cruel—reflected prevailing attitudes about race and culture that continually confronted Mexican Americans as they tried to make better lives for themselves and their children in the United States. In 1931, in a Mexican-American community in the El Monte section of Los Angeles, police authorities conducted a raid in which individuals were rounded up to be sent out of the city and the country. It was only the beginning.

Throughout the 1930s there were other raids that terrorized communities; split families apart; humiliated men, women, and children; and generally created a climate of hysteria within Mexican-American communities.

1

In August 1931, at the Los Angeles train station, relatives and friends wave goodbye to individuals being "repatriated" to Mexico during the Great Depression. The so-called Mexican Repatriation was simply a government action to send as many in the "Mexican" communities in the United States back to Mexico in order to open up jobs for other Americans during a time of economic collapse. The unjust and cruel enterprise involved raids that split families apart and generally created a climate of hysteria within Mexican-American communities. Although the targets were supposed to be illegal immigrants, later evidence indicated that more than half of those sent to Mexico were actual U.S. citizens. (NY Daily News Archive/Getty Images)

Individuals were arrested without warrant as suspected aliens, held incommunicado without opportunity to seek counsel, and subsequently deported. Entire barrios virtually disappeared. Thousands of Mexican-American immigrants were forced out and their property was seized. Although the targets were supposed to be illegal immigrants, later evidence indicated that more than half of those sent to Mexico were actual U.S. citizens. In California alone, nearly half a million individuals were forced from their homes.

When Carlos Guerra was three years old, Los Angeles law enforcement officials came to his family's house in Azusa and ordered his mother, a legal U.S. resident, and her six children, all born in the United States, to leave the country. He later remembered the train ride to Guanajuato, Mexico, and the 13 years of exile from his native country, years in which he had to learn a new language amid Mexican neighbors who distrusted those who had been moved in from the United States. He also remembered with much sadness the forced estrangement from his father, who stayed behind because California agribusiness still needed Mexican Americans to pick oranges. "The saddest thing of all," Guerra said later, "is that I lost my country. This is where I was born. I'm a California native. But it took me years to be able to call myself a so-called 'Americano'" (Hecht 2005).

Although the exact numbers are impossible to trace, most historians now believe that approximately 60 percent of the people sent to Mexico were adults of Mexican descent who were citizens and children born in America. So egregious were the violations of civil liberties and constitutional rights during the repatriation years that the state of California eventually apologized, passing the "Apology Act for the 1930s Mexican Repatriation Program." The apology was made in the year 2005.

Unfortunately for Mexican Americans living in the early 1940s, that apology was over a half century in the future. Instead, the racial and cultural denigration continued. Their schools were segregated and given inadequate facilities. Mexican Americans in the 1940s faced signs in front of certain businesses that read "Whites Only—No Spanish or Mexicans." They could not use many of the public facilities available to whites, such as certain skating rinks and swimming pools. Often, Mexicans and blacks could swim only one day of the week, after which the pools would be cleaned.

A Mexican consul working in the United States reported to his diplomatic superiors that the discrimination against Mexican Americans was not only invidious but was also out in the open for all to see. Some churches would not allow Mexican Americans to use churches on certain days. Many cemeteries, even those that publicly operated, reserved special sections specifically for Mexican Americans, thus separating them from Anglos in death just as they had been during life.

Some theaters did allow Mexican Americans and African Americans access but only on certain nights. "Mexican Night Every Wednesday" and "Colored Night Every Thursday," read the advertisement for one Los Angeles theater in 1942 (Alvarez 2009, 19). Some theaters allowed Mexican Americans but only in the balconies.

A young Mexican American named Cesar Chavez, who would later rise to international prominence by forming a union of farmworkers, remembered a time in the early 1940s when he went to a theater with a girlfriend who would later become his wife. The theater had a special section reserved for Mexicans. Chavez later remembered that even as a teenager he was already acutely aware of the low social status of Mexican Americans and was already tired of the boundaries, restrictions, insults, and the taboos. He decided to take a stand. He sat in the section reserved for Anglos. "The assistant manager came," he remembered. "The girl who sold the popcorn came. And the girl with the tickets came. Then the manager came. They tried to pull me up, and I said, 'No, you have to break my arms before I get up.'" The police then came. He was hustled off to jail and given a lecture on the proper behavior for Mexican Americans ("The Little Strike" 1969, 205).

Mexican Americans read stories in Los Angeles newspapers that called them undesirables. They were accused by law enforcement officials and political leaders of being inclined to engage in criminal activities and were, therefore, a threat to law and order. When arrested for petty crimes, many were subjected to what was euphemistically called the "third degree"— from beatings with rubber hoses to "three-day hunger tests."

All of this happened at a time when the United States was now officially at war against foreign enemies. It was a small step, indeed, to assume that some of those foreign enemies were already within the confines of the neighborhoods of Los Angeles. Now that steps were under way to segregate the Japanese Americans into relocation camps, what about the other suspicious foreign presence, especially those wearing the suspicious-looking Zoot suit clothes—the Mexicans?

The Zoot Suit Culture

Who were these people in Los Angeles, mostly with long, black hair, swaggering around wearing those outlandish-looking oversized coats with broad shoulders and ballooned pants, and those large broad-brimmed hats, with watch chains dangling down their sides? Thick-soled shoes called Calcos added to the look. Mostly, they were Mexican-American youngsters born in the United States to parents who had immigrated. Although the exact origins of the Zoot suit are unclear, certainly the Mexican-American youth of Los Angeles had adopted the so-called drape look worn by African Americans they had seen in pictures and movies, especially in eastern cities and, most especially, in Harlem. And the jazz music and the jitterbug dance craze had made their way to the West Coast along with the clothes that spoke of youthful rebellion and urban identity. Along Central Avenue and other locations a number of new jazz clubs began to attract popular bands. A couple of clothing stores on Central and Main streets began to specialize in the drapes. Although most Anglos in Los Angeles began to see the clothing as gang-related, the Zoot look was the uniform of jazz and its hot music dances.

But the Zoot suit also represented a stark visual expression of culture for Mexican Americans, about making a statement—a mark of defiance against the place in society in which they found themselves. Walking around the streets wearing the drapes with friends from their neighborhoods gave them, both young men and women, a group identity—admiration from some in their own community; disgust and ridicule from others, especially the Anglos.

Many young men took on the name "pachucos" and women "pachucas," terms of uncertain origins that mostly came to mean those in adolescent gangs wearing Zoot suits. Not every pachuco wore a Zoot suit, however, and certainly most members of the Mexican-American community did not consider themselves part of the pachuco rage. Indeed, the parents of many of those adolescents involved were unquestionably anxious and concerned about the fidelity of their sons and daughters to this new cultural phenomenon.

But the Zoot suit rage grew. Many pachucas also wore a form of Zoot suit, usually black or gray men's jackets with short-pleated skirts and bobby socks or fishnet stockings with platform heels or saddle shoes. They often wore their hair high in a kind of high bouffant style and used heavy amounts of makeup. Sometimes, they also carried the pocket chain.

The Zoot suiters spoke in slang they called "Chuco," much of it from a Caló dialect that could be traced to early Spanish wanderers and outcasts. Among the young boys and girls wearing the drapes one would hear such terms as homeboy or homie (a close friend from one's neighborhood), sancha (girlfriend), vato (dude or guy), machín (excellent or outstanding), and many others. For pachuco and pachuca youth, Chuco was hip and stylish. In intermixing English, Spanish, and Caló, they invented an argot especially for their time and place.

They gathered in groups that carried names of Mexican-American neighborhoods—39th Street, White Fence, Alpine Street, and Happy Valley. Many wore tattoos on the left hand between the thumb and index finger.

Various scholars, historians, and social scientists have long wrestled with the nature of the pachuco culture. Octavio Paz, a Mexican progressive liberal poet and writer, traveled to the United States in 1943 on a Guggenheim Fellowship. A few years later he authored a celebrated study of Mexican cultural and identity titled *The Labyrinth of Solitude*. In that work he reflected on the pachuco movement he had witnessed during his stay in the United States. He talked about the "furtive, restless air" of the pachuco: "They are instinctive rebels," he wrote, "and North American racism has vented its wrath on them more than once. But the pachucos do not attempt to vindicate their race or the nationality of their forebears. Their attitude reveals an obstinate, almost fanatical will-to-be, but this will affirms nothing specific except their determination . . . not to be like those around them" (Paz 1961, 13).

Other writers would argue that the pachuco phenomenon was an affirmation of their heritage, not a denial of it.

George Isidore Sánchez, who became a professor at the University of Texas in 1940 and who was a staunch Latino civil rights activist, traced the growth of the pachuco culture to the racial and social discrimination and exclusion under which young, first-generation Mexican Americans were forced to grapple: "The seed for the pachucos was sown," he said, "by unintelligent educational measures, by discriminatory social and economic practices, by provincial smugness and self-assigned 'racial, superiority. Today we reap the whirlwind in youth whose greatest crime was to be born into an environment which, through various kinds and degrees of social ostracism and prejudicial economic subjugation, made them a caste apart" (Sanchez 1943, 15).

Vicente Morales, a young Mexican American in Los Angeles who donned the Zoot look, later said that he and his friends encountered much open disgust on the downtown streets. "They didn't like us," he said, "and I remember when I used to go downtown to the stores and the restaurants usually I'd get dirty looks like I was going to rob something from them, and they didn't like the way I dressed or the way I looked" (Alvarez 2009, 129). Most citizens of Los Angeles became increasingly wary of the Zoot look of Morales and his friends; to Morales, however, it gave him a sense of pride.

In 1942, the War Productions Board, in an effort to cut back on the use of fabric material in the clothing business, passed a regulation that prohibited the production of Zoot suits. Not surprisingly, the action merely launched a new underground source of bootleg Zoot suits. Thus, the Zoot suit became even more a symbol of resistance and rebellion, a product of discontent with second-class citizenship.

Wartime Tensions in Los Angeles

As the United States entered World War II, the city of Los Angeles was not only heavily fortified against possible Japanese attacks but was also a central launching site of troop deployments to the Pacific Theater. The U.S.

Naval and Marine Corps Reserve Armory served as an induction, separation, and training center. In 1941 the new armory was in Chavez Ravine, the site where two decades later the Los Angeles Dodgers would build its baseball stadium. It was also adjacent to a predominantly Mexican-American neighborhood.

Also in Los Angeles was Fort MacArthur, a U.S. Army post that guarded the city's harbor and had major responsibility for protecting the American continental coastline from invasion. At the time of the attack on Pearl Harbor on December 7, 1941, the post had approximately 2,000 men. Those numbers immediately increased as the U.S. government, understanding the critical importance of Los Angeles as a prime military target by the Japanese, began to brace the coast for any possible attacks, bringing in new recruits and fortifying the batteries.

More than any other Americans on the U.S. mainland, those on the West Coast, especially in Los Angeles, saw themselves almost on a frontline in the battle with Japan. City leaders, aided by the military, established civilian patrols. On any given weekend in Los Angeles, up to 50,000 servicemen might be in the city.

Early in 1942, the Army began receiving conflicting but unnerving reports about not only possible submarines lurking off the coast but also about sightings of surface ships and unidentified planes. It was after one of these reports in late February 1942 that the infamous "Battle of Los Angeles" ensued in which anti-aircraft fire lit up the skies around the city like fireworks seeking out reported enemy planes.

Some attacks were not fanciful. The *SS Montebello* was sunk by torpedo and shell fire off San Simeon. The freighter *Absaroka* took torpedo fire off Point Fermin. Another Japanese submarine fired several rounds into an oil field installation at Elwood, destroying one oil derrick and damaging some other installations.

And so the city of Los Angeles in 1942 was buzzing with wartime mobilization and coping with threats—real, imagined, and exaggerated.

In the early 1940s, the California Senate established a Committee on Un-American Activities. Chaired by Senator Jack Tenney, the committee investigated activities of groups and individuals suspected of subversive activities. Much of the impetus for the work of such an investigative body had been fueled by fear of Communist, Fascist, Nazi, and other foreign-dominated groups gaining influence and power in the state.

Along with the supposed Japanese-American threat that was now being handed by relocation proceedings, the Mexican-American community represented another source of concern about foreigners. Tenney's committee, for example, began to investigate the Sinarquistas, a Fascist group that had tried to influence politics in Mexico and was seen as having possible connections to the barrios of Los Angeles. The committee would also closely investigate the activities of Hollywood actors, writers, and producers who had ties with Communist organizations and activists who worked for the amelioration of economic and race prejudice against Mexican Americans. Could they be secretly in league with menacing Communist infiltration? Thus, the focus on the Mexican-American community as a possible seedbed for anti-American sentiment and a threat to national security further exacerbated growing tensions.

Stoking Fear of a Mexican Crime Wave

On June 12, 1942, a 19-year-old Mexican American named Frank Torres was shot to death outside a high school track meet held at the Los Angeles Memorial Coliseum. As the assailant disappeared among the large crowd, the ensuing panic and near-stampede among the frightened groups of people was large enough for the Los Angeles police to call for help from nearby armed soldiers to help quell the confusion and stem any further injuries or loss of life. The violence at the Coliseum and the ethnic makeup of the victim and many of the spectators began to fuel increasing attention to the pachuco gangs and their rivalries.

In late July, another incident grabbed attention. When four plainclothes policemen attempted to break up a craps game at the corner of Pomeroy and Mark Streets in Boyle Heights, the largely Mexican-American crowd resisted. When the police attempted some arrests, a melee broke out. Some in the crowd seized the radio in the police car; others doused the police with water.

The incident became an embarrassment to the police force and fodder for Los Angeles newspapers that demanded that aggressive action be undertaken to stop out-of-control Mexicans. Media mogul William Randolph Hearst, owner of the *Los Angeles Herald-Examiner*, and Harry Chandler of the *Los Angeles Times* both had deep-seated hostility toward Mexicans. Hearst had lost 6.5 million acres of land in Baja, California, that had been expropriated by the Mexican government, and Chandler had been indicted in 1915 for conspiracy to overthrow the Mexican government in order to hold onto his own holdings in Baja. Chandler's paper often referred to Mexicans as "ignorant" and "peons" and Hearst suggested that Mexicans who had immigrated to the United States were either communists or supporters of Hitler. Either way, they were here to stir up insurrection.

And now, in 1942, headlines in the press talked about a "crime wave" and "gangsters." Coverage concerning Mexican Americans grew even more negative in tone than ever, thus bolstering the sense that there was this community within the confines of the city that was uncontrollable, alien, and a threat to the war effort. When discussions about minority adolescents occurred, it was almost always presented in terms of gangs. In fact, only a small portion of the Mexican-American population could be considered in any way a part of a so-called gang. Indeed, even among pachucos and pachucas, most did not consider themselves members of gangs.

Nevertheless, the xenophobia toward Mexican Americans spiraled upward in the spring of 1942. And with all of the talk about teenage crime and violence, another problem began to take hold—increasing confrontations between servicemen and Mexican-American youth downtown and in certain barrios.

Animosity between the groups wearing the opposite suits—the whites of the naval servicemen and the Zoot suits of the pachucos—seems, in retrospect, inevitable. Military men off base looking for some carousing in the territories of Mexican-American youth led to increasing numbers of skirmishes. Servicemen saw the Zoot suit as an offensive affront to their roles in the military. Few realized that Mexican-American youths actually saw service in World War II in numbers larger than their percentage of the population. On the other side, Zoot suiters resented an invasion of their neighborhoods, especially when military men made moves toward young Mexican-American women. With increasing frequency, small groups clashed, armed usually with bottles, clubs, and knives. Servicemen frequently returned to base with cuts and scrapes; Zoot suiters went home with similar injuries.

All of this was a prelude. All of the elements were in place for an explosion. Carey McWilliams, noted progressive writer and activist, a man who would be in the epicenter of the explosion to come, wrote, "With the backdrops all in place, the curtain now rolls up on an interesting tableau on Our City the Queen of the Angels which was founded in the year 1781 by Mexican *pobladores* under the direction of Spanish officers who wore costumes far more outlandish than those worn by the most flamboyant *pachucos*" (McWilliams 1990, 219).

References

Alvarez, Luis. 2009. *The Power of the Zoot: Youth Culture and Resistance during World War II*. Berkeley: University of California Press.

Hecht, Peter. 2005. "Mass Deportations to Mexico in 1930s Spur Apology." *The Sacramento Bee*, December 28. http://clubs.asua.arizona.edu/~mecha/pages/Mass DeportationApology.html.

"The Little Strike That Grew to La Causa." 1969. *Time*, July 4, 20.

McWilliams, Carey. 1990. *North from Mexico: The Spanish-Speaking People of the United States*. New York: Praeger.

Paz, Octavio. 1961. *The Labyrinth of Solitude*. New York: Grove Press.

Sanchez, George. 1943, "Pachucos in the Making," *Common Ground*, Autumn. http://historymatters.gmu.edu/d/5155.

TWO

The Death at Sleepy Lagoon

"SLEEPY LAGOON" WAS BEST KNOWN as a hit song made popular by trumpet player Harry James. It made the best-seller chart of *Billboard* magazine in April 1942 and, at one point, reached No. 1. From the night of August 1, 1942, forward, the name "Sleepy Lagoon" would also take on a new and very different connotation. It would become the place of a famous murder. It would be remembered as the name of one of the most infamous trials in the history of California jurisprudence. It would also be a symbol to the Mexican-American community, not only in Los Angeles but also across the country, of racial and cultural injustice.

Sleepy Lagoon was one of two reservoirs located in an area in southeast Los Angeles near what is now Commerce, off the east bank of the Los Angeles River, that served to irrigate crops on the Williams Ranch. Nestled amid a grove of trees and shrubs with a grassy incline, it was also a natural swimming hole and a gathering spot for groups of young Mexican Americans.

On this warm, pleasant August evening, there was to be a cheerful occasion at the home of Amelio and Angela Delgadillo about a quarter of a mile to the east of the reservoir. Their daughter Eleanor was celebrating her 20th birthday. About 30 families had been invited to the weekend festivities and a four-piece band was there to entertain.

One of the guests was a 22-year-old neighbor named José Díaz. Born in Durango, Mexico, his family fled in the aftermath of the Mexican Revolution and headed north across the Texas border. In 1928, the Díaz family settled in one of the bunkhouses on the Williams Ranch southeast of Los Angeles and, along with other immigrant families, began work picking fruit and vegetables. On the Williams Ranch and in the immediate vicinity, the Díaz family was among a small, close-knit community where immigrant families settled to build new lives.

11

José finished his eighth grade, left school, and joined a brother and sister working at the Sunny Sally Packing Plant processing vegetables and began to help support the Díaz family with his earnings. Like other young Mexican Americans, he began to wear a white shirt and peg pants that were part of the growing "drape" look and took a lively interest in jazz music.

In the summer of 1942, Díaz decided to seize an opportunity to get ahead. Along with other Mexican Americans, he decided to enlist in the U.S. Army. Here was a way, he believed, he could break away from the lower-class, segregated life of the immigrant class and could make a better life for himself. For Díaz, the birthday party was a chance to get together with his friends before the next chapter of his life. A few days before the party, he had posed before a camera for his Army induction photograph and was to report to the recruitment center on Monday.

During the evening, a small group of mostly Anglo boys from the suburb of Downey, a few miles southeast of the Delgadillo house, crashed the party. Around 11:00 P.M., the hosts insisted that the rowdy boys from Downey leave the premises. As they left, they drove through the area of the Sleepy Lagoon reservoir. A few cars were parked in the area. At night, it was a popular lover's lane gathering place.

As the Downey boys slowly drove into the area, they stopped next to one of the parked cars. They could not resist the temptation for more harassment. Inside the car was a Mexican American from the 38th Street neighborhood, northeast of Sleepy Lagoon. His name was Henry Leyvas and he was with his girlfriend, Dora Baca, and a friend, Bobby Telles. They, along with a few others from the 38th Street neighborhood, were about to get a beating. They were also about to sink into a chain of events that would result in much more than some scrapes and bruises.

Unlike José Díaz, who had been born in Mexico, the 19-year-old Leyvas was born in Tucson, Arizona, the third of 10 children of parents from Mexico. He befriended a number of other Mexican-American teenagers who lived in or near a residential neighborhood around 38th Street. The youngsters hung out at places around the intersection of Vernon and Long Beach Boulevard—a pool hall called Los Amigos, the Dorkel movie house, and a malt shop. As had most of his friends from the 38th Street neighborhood, Hank had several confrontations with the police as a teenager. He was once held for three months on an assault charge before being released. Another assault case brought a sentence of three years of probation. Hank had a love of cars, liked fast driving, and gained the skills of a mechanic. He frequently could be seen helping fix the cars of friends. Intelligent, a natural leader, many said, he was also fiercely independent and defiant of authority.

Police began to notice his attitude and on a number of occasions he had been rounded up on suspicion of petty crimes for which he was in no way connected. He and his brother were once held on suspicion of car theft. It took the police three days to conclude that the car actually belonged to the family. In some instances, he had been treated roughly, which made his defiance even more pronounced. Like José Díaz, Leyvas had decided to break away from the grinding life in southeast Los Angeles and join the armed services. He made plans to enlist in the Merchant Marines. The night of August 1 at the Sleepy Lagoon dashed those plans.

The Downey boys not only gave Leyvas a beating, but they also attacked his girlfriend, Dora, who was in the car. Leyvas, who had been in a car accident a few weeks earlier, was nursing an injured leg. When several of the attackers at the Sleepy Lagoon opened the door and began beating Leyvas, Dora tried to stop them. She said later, "I put myself on top of him so they wouldn't hit him, because he couldn't do anything" (*People v. Zammora* 1942, 4493).

Although a few of Leyvas's friends were in other cars in the Sleepy Lagoon area—youngsters such as Gilbert Mendoza, Manny Delgado, and Gus Zamora—they were badly outnumbered and also incurred cuts and bruises. Fights between neighborhood groups were not unusual in the world of José Díaz and Hank Leyvas. But roughing up girlfriends went beyond the bounds. Leyvas quickly looked for revenge.

His face bloodied, he, along with his friends in the other cars, drove the five miles back to the 38th Street neighborhood and gathered a number of additional friends—reinforcements to give some payback to the Downey boys.

Meanwhile, at the Delgadillo house, the party was still going on after midnight. When the band left, the guests used a radio to provide music. Around 1:00 A.M., some of the partygoers decided to leave. Eleanor Delgadillo later said that she saw José Díaz leaving with two other guests.

Shortly afterward, the caravan of cars carrying young men and women from the 38th Street neighborhood—one as young as 14—arrived at Sleepy Lagoon looking for their earlier tormentors from Downey. The area was deserted but the sounds from the Delgadillo party could be heard in the distance. Were the Downey boys at the party? The contingent from 38th Street decided to find out.

The next few minutes, as later recounted by those still at the party and the group newly arrived from 38th Street, were filled with harried screams and shouts and the sickening sounds of clubs hitting their targets, glimpses of waving knives, flying bottles, and the sight of blood streaming down faces and arms. Ironically, the melee apparently involved none of the boys from Downey who were the target of revenge. Nevertheless, amid confusion and chaos and charges and denials, a birthday party had turned truly ugly. Shortly afterward, it turned tragic.

As the fight broke up and as partygoers and intruders alike left the Delgadillo home, a few young men and women heading across the area near the Sleepy Lagoon came upon a pitiful sight—José Díaz lying face up in the middle of the road, barely breathing, bleeding from knife wounds, his face swollen, and his pockets turned inside out.

The youngsters who found Díaz ran to find José's younger brother, Lino, who was home at the time. José's father and other family members were away from Los Angeles in Central California working in the fields during the prune harvest. Lino and others managed to get to a main road and flag down an ambulance. It took 45 minutes for the ambulance to reach the Los Angeles General Hospital. An hour-and-a-half later, José Díaz died from a brain hemorrhage caused by a fractured skull.

The Roundup

The front page headline in the *Los Angeles Times* on August 3, 1942, trumpeted the news on the war: "Russians Stop Nazi Tank Attacks . . ." The story just under the lead was "One Killed and 10 Hurt in Boy 'Wars.'" In the coming months, for the *Times* as well as other Los Angeles dailies such as the *Examiner*, there were two wars now worth reporting—one of them local. The story about the Sleepy Lagoon murder used the term "Boy Gang Terrorists."

The concern about juvenile delinquency among Mexican-American youth in Los Angeles intensified following the death of José Díaz. In fact, the police department's own records showed that crime among those in the Mexican-American community was actually decreasing during this period. It is true that neighborhood groups of pachucos and Zoot suiters often engaged in turf skirmishes and petty crime. And now the press increasingly reported on what writers and editors began generally to call a Mexican crime wave. California governor Cuthbert L. Olson pledged to eradicate gang violence.

Following the death of Díaz, city authorities reacted swiftly. A large force from the Los Angeles Police Department swept into the general area of Sleepy Lagoon. It was augmented by county and state law enforcement agencies. After blocking off a number of streets, they began a general dragnet of homes and a search of cars coming and going from the nearby barrios. They were especially looking for the youths with whom they had previously encountered on the streets, especially Henry Leyvas and his 38th Street friends.

Every boy or girl wearing a Zoot suit was of particular interest, under special suspicion. And many of the police who confronted the Zoot suiters were armed with pokers to which were attached sharp razor blades. Their purpose was to cut and rip the peg-top trousers and other parts of the Zoot suits. This was not just a search for suspects. This was already a punishment for being a Mexican-American kid with long hair, for being one of those pachucos or whatever they called themselves.

After several days of the dragnet, Joseph Reed, an assistant to the chief of police, reported to his boss:

The Los Angeles Police Department in conjunction with the Sheriff, California Highway Patrol, the Monterey, Montebello, and Alhambra Police Departments, conducted a drive on Mexican gangs throughout Los Angeles County on the nights of August 10th and 11th. All persons suspected of gang activities were stopped. Approximately 600 persons were brought in. (McWilliams 1990, 213)

Every one of the estimated 600 people arrested during the dragnet had a Spanish surname. Not even the Downey boys ended up on the suspect list, even though they had not only been uninvited intruders at the Delgadillo party but had also been involved in a clear case of assault at the Sleepy Lagoon.

This was not merely an investigation into the murder of one young man but a major raid of the Mexican-American community. The jail cells filled with Mexican-American youngsters as the police tried to sort out what they had uncovered. And as the law enforcement officials began to narrow down their suspects in the Díaz case—those who had been at the party and at the Sleepy Lagoon and their friends—the interrogations began.

Rough treatment by law enforcement was not new to a number of the suspects brought in for questioning. But some of the 38th Street neighborhood youths said later that the vicious battering they suffered at the hands of the police in the aftermath of the dragnet of 1942 had not only been intense but had also been humiliating in the extreme. Not only Leyvas talked about slaps and crushing punches to the head in the interrogation room along with the racial slurs but so did Joseph Valenzuela, Benny Alvarez, Eugene Carpio, Manuel Reyes, and a number of others.

Angel Padilla, one of those who had been at the Sleepy Lagoon on the night of the murder, later said that when he arrived at the police substation, officers surrounded him and began a rapid-fire interrogation. When he refused to answer some of the questions, they began to punch him, at one point knocking him off his chair. He remembered one of the officers saying, "Sit down so we can hit you some more. You Mexicans think you are smart: you guys never fight fair." Another yelled, "We ought to shoot every Mexican dog like you" (Pagán 2003, 72).

A photograph of one of the suspects had been taken before his questioning and another shortly afterward. The blood on his face and shirt that stood out in the second photograph was not present in the first.

The newspapers continued to ratchet up the sensationalist rhetoric demeaning to all in the Mexican-American community. Reacting to the newspaper slurs, a young man named Pete Vasquez said,

> The fellas down in our section—there's nothing bad about them, no more than anywhere else. But things are tough. There's nowhere to go—no place to play games—or nothing—. If the cops catch you on the street after 8 o'clock, usually they run you in—or rough you up, anyway. If you look like a Mexican you just better stay off the street, that's all—. And where can you go? It's real bad. I'm going into the Army, and it's all right with me. I'm glad to be going. Things'll be better in the Army, and I'm glad of the chance to fight. It makes it hard, though, for a lot of our fellas to see things that way. They want to fight for their country, all right—but they want to feel like it's their country. ("The Sleepy Lagoon" 1943)

After a grand jury began to hear evidence about a number of individuals suspected of involvement in the death of José Díaz, the Los Angeles Police Department submitted a report designed to help the members of the jury better understand the issues of youth gangs and ethnicity. It was prepared by Captain E. Duran Ayres, chief of the Foreign Relations Bureau of the sheriff's office. Filled with pseudo-scientific racial and cultural assertions, the "Ayres Report" represented in large measure the prevailing attitudes about the Latino immigrant community held not only by law enforcement but also by the mainstream media, the judiciary, and others who would determine the fate of those charged with Díaz's death.

To get a true perspective of the Mexican culture and nature, Ayres wrote that one had to look for fundamental, biological factors: "Although a wild cat and a domestic cat are of the same family," he said, "they have certain biological characteristics so different that while one may be domesticated the other would have to be caged to be kept in captivity; and there is

Mexican-American soldiers in the U.S. Army at Fort Benning, Georgia, February 1943. At the time of the Zoot Suit Riots, several hundred thousand Mexican Americans and Mexican nationals who grew up in the United States were serving for the United States in the military during World War II. They fought in almost all major battles during the war and served in every branch of the armed forces. Thirteen Latino servicemen earned the Medal of Honor. Unfortunately, on their return after the war, they still faced degrading segregation and such signs as "No Mexicans Allowed." (Bettman/Corbis)

practically as much difference between the races of man as so aptly recognized by Rudyard Kipling when he said when writing of the Oriental, 'East is East and West is West, and never the twain shall meet,' which gives us an insight into the present problem because the Indian, from Alaska to Patagonia, is evidently Oriental in background—at least he shows many of the Oriental characteristics, especially so in his utter disregard for the value of life" (Ayres 1942).

By linking the biological nature of the Mexican Americans to those of Orientals at a time when the United States was in a bloody war with Japan and had begun to remove Japanese Americans to relocation camps, Ayres did nothing to reassure the grand jury members of the possible innocence of those rounded up in the police dragnet. Indeed, Ayres continued that extreme violence was in their very nature: "One cannot change the spots of a leopard," he wrote. "The Caucasian, especially the Anglo-Saxon, when engaged in fighting, particularly among youths, resort to fisticuffs and may at times kick each other, which is considered unsportive, but this Mexican element considers all that to be a sign of weakness, and all he knows and feels is a desire to use a knife or some lethal weapon. In other words, his desire is to kill, or at least let blood" (Ayres 1942).

Ayres said that Mexican Americans had inherited their naturally violent instincts from the bloodthirsty Aztecs of ancient Mexico, who practiced human sacrifice. He suggested that even with earnest attempts at assimilation through the efforts not only of government but also of social agencies, their wild instincts would likely remain and need, in some fashion, to be tamed.

The Los Angeles Police Department was out to tame those instincts in the summer and fall of 1942. The grand jury was about to offer help.

The Indictments

After sifting through the welter of stories and recollections of those at the Delgadillo party and those involved in the fight at the Sleepy Lagoon, the grand jury was left with nothing substantial to tie any one particular individual with the actual murder of José Díaz. After narrowing its focus to 24 individuals, the grand jury decided to charge all of them with murder. Most but not all of the young men charged had some previous run-ins with law enforcement. All but two were of Mexican descent.

In addition to Henry Leyvas, they included, among others:

Manuel "Manny" Delgado, 18, married at the time of his arrest with his wife expecting a child;

John Matuz, 20, of Hungarian descent, who had worked for a time for the U.S. Engineering Department in Alaska and had no criminal record;

Jack Melendez, 21, already sworn into the Navy and ready to report for duty;

Angel Padilla, 18, had worked in a number of jobs and had also spent time at a work camp for robbery and assault;

Ysmael "Smiles" Parra, 20, nicknamed for his usual facial expression, had worked at a Civilian Conservation Corps (CCC) camp;

Manuel "Manny" Reyes, 17, at the time of his arrest scheduled for a physical examination for possible enlistment in the Navy;

José "Chepe" Ruíz, 18, an aspiring baseball player but a youngster with a record of arrests;

Robert "Bobby" Telles, 18, the young man in the car with Leyvas when they were attacked at the Sleepy Lagoon, was working at the North American Aviation defense plant;

Victor "Bobby Levine" Thompson, 21, from one of the Anglo families in the predominantly Mexican-American 38th Street neighborhood, had also worked for a time at a CCC camp;

Henry "Hank" Joseph Ynostroza, 18, married and the father of a young girl;

Gustavo "Gus" Zamora, 20, was Mexican-born and could not join the military and had begun a job at a furniture factory.

Thus, 22 defendants would face a murder trial en masse. In the heated racial atmosphere of Los Angeles in the summer of 1942, charging over 20 individuals with one murder did not seem to the press, the courts, the police, or the wider population as bizarre.

References

Ayres, Edward Duran. 1942. "Statistics: The Nature of the Mexican American Criminal." Online Archive of California, Department of Special Collections, Charles E. Young Research Library, UCLA. http://www.oac.cdlib.org/view?docId=hb6m3nb79m&brand=oac4&doc.view=entire_text.

McWilliams, Carey. 1990. *North from Mexico: The Spanish-Speaking People of the United States*. New York: Praeger.

Pagán, Edwardo Obregón. 2003. *Murder at the Sleepy Lagoon: Zoot Suits, Race, and Riot in Wartime L.A.* Chapel Hill: The University of North Carolina Press.

People v. Zammora, 1942. "Transcript of Testimony." October 13–22. http://content.cdlib.org/view?docId=hb6199p2dh;NAAN=13030&doc.view=frames&chunk.id=vol1&toc.depth=1&toc.id=vol1&brand=calisphere.

"The Sleepy Lagoon Case: Prepared by the Sleepy Lagoon Defense Committee." 1943. Online Archives of California, Department of Special Collections, Charles E. Young Research Library, UCLA. http://www.oac.cdlib.org/view?docId=hb7779p4zc&brand=oac4&doc.view=entire_text.

THREE

The Trial

On October 13, 1942, in Superior Court of Los Angeles, the trial of *People v. Zammora* began. Even the name of the case was wrong. A clerk typing the names of the defendants listed Gus Zamora as the first. The clerk misspelled his name. The name of the case was never changed.

Three months after the Los Angeles police dragnet had rounded up 600 individuals from the Mexican-American community, questioned them, and, in some occasions, beaten information out of them, the number of defendants had been narrowed to 24 young Mexican-American men from the 38th Street neighborhood who stood accused of murder even though there was no definite evidence linking any one of them to the crime.

As defined by the grand jury, the case revolved around the charge that this group of 24 had engaged in a conspiracy to commit murder. In fact, José Díaz died from injuries suffered at the hands of an unknown assailant during fights at a party that involved both men and women. The charge of conspiracy, nevertheless, allowed the prosecution to indict an entire group of individuals for murder even though no one seemed to have the vaguest idea of who actually delivered the fatal blows or why, if there were such a conspiracy, José Díaz was the victim. Two of the young men, through the efforts of their families in securing separate trials, were eventually acquitted, leaving 22 to face a jury en masse.

The perfunctory jury selection, with neither side offering any significant challenges, resulted in eight women and two men who would decide the fate of the accused. Not one of the jurors was Latino. None were parents of youngsters about the age of the defendants. From the onset of the trial, the jury, after each day of testimony, continued to have access to magazine and newspaper articles that commonly referred to the defendants as mobsters and hoodlums.

In the courtroom, the 22 defendants sat in two rows of chairs in alphabetical order along one side facing the jury. Their lawyers sat at a defense table. Because of the separation, the boys could speak personally with their counsel only after the day's proceedings. They could not even meet during recesses. To any observer of usual courtroom procedures that allowed defendants the right to counsel at all times during a trial, the seating arrangement for the 22 Mexican Americans seemed breathtakingly prejudicial from the onset of the proceedings.

In addition, while the boys were in the Los Angeles County Jail awaiting trial, defense attorneys requested that they be given permission to get fresh clothes and haircuts before the trial, as was usual for defendants about to face a jury. The request was denied. The district attorney, the police, and the prosecuting lawyers all insisted that the jury be able to see the gang members in their Zoot suit clothing, to see them in their actual character as antisocial misfits. Despite the strong and persistent objections raised by defense counsel, the young men marched into the courtroom as a disheveled lot, just as the prosecution wanted them to look. As the trial continued, their appearance became even more haggard. Sitting directly across from the jury, they certainly appeared not to be a group of mostly scared teenagers but a small motley army of invading hoodlums.

Who was it then that was ready to orchestrate what promised to be a judicial monstrosity?

The Judge: Charles Fricke

Judge Charles W. Fricke, a noted jurist with a distinguished career on the bench as well as the author of a number of influential law treatises and procedure manuals, quickly became an archenemy of the Mexican-American defendants who sat before him and his gavel at the Sleepy Lagoon murder trial. To many observers it seemed as if Fricke had joined the mission to destroy the evils of the Zoot suit culture and that he had brought to the trial all of the racial and cultural stereotypes rampant in the press and prevalent in a predominant part of the Anglo community in Los Angeles.

A native of Milwaukee, Wisconsin, Fricke was educated at New York University, served as a district attorney and municipal judge in Wisconsin, and moved to Los Angeles where he steadily moved up in the judicial system to become a superior court judge known for his toughness and numerous harsh sentences. Some called him "San Quentin Fricke" because he had reportedly sent more convicts to the infamous prison than any other judge in history.

With his experience, Fricke seemed uniquely capable of finding a solution to the problems inherent in the case, especially the logistical situation involving the separation of the defense counsel and the defendants during testimony. Nevertheless, from the beginning of the trial, Fricke seemed more intent on putting the defendants and their counsel in their place than in establishing a solid judicial proceeding. In the case of the seating arrangements, for example, Fricke had no answer to the vexing problem except to say that the courtroom simply lacked the space to accommodate normal procedures. To experienced court reporters and others who were familiar with trial proceedings, the Sleepy Lagoon case began to take on a surreal quality, bereft of fairness and equity, explainable only in terms of the tensions and xenophobia plaguing the city of Los Angeles during wartime.

The Court Battle Begins

At the beginning of the trial, the defense team consisted of a number of lawyers hired by the families of the defendants. Because the families had little money, the lawyers had no extensive experience, especially involving a trial of this notoriety. Some of the defendants, whose families could afford no legal representation, were served by a court-appointed public defender.

The prosecution was handled by two deputy assistant district attorneys—Clyde Shoemaker and John Barnes—both of whom had been at the center of other cases in Los Angeles and Hollywood that involved issues of public fascination and scrutiny. They also had whatever public resources at their disposal to prosecute the case in any manner they judged to be most formidable.

As the prosecution called its first witness on October 19, it became clear to everyone in the courtroom that the defense team faced an intimidating task. Judge Fricke continually interrupted the defense lawyers in their cross-examination of the first witnesses, admonishing them about rules and procedures. From the beginning, most observers realized that those 22 defendants faced weeks of bleak courtroom drama.

LaRue McCormick and the Citizens' Committee for the Defense of Mexican-American Youth

In the early days of the trial, labor organizer and left-wing activist LaRue McCormick began a vigorous attempt to help counter the anti-Mexican hysteria surrounding the Sleepy Lagoon trial. She was a member of the

International Labor Defense (ILD), a legal arm of the Communist Party of the United States that had been formed in 1925 to help fight groups such as the Ku Klux Klan and to defend high-profile defendants the organization considered unjustly charged with crimes. The Sleepy Lagoon case seemed to be a prime example.

For a decade, McCormick had worked to help agricultural workers, labor union members, and African Americans in civil liberties cases and in arrests relating to strike activities. She had close ties with "El Congreso del Pueblo de Habla Española" ("The Congress of Spanish-Speaking Peoples"), a pioneering civil rights organization, based in southern California, devoted to Latinos and other minorities.

Outraged by the blatant racism and the obvious injustice of the Sleepy Lagoon case and the humiliating attacks against the young Mexican Americans, McCormick decided to form a group called the Citizens' Committee for the Defense of Mexican-American Youth (CCDMAY). "They [Sleepy Lagoon defendants] were all charged with first degree murder," she said later. "We waited around thinking that somebody was going to come to their defense. But they didn't. So I finally called a conference and we had several hundred people turn out to it and set up a Sleepy Lagoon Defense Committee" (Barajas 2006, 40).

Led by McCormick, the group began to raise funds and to ally itself with other progressive groups and individuals in Los Angeles. It enlisted the assistance of some of the family members of the defendants, especially Lupe Leyvas, mother of Hank. It handed out leaflets encouraging public-spirited citizens to try to ensure a vigorous defense and fair trial. To that end, McCormick called on an attorney with the experience and courtroom savvy to represent the rights of the accused.

For the Defense: George Shibley

George Shibley's wife, Eleanor, said of her husband, "He took cases that no one else would." He defended African Americans and Mexican Americans fighting injustice, homosexuals, members of striking labor unions, and left-wing individuals and groups accused of anti-American and subversive activities. When McCormick and her new group approached Shibley about the case, he signed on and joined the defense team after the first week of testimony. "Everyone knew the case would last for months" he said, "and it sounded like a loser, but it interested me" (Zoot Suit Riots, 2001).

Born in New York City, the son of Syrian immigrants, Shibley grew up in Long Beach, California, attended Stanford University, and graduated from

Stanford Law School in 1934. Beginning his practice in Long Beach, a place that would remain his home, he quickly earned a reputation as a fighter for those with little chance and most of whom had little money. In this courtroom, at this time, faced with this judge, Defense Attorney Shibley faced nearly impossible obstacles.

Shibley realized from the beginning that winning the case outright would be nearly impossible, given the bizarre conditions, the obvious bias of Judge Charles Fricke, and the outrageous yellow journalism coverage in the press. He later spoke of the fact that it was, at that time, an "open season" on Mexicans in Los Angeles.

When he looked back on the trial years later, Shibley reflected on the lunacy of the entire proceeding: "The conspiracy," he said, "was a conspiracy or an agreement to commit a trespass. In other words, when these twenty-two or forty-two young men and women said, 'let's go crash the party,' or 'let's go to the Williams ranch,' whether they said it in words or by assent in just joining the group, they were agreeing or conspiring to commit a misdemeanor" (Mazón 1984, 21).

And yet, here were Shibley and his fellow defense lawyers up against a court and system that was seemingly intent on proving all 22 guilty of murder. Nevertheless, he was a battler and, at every turn in the trial, began to raise objection after objection to the proceedings.

Shibley's strategy was to aggressively challenge and put on the record every egregious judicial outrage displayed in the courtroom—the racist slurs, the demand by the judge that the defendants wear the same clothes they wore when arrested, the prohibition that the accused could not consult with their individual lawyers during the proceedings, and many other defamatory actions against the young men. Through his tactics and legal challenges, the shrewd Shibley, realizing the long odds of winning the case, began to leave a record upon which a strong appellate case could be made.

Upon entering the case, Shibley soon turned to the issue of the right of the accused to confer with counsel during the trial. Fricke, citing the congestion in the room and too few bailiffs, said that opening up frequent consultations between the lawyers and each of the defendants during the proceedings would hopelessly mire the case in endless delays and disturbances. Undeterred by Fricke's response, Shibley demanded that some arrangement be made through which each of the defendants could have easy access to their attorney. After all, changing the seating arrangements in the room would not actually add additional individuals to the room or take up more space. Fricke remained undeterred by the defense counsel's demands.

Shibley continued to argue that the boys should have been allowed to change clothes and get haircuts. On October 26, they were again in court, looking even more ragged than they were apprehended months earlier. Judge Fricke, as he would do throughout the proceedings, cut off Shibley with undisguised condescension:

MR. SHIBLEY:	If your Honor please, before counsel proceeds further, counsel wishes to bring something to the attention of this court, the appearance of these boys. For the past two weeks we have been trying to get money to them so they can get haircuts and have clothes—
THE COURT:	I will take that matter up outside of the presence of the jury, however. We have spent 10 minutes getting started and we are ready to take testimony. Those matters should be taken up during the recess . . .
MR. SHIBLEY:	If your Honor please, if I just may say this, this bears upon something the district attorney has done—
THE COURT:	I will take it up outside of the presence of the jury at recess. I hope counsel understands the English language. (*People v. Zammora* 1942, 750)

Young Women on the Stand

Twenty-two young Mexican-American men stood trial on the charge of conspiracy to murder in the death of José Díaz. Yet, a number of individuals accompanying those men that fateful night at the Williams house and the Sleepy Lagoon were young women. Along with the boys, they were in the caravan of cars that rode to the Williams house looking for the Downey boys. They were actively involved in the ensuing fighting. Like the young men, the women wore long hair and wore Zoot suit–like clothes. Yet, the conspiracy to murder was not directed to the females. Perhaps, the grand jury and the prosecutors realized that a jury would be reluctant to convict young women of such a severe charge in the case.

Nevertheless, as they started to present the facts to the jury about the night that Díaz lost his life, the prosecutors decided to set the scene with a parade of the women to the witness stand. One among them was the 20-year-old Lorena Rosalee Encinas.

Born in Nogales, Arizona, Lorena was the third child to her parents who had recently immigrated to the United States from Mexico. Besides the unremitting challenges facing a poor immigrant family, Lorena, at the age of 13, faced additional emotional trauma—her father passed away from cancer. In addition, her younger brother Louis began a life of petty crime that would lead him to a number of incarcerations and later to suicide after a bank robbery. On August 1, 1942, Lorena, now the mother of a child, was one of those involved at the birthday party at the Williams ranch.

Although Lorena and the other young women had testified at the grand jury proceedings prior to the trial, this time they decided to give no details of what they had seen or heard on the fateful night. By the time of the trial the girls had seen the fierce reporting in the press that referred to their friends in vile and repulsive ways. They had been informed by defense counsel that the U.S. Constitution gave them the right not to incriminate themselves in a courtroom. They decided to exercise that right.

Judge Fricke, with all his years and experience on the bench, could not move the young women to implicate themselves or give evidence against their friends. Even under constant pressure from Fricke, Lorena Encinas and the others held firm.

On October 28, 14-year-old Bertha Aguilar faced the court. When she refused to give details, Judge Fricke snapped at the youngster:

THE COURT: Answer the question. This is a court. You cannot sit back here and say you won't answer questions just because you won't. It is against the law for you to do that. The law says if you are asked questions and they are proper questions and there is no legitimate reason why you should not answer them, you have to answer the question.

A: Well, I don't have to answer all the questions.

THE COURT: No, there might be some questions you don't have to answer.

A: I don't want to answer that.

THE COURT: You cannot pick out which questions you want to answer. (*People v. Zammora* 1942, 1193)

Meanwhile, the publicity assault of the press and the Los Angeles Police Department about the threat of Mexican-American juvenile delinquency was becoming something of a self-fulfilling prophecy. The number of Mexican-American minority teenagers in Los Angeles jail cells increased as police frequently arrested entire groups of youngsters who were socializing on street corners and charged them with vagrancy.

In addition, clashes between military personnel and Zoot suit teenagers were becoming more frequent. Military servicemen saw the Zoot suit as an anti-American symbol; Mexican Americans saw the servicemen wandering in their neighborhoods looking for dates not only as an invasion of territory but also as a blow to their self-respect and an insult to their community.

Both inside and outside the courtroom, the assault against Mexican-American culture and values became even more vocal. Clem Peoples, a deputy sheriff for Los Angeles County for 20 years, a chief investigator at the center of the Díaz murder investigation, and the ensuing dragnet that brought 600 suspects into custody, suddenly became an author in the middle of *People v. Zammora*.

Somehow rejecting the idea that an article on Mexican-American youth crime would not be prejudicial or his actions unethical, Peoples published a piece called "Smashing California's Baby Gangsters" in a second-rate, pulp tabloid called *Sensation* magazine. Peoples' article fit perfectly into the lurid nature of the publication. The young men were, he breathlessly penned, "reckless madbrained young wolves" (Pagán 2003, 91).

Because Peoples' article had not come from one of the usual pulp authors normally featured in *Sensation*, it carried a measure of credibility. It further sensationalized the already prevalent theme proclaimed in the press and from statements issued by law enforcement officials that Mexican gang violence was dangerously on the rise and that the gangs of "wildcats" and "wolves" prowling the city's downtown streets had to be taken down.

As the testimony proceeded, a number of things became clear to the jury members listening to the parade of witnesses. There had been a birthday party held by a Mexican-American family in East Los Angeles to which a large number of family friends had been invited. At the party, a group of uninvited Anglo youths from the Downey Street area had caused some trouble and had been asked to leave. At the same time, a few Mexican-American youths from a neighborhood around 38th Street had gathered at a reservoir location called Sleepy Lagoon and had been attacked by the Downey Street boys.

Later, in an attempt at retribution, the 38th Street youths gathered reinforcements and searched for the Downey Boys, first at the Sleepy Lagoon and then at the location of the party. When they arrived well after midnight, a major fight began, in which a number of individuals were injured. Shortly afterward, a young man was found nearby, suffering from injuries that would cause his death a few hours later.

No one who testified gave any information about how the young man sustained his injuries. As a matter of fact, throughout the entire trial, someone very significant to the case almost seemed to be missing in the story—the youth who died—José Díaz. Little was asked about his activities at the party, his background, his friends, whether he had enemies, whether he was engaged in fighting, or indications of how he might have been attacked. No one saw him at the party after 11:00 P.M. Those at the party gave no evidence as to the cause of his death or who might have been involved. Indeed, some witnesses suggested that Díaz's injuries might have resulted from a fall or being hit by a car. The prosecution simply was painting a picture of a group of gang members engaging in a brawl in which a young man was killed. The prosecution was asking the jury to find them all responsible for his death through a conspiracy.

In painting this picture, the prosecution had no difficulty showing that serious violence had, indeed, taken place at the Williams house. On November 8, the court called to the stand Eleanor Coronado, the married daughter of the Delgadillos whose birthday was the occasion for the party. Through her testimony and those of others it was clear that the mayhem at the house in the early hours of August 3 was vicious and that it included both young men and women:

Q BY MR. BARNES: Who had the knife?

A: Ysmael Parra, and he stabbed Joe. So I thought he was going to kill him, so I grabbed a beer bottle that was lying on the kitchen floor there, and I was going to hit him over the head with it—I was going to hit Ysmael Parra over the head with it, and then some girl from behind me—she was Delia Parra—she grabbed me from behind and she said, "You can't hit my old man like that." Then I started fighting with Delia.

Q: Did you get to swing that beer bottle on the head of Mr. Parra?

A: No, I did not.

Q: Somebody caught it before you could swing it; is that right?

A: Delia Parra caught me from behind and she made me drop the bottle.

Q: Then what happened?

A: Then I started fighting with Delia Parra, and then Ysmael Parra turned around and he saw us, and then he said, "My wife." Then Parra turned around and he hit me and he knocked me down. (*People v. Zammora*, 1942, 2146)

On November 12, the simmering mutual contempt between Fricke and Shibley burst into full flame. Fricke had explicitly given orders on a number of occasions that during recesses, the defendants were not to talk with their attorneys. During an afternoon recess, either Fricke had seen some communication between the defendants and their counsel or someone had told him about it. During the afternoon testimony on November 12, the following exchange ensued:

THE COURT: . . . I want counsel to sit down here a minute. I am just getting thoroughly tired of this situation. I am going to ask counsel to just listen for a moment while the court reads something. I referred on October 21st to the difficulty we were having, by a confusion that was caused—I made this statement: "There is another thing I want stopped very definitely, and that is when we take a recess I want these defendants—there are a large number of them—taken to the prisoners' room and I do not want anybody to stop those prisoners and try to talk to them. If counsel want to talk to their clients they will have to do it at some other time."

Now, I said that and I meant it. I am not going to tolerate any violation of the orders of this court. Counsel who disobey that injunction are guilty of contempt of court. I am not going to proceed in that matter, but if it happens again I am going to take very severe action. I want to call attention to the fact this is the third time I have had to mention it, and it is going to be the last.

While I am talking I want to call counsel's attention to something else, and that is to huddles in the hallway between counsel and witnesses and counsel and members of the families, and also to conversations on the elevators. To my own knowledge that has also been violated, and if that order is violated something is going to happen. . . .

MR. SHIBLEY: If your Honor please, I still make the request, and I do wish to make a showing in the record here, that it is relatively impossible for me to conduct my defense of my defendants without being able to consult with them and sit with them, and talk with them during the presentation of the prosecution's case. I am also going to say this for the record: That the defendants in the position in which they are seated are seated in a column of seats in very much the fashion as prisoners in a prisoners' box, and the jury are looking at them all the time sitting in that prisoners' box. And I say, for the record, that seated as they are, the purpose of it or, at least, the effect of it is to prejudice these defendants in the minds of the jury. And I am going to cite your Honor's action in having them seated there and in refusing them the right to consult with counsel during the trial and talk with their attorneys during the trial in the courtroom, as misconduct, and ask the jury be admonished to disregard the fact that they are seated in the place that they are, and ask your Honor to point out to the jury the fact they are seated there does not impute that they are guilty or that there is any suspicion that they are guilty of a crime. (*People v. Zammora*, 1942, 2799–2800)

Following Shibley's statement, a burst of applause broke out among some of the spectators. An infuriated Fricke immediately ordered the bailiff to sort out which members of the audience had applauded. They were held for contempt of court.

National and International Concerns

As the news of the trial reached out from Los Angeles, it began to cause increasing consternation among officials of the Roosevelt administration in Washington. The building anti-Mexican hysteria surrounding the Sleepy Lagoon case and its carnival-like atmosphere clearly had possible implications for the U.S. war effort and its need to keep close alliances in Latin America. The growing animosity toward Mexican Americans ran directly counter to Roosevelt's so-called Good Neighbor Policy that the president and his diplomatic team had been cultivating for nearly a decade.

When Roosevelt took office in 1933, he was determined to improve relations with the nations of Central and South America. Under his leadership, the United States emphasized cooperation and trade rather than military force to maintain stability in the hemisphere. It was an overt attempt to distance the United States from earlier interventionist policies.

In his inaugural address on March 4, 1933, Roosevelt declared: "In the field of world policy I would dedicate this nation to the policy of the good neighbor—the neighbor who resolutely respects himself and, because he does so, respects the rights of others." Roosevelt's secretary of state, Cordell Hull, participated in the Montevideo Conference of December 1933, where he backed a declaration favored by most nations of the Western Hemisphere: "No state has the right to intervene in the internal or external affairs of another" ("Good Neighbor Policy" 1933).

The issue of relations with Mexico was especially critical as the United States entered World War II. Damaging labor shortages affected many areas of the economy, especially agriculture production and the workforce necessary to pick crops in the harvest fields. On July 23, 1942, a week before the death of José Díaz, the United States and Mexico signed an agreement that became Public Law 78 to enable temporary workers to cross the border into the United States during harvest seasons and then be returned to Mexico. It was called the Bracero Program.

A boon to American growers, the system was fraught with harsh treatment to the migrant workers. But Mexican nationals, eager for work, were willing to take those jobs for meager pay and many looked back on the experience as an opportunity they would not have otherwise had in Mexico. Although, many would also look back on their experiences with much bitterness, in 1942 the new program represented a high diplomatic mark for the two nations allied in the war effort.

Thus, the Sleepy Lagoon trial stirred special interest in Washington, especially at the newly created Office of War Information (OWI). One of the OWI's central missions was to coordinate the release of war news and to disseminate a propaganda campaign to inspire patriotic fervor in the American public for the war effort. Led by Elmer Davis, the OWI, since its inception in the summer of 1942, already had concerns about the building animosity in Los Angeles between the city officials and the press toward the Mexican-American community. Worried that such civil distress might result in adverse publicity for the United States, not only in Mexico but also in other Latin American countries, OWI officials sent to Los Angeles a young journalist named Alan Cranston who had worked for the International News Service covering events in a number of European countries. Cranston would later become a U.S. Senator from California.

Cranston traveled in the summer of 1942 in an effort to cool tensions. He met with city officials. He visited managing editors and publishers of all four of the major newspapers in the city and encouraged them to stop using the term "Mexican" to describe the so-called crime wave that they were trumpeting in the pages of their dailies. Although Cranston was encouraged by their expressed willingness to tone down the racial and cultural angle of the Sleepy Lagoon case and the incidents of Mexican-American youth delinquency, his efforts did not yield the desired result. As they had promised, the papers now rarely used the term "Mexican" to refer to the defendants and other Mexican Americans involved in incidents in the city. Instead, they increasingly used the words "pachuco" and "Zoot suiters." The change did not help the escalating tensions. It may have made them worse.

Cranston also met with District Attorney John Dockweiler and expressed his concern that the trial could have deleterious propaganda effects on the war effort if it became clear that the defendants had not been given due process. After all, this was the first time in the history of California, he pointed out that "so many people have been charged with first degree murder for the death of one person." If all of the boys received stiff sentences, Cranston told Dockweiler, the repercussions of outrage from the Mexican government and the rhetorical ammunition that the trial would give the enemies of the United States would be extremely unfortunate. Dockweiler seemed agreeable. Cranston wrote back to Washington: "He eagerly agreed, said that he was personally avoiding the courtroom to keep publicity of the trial to a minimum, and that he had decided to narrow the real case down to two of the youths. He said that before the case goes to the jury they might ask for a general reduction in the charges, and that in any case he would tell the Judge about the dangerous consequences of too stiff a verdict. I am convinced that this takes the trial out of the danger zone." Unfortunately, Dockweiler's assurances to Cranston meant nothing. The charges were not reduced. The trial was in no way out of the danger zone (Cranston 1942).

Henry Leyvas on the Stand

On December 4, 1942, Henry Leyvas took the stand. In the eyes of the prosecution and through its presentation in the case, Leyvas was the ringleader, the brains behind both the gang from 38th Street and the conspiracy to commit murder. No one from 38th Street had admitted that an organized gang even existed or hinted that Leyvas was a gang leader. Nevertheless, the prosecution, the police, and the Los Angeles newspapers had all anointed him as the sinister kingpin of a band of vicious criminal thugs.

Through a laborious questioning and cross-examination, Leyvas insisted
he had been severely beaten by the police during his original interrogation,
that he feared he was being singled out as a murderer, and that he lied to
protect himself before the grand jury. And now at the trial, he took question
after question about his lies before the grand jury, about the injury to his
leg a week before José Díaz's death, about the beating he and his friends
took from the Downey boys at the Sleepy Lagoon, and about the fight that
ensued at the Delgadillo house when the 38th Street youth went back looking for revenge.

In all of this questioning, throughout the seemingly interminable objections and judicial rulings and lawyerly wrangling, something continued
to be clearly missing—any vigorous effort to discuss the victim of the
murder—José Díaz—whether Leyvas had seen him that night, if he was
involved in any violence directed toward Díaz, or if he had heard comments
from others about the fatal attack on the victim.

The entire examination of Leyvas, as it had been for others involved
in the fateful night at Sleepy Lagoon, was simply to place Leyvas and the
others at the general scene of the homicide. The prosecution seemed to believe that it was enough to show that Leyvas with his gang from 38th Street
was involved in violence in the vicinity of the murder and that the entire
gang could be held responsible for it. Given the overlying factors influenc-
ing the trial, that strategy appeared destined for success.

The Convictions

The trial lasted 13 weeks. The transcript of the testimony had grown to
over 6,000 pages. On December 15, 1942, both sides closed their arguments
in the case of *People v. Zammora.*

After the court adjourned for three weeks over the holidays, on January 7, Judge Fricke gave his summation to the jury. His instructions included the following:

> I would suggest this to the jury: That upon first arriving in the jury
> room, instead of endeavoring to immediately decide the ultimate
> question of guilty or not guilty, that you discuss among yourselves
> the basic, outstanding and principal facts of the case. I think you will
> find that your duties will be simplified if you take those matters as
> to which there can be no dispute. There seems to be no particular
> disagreement but what certain defendants went out to the Sleepy La-
> goon earlier in the evening, that they there suffered punishment and

that they went back thereafter, a larger crowd, and went up in the vicinity of the Williams ranch when certain things occurred there. One of the questions, of course, you are going to have to decide is whether there was any conspiracy. I think if you will take the matter step by step—I am not going into the matter in detail with you—and try to follow it out in the way in which it is claimed this occurred, you will find you can agree on one subject and then another: you will find it will simplify your conclusions in agreeing upon your verdicts. (*People v. Zammora*, 1942, 5926–5927)

On January 12, 1943, after deliberating for five days, the jury returned verdicts. Seventeen young Mexican Americans were convicted. Three of the defendants were found guilty of first-degree murder: Henry Leyvas, Jose "Chepe" Ruiz, and Robert Telles. They were sent to San Quentin Prison with a life sentence. Nine were found guilty of second-degree murder: Ysmael Parra, Manuel Reyes, Victor Thompson, Henry Ynostroza, Gus Zamora, Manuel Delgado, John Matuz, Jack Melendez, and Angel Padilla. They were sent to San Quentin for five years to life. Five of the 17 defendants were found guilty of assault. Andrew Acosta, Eugene Carpio, Victor Segobia, Benny Alvarez, and Joe Valenzuela. They would serve time in a county jail. Five of the 22 individuals indicted were acquitted: Joe Carpio, Richard Gastelum, Edward Grandpre, Ruben Pena, and Daniel Verdugo.

Five young women of the 38th Street neighborhood who were with the boys on the night of the murder at Sleepy Lagoon and who refused to testify against the boys in the trial were sent to the Ventura School for Girls, a women's reformatory, without benefit of trial or jury. They included Lorena Encinas and Bertha Aguilar.

Following the verdicts, the defense attorneys began to make a plea for a retrial based on the flood of prejudicial and racial publicity surrounding the case, on dubious judicial rulings, and on a host of other issues. Judge Fricke defiantly waved off the criticism: "I haven't the slightest doubt in my own mind," he declared, "not only that the evidence fully sustains all of the verdicts but would sustain the conviction of offenses of higher grades than those cases in which the jury returned verdicts of less than first degree murder and less than assault with a deadly weapon with intent to commit murder." Glowering at Shibley and the other attorneys for the defense who wanted to continue their plea, Fricke said simply, "I am afraid you are running into a brick wall" (Weitz2010, 109).

Years later, reflecting on the trial and its legacy, George Shibley said, "Its effect on constitutional law was felt throughout the United States. . . . This has got to be one of the most outstanding cases of open police brutality ever recorded in this country. "Shibley pointed out that *People v. Zammora* would lead to subsequent court actions that would overturn the kind of outrageous judicial actions displayed in the case, especially in one particular. "As a result of this case," Shibley said, "the court held that a defendant had a right to participate in his own defense. . . .[T]he court said that if the courtroom was not big enough to enable defendants to sit with their attorneys, then some place must be found that is big enough. In short, it has made it almost impossible to hold mass trials" ("George Shibley," PBS 2002).

References

Barajas, Frank. 2006. "The Defense Committees of Sleepy Lagoon: A Convergent Struggle against Fascism, 1942–1944)." *Axtlan: A Journal of Chicano Studies* (Spring). http://history.msu.edu/hst327/files/2009/05/Defense-Committees-of-Sleepy-Lagoon.pdf.

Cranston, Alan to Elmer Davis. November 28, 1942. Record Group 208: Records of the Office of War Information, Records of the Director, Subversive Activities, 1942–1943, National Archives and Records Administration, College Park, MD.

"George Shibley." 2002. "Zoot Suit Riots, PBS American Experience." http://www.pbs.org/wgbh/amex/zoot/eng_peopleevents/p_shibley.html.

"Good Neighbor Policy." 1933. http://history.state.gov/milestones/1921–1936/GoodNeighbor.

Mazón, Mauricio. 1984. *The Zoot-Suit Riots: The Psychology of Symbolic Annihilation*. Austin: University of Texas Press.

Pagán, Edwardo Obregón. 2003. *Murder at the Sleepy Lagoon: Zoot Suits, Race, and Riot in Wartime L.A.* Chapel Hill: The University of North Carolina Press.

People v. Zammora. 1942. "Transcript of Testimony." October 13–22. http://content.cdlib.org/view?docId=hb6199p2dh;NAAN=13030&doc.view=frames&chunk.id=vol1&toc.depth=1&toc.id=vol1&brand=calisphere.

Weitz, Mark. 2010. *The Sleepy Lagoon Murder Case: Race Discrimination and Mexican-American Rights*. Lawrence: University Press of Kansas.

Zoot Suit Riots. 2001. PBS American Experience. http://www.pbs.org/wgbh/amex/zoot/eng_peopleevents/e_murder.html.

FOUR

The Sleepy Lagoon Defense Committee

As the young Mexican-American men convicted of the Sleepy Lagoon murder were sent to jail—nine of them to San Quentin prison—the poisonous atmosphere against pachucos and Zoot suiters in Los Angeles grew ominous. Stories continued to appear in the newspapers and pulp tabloids about the Mexican crime wave, and about Zoot suit "Goon Squads" and "Pachuco Killers." The scope of the reporting suggested a surge of gang violence. Some police officers fed stories to reporters about confrontations with Zoot suiters and the dangers they represented. The reporters took it all down with little or no corroborating evidence. An editor at the *Los Angeles Times*, later reflecting on the coverage, said, "At the time, we thought we were objectively covering the news" (Peiss 2011, 114).

The trial itself exacerbated tensions already high between U.S. servicemen who often ventured into areas of the city where the Zoot suiters also hung out. The occasional incidents of harassment and minor fighting between small groups became more frequent.

Servicemen saw the verdicts in the trial as vindication of their notions that pachucos were nothing but thugs and criminals. Among youngsters in the Mexican-American community, the trial was further evidence that the entire system was rigged.

For the convicted young men, a dreaded uncertainty awaited. Attorneys tried to assure them that they had good reason to hope that the outcome of the trial could be overturned on appeal. But the youngsters had seen the glares from the jury box and heard the hate-filled words of the prosecution. They already knew about the general attitudes of the Anglo community—the usual epithets, the exclusion, the derision. The teenagers and young men in their early 20s who faced long prison terms saw their lives shattered. Confused and scared, they needed friends.

Alice Greenfield

In the early 1990s, Alice Greenfield McGrath told the prize-winning author, historian, and radio broadcaster Studs Terkel about her early life. When she was 23, she volunteered at the Congress of Industrial Organizations (CIO) with ambitions to become a labor organizer. Soon, she was suffering from pleurisy. In the days before antibiotics, she said later, "they put you in a hospital and hoped you would live." She did. She told Terkel that while she was recovering "a CIO lawyer working on the Sleepy Lagoon case asked me to help him summarize the day's testimony. As I read it, I became so enraged, so appalled by the hatred of this judge for the defendants, his insulting of the defense attorneys, his helping the prosecutor, that I decided to go down and sit in at the trial. It was even worse than what I read" (Terkel 1996, 361). Thus began her tireless advocacy on behalf of 22 Mexican-American young men. The lawyer she referred to in her interview with Studs Terkel was George Shibley.

The daughter of Russian Jewish immigrants, she was born Alice Greenfield in Calgary, Canada, in 1917. She never finished community college because her family could not afford it. After taking a series of low-paying jobs, including one at a candy factory where she earned 25 cents an hour, she managed to find work at the CIO, where she met Shibley. For Greenfield, this young, progressive reformer, the Sleepy Lagoon murder case represented everything that drove her passion for the underdog—an obvious witch hunt against poor, Mexican-American youngsters who had been vilified by the public, the press, and the police; a trial that reeked of injustice; and the incarceration of an extraordinarily large number of young men in a single trial for long prison sentences. She committed herself to helping them win their freedom on appeal. She began to visit them in prison, giving assurances that many people were rallying to their cause.

Xenophobia: A Peril to Wartime Alliances

In April 1943, Franklin Roosevelt became the first U.S. president in 34 years to meet face to face with a president of Mexico. So vital did Roosevelt consider the wartime alliance with Mexico that he traveled to Monterrey and met with Mexican president Manuel Ávila Camacho.

In his remarks, Roosevelt compared such Mexican heroes as Benito Juárez and Miguel Hidalgo to America's founding leaders, George Washington and Thomas Jefferson. Roosevelt spoke of the common values shared by the two countries and the need to remain tied in mutual determination and respect in combating Axis aggression and atrocities. The attacks against the Allies, Roosevelt declared,

> did not find the Western Hemisphere unprepared. The twenty-one free republics of the Americas during the past ten years have devised a system of international cooperation which has become a great bulwark in the defense of our heritage and our future. That system, whose strength is now evident to the most skeptical, is based primarily upon a renunciation of the use of force and the enshrining of international justice and mutual respect as the governing rule of conduct by all nations. (Roosevelt 1943)

It is time, Roosevelt said, that every American citizen and every citizen in Mexico realize the common bonds between the two countries (Roosevelt 1943).

The Sleepy Lagoon case and the anti-Mexican hysteria raised in Los Angeles threatened to damage those common bonds. During the trial the Citizens' Committee for the Defense of Mexican American Youth (CCDMAY), started by labor activist LaRue McCormick, worked to raise money in an attempt to counteract the one-sided adverse publicity, the stories that day after day portrayed to the public a scathing portrait of the defendants. The CCDMAY hosted numerous gatherings to raise money for them.

From the earliest days after the verdicts and sentences rocked the world of the convicted boys, the CCDMAY focused on establishing a team to prepare the appeal. It published a short pamphlet called "We Have Not Yet Begun to Fight." Proclaiming that the Sleepy Lagoon boys had been railroaded by anti-Mexican hysteria and judicial misconduct, the document also stressed another theme that would add to the arsenal of charges to be used in the appeal—that the trial itself and the anti-Mexican xenophobia rampant in the city could hurt the war effort. "The effect of these convictions, like the effect of the long series of mass arrests, persecutions, and police brutalities against the Mexican-American people," the CCDMAY declared, "may have very serious consequences. . . . [M]istreatment of minorities is an Achilles' heel vulnerable to all manner of Axis insinuation" (Weitz 2010, 115).

That insinuation had already begun. On January 13, Axis radio carried a message in Spanish to a number of Latin American countries, especially Mexico. It told of the guilty convictions of 17 Mexican boys for one crime. It talked about the detention camps in which Japanese Americans were languishing. It asked whether this was the kind of justice that a "Good Neighbor" such as Uncle Sam dispenses to his own people. This kind of attack by the wartime enemies of the United States worried the Roosevelt administration determined to keep unity among Latin American allies.

In Mexico, a fascist group known as the Sinarquistas, had been organized by Adolph Hitler's German government in 1936. It had a membership estimated at nearly 2,000 in Mexico as well as operatives in several southwestern states of the United States. The Sinarquistas seized on the defamation of the press against Mexican Americans in Los Angeles as well as the Sleepy Lagoon trial as evidence that democracy in the United States was a sham. Why should the Mexican government support the U.S. war effort if Mexican Americans in the United States were treated so shamelessly?

Racial intolerance against Mexican Americans, the CCDMAY charged, emboldened the Sinarquistas and its fascist and Nazi supporters. If the United States valued its support of its Mexican and Latin American allies in the war effort, the CCDMAY argued, the debasement of the Mexican-American population in the press, in the courts, and on the streets must cease.

On March 3, 1943, the CCDMAY issued a press release explaining the hostility and discrimination which the Mexican-American community had faced. "Despite all the obstacles and difficulties," the statement read, "the Mexican-American population is participating in the war program. Hundreds of thousands of Mexican-American youths have gone as volunteers into the armed forces of the United States. Other hundreds of thousands are now at work in factories, shipyards, and fields, producing for war. They are entering the State Guard, American Red Cross, and other civilian defense organizations" ("Social Conditions" 1943).

Soon, the CCDMAY sponsored a conference in Los Angeles to discuss the trial and the racial tensions in the city. Both Mexican consuls in Los Angeles attended as did a number of diplomatic and civil liberties spokesmen. George Shibley gave a firsthand view of the trial proceedings. Since the advent of the CCDMAY during the trial, the organization had solicited support from over 50 organizations, including unions, churches, and fraternal and youth groups. One central figure at the conference was a determined and fierce fighter against the racism reflected in the trial and its publicity.

Carey McWilliams

One of the most notable muckraking progressive writers of the 20th century, Carey McWilliams wrote over 200 articles and nine influential books between 1939 and 1950 alone. His writings and activism on issues relating to labor, race, and ethnicity made him a celebrated nemesis to right-wing, conservative political leaders and business interests, especially after the Sleepy Lagoon murder case.

Born in Steamboat Springs, Colorado, McWilliams earned a law degree in 1927 from the University of Southern California and began a legal career that introduced him to individuals and cases involving the rights of the powerless. From 1939 to 1942, he headed California's Commission of Immigration and Housing where he fought to increase inspections of labor camps and other reforms. Soon, McWilliams became the growers' most persistent critic, a man many of California's growers acidly called "Agricultural Pest Number One." His research and work on California migratory labor, especially the books *Factories in the Field* and *North from Mexico*, mightily influenced a young community organizer named Cesar Chavez as he began his quest to form a union of farmworkers.

At the CCDMAY conference, many speakers emphasized the need to further broaden the number of groups, organizations, and members who could actively support the efforts to free the young men not only with financial donations but also with much-needed publicity. Soon after the meeting, the organization changed its name to the Sleepy Lagoon Defense Committee (SLDC). Carey McWilliams, whose term in California state government was coming to an end, agreed to act as its national chairman.

McWilliams took the job saying that the new SLDC should seek the help of not only the labor, business, and the motion picture industry but also the African-American supporters who understood the challenges ahead for a large portion of the American population facing prejudice and discrimination. He also demanded a clean accounting of donations and expenditures and the use of auditors to ensure that there would be no financial irregularities that could compromise the committee's efforts.

Soon after the reorganization under the leadership of McWilliams, he asked Alice Greenfield to become executive secretary. She said later, "I came to the [Sleepy Lagoon Defense] Committee having no recognizable or apparent skills for doing anything except running the mimeograph machine, stuffing envelopes. . . . But I dealt myself in. I just wanted to be part of this" ("Alice McGrath" 2002).

"I was very timid but very committed," Greenfield recalled later about McWilliams's offer. "I told him, 'I've never done anything like that before.' And he said the four words that changed my life: 'And now you will'" ("A Voice for Those without" 2003).

Greenfield began to visit the prisoners regularly at San Quentin. On May 3, 1943, Henry Leyvas wrote to Greenfield:

Am writing these lines to express my appreciation for the efforts you and the committee have taken in the behalf of our defense. And I wish that you would thank each and every one for me, for all they have been doing for us, also tell them that I love them all because they are helping me, and for putting their hand into my heaped-up heart and passing over all the little foolish weak thing, that you can't help dimly seeing there. And for bringing out into the light all the beautiful thing about me, that no one had cared to look quite far enough to find. (Leyvas 1943)

Following the trial, the able George Shibley, who had proceeded in his defense in preparation for an appellate case, was eager to continue, convinced that the court's actions had violated numerous legal demands and precedents. Unfortunately, shortly after the court's decision, Shibley was drafted to serve in the military. McWilliams and his fellow SLDC leaders looked for a replacement. They struck appellate gold.

Ben Margolis

Prominent and highly skilled, 33-year-old Ben Margolis was the son of Russian immigrants who spent his early years on New York's East Side. His father, a house painter, was a member of the International Workers Order (IWO), a socialist organization. Margolis followed in the family's political bent, becoming a leading labor and civil rights attorney. With a law degree from Hastings School of Law, University of California, Margolis began to practice in San Francisco and was in the process of moving to Los Angeles when he was contacted by McWilliams.

After examining the transcripts of the original trial, Margolis said that in his entire career he had never seen such unremitting bias and persecution of defendants. With deft precision, Margolis began to slice the case against the men into the bits of sloppy police work, unsubstantiated rumors, judicial improprieties, and racism that put 17 young men behind bars. Aggressive and combative, he became strongly committed to the defense of the imprisoned Mexican Americans.

As Margolis began to immerse himself in the details of the case and to build upon the groundwork for the appeal laid by George Shibley, McWilliams and others went to work building the structure of the SLDC.

Josefina Fierro de Bright was especially active in establishing the committee. Born in Mexico in 1920, the daughter of a bordera who served meals to migrant workers in Madera, California, she briefly studied at UCLA. But soon her passion and energy drove her into community organizing activities. She became executive secretary of El Congreso, the first national Latino civil rights organization. She fought against racism in public schools, against the numerous bans against Mexican Americans in using public recreational facilities, and against prejudicial mistreatment by law enforcement against the Mexican-American community, especially its young people and especially those who wore Zoot suits.

Humberto Noé "Bert" Corona, the son of Mexican immigrants, also joined the cause. Active in Mexican-American civil rights activities while a student at the University of Southern California, Corona, by 1941, had been elected president of the Los Angeles chapter of the International Longshoremen's and Warehousemen's Union Local 26. McWilliams, Fierro de Bright, Corona, and others helped persuade groups such as the California executive committee of the CIO to join the Sleepy Lagoon defense effort. Union members began to circulate information and solicit contributions to help defray the expenses of the appeal. Following the lead of the SLDC, the CIO appealed to the patriotic fervor of its members, pointing out that the Sleepy Lagoon trial was being used as ammunition by enemies of the United States to persuade Latin American allies that U.S. democracy was a shameless misnomer and that the mistreatment of Mexican Americans in Los Angeles was hard evidence. McWilliams and other SLDC members soon gained support from church groups and leftist organizations and individuals.

In early April 1943, Alice Greenfield produced the first issue of a newsletter for the SLDC called *Appeal News*. The paper not only began to spread the word about the injustice of the trial and the efforts of the SLDC to prepare for the appellate challenge but it also became a vehicle to let the young men in prison know of the determination of the organization to right the wrong committed against them. She told them that it was essential that they maintain a spotless record while incarcerated and encouraged them to begin a correspondence with her and others.

Shortly after the first issue of the newsletter was printed, Greenfield received a letter from Henry Ynostroza from San Quentin. "I had gave up hope," Ynostroza said, "but when I received this letter I said if the people are trying to help well I got to have hope . . . I know that all of us up here will try and make a good record" (Weitz 2010, 127).

As Greenfield began to make visits to San Quentin and began a correspondence with the imprisoned young men, and as McWilliams and others aggressively sought increased support from local labor unions and Mexican-American groups, the city of Los Angeles was about to experience an eruption of racial and cultural antagonism and hatred that epitomized the issues grounded in the Sleepy Lagoon murder case.

References

"Alice McGrath." 2002. Zoot Suit Riots, PBS American Experience. http://www
.pbs.org/wgbh/amex/zoot/eng_peopleevents/p_mcgrath.html.

Leyvas, Henry to Alice Greenfield. 1943."Mat 3." Zoot Suit Riots, PBS American
Experience, Primary Sources.http://www.pbs.org/wgbh/amex/zoot/eng_filmmore/
ps_03.html.

Peiss, Kathy. 2011. *Zoot Suit: The Enigmatic Career of an Extreme Style*. Philadelphia: University of Pennsylvania Press.

Roosevelt, Franklin. 1943."United Effort for a Better World: Interdependence of
all Nations." Broadcast from Monterrey, Mexico (April 20). http://www.ibiblio.org/
pha/policy/1943/1943–04–20a.html.

"Social Conditions of Mexican-American Youth. March2, 1943. http://www.oac
.cdlib.org/view?docId=hb1m3nb420&brand=oac4&doc.view=entire_text.

Terkel, Studs. 1996. *Coming of Age: The Story of Our Century by Those Who've
Lived It*. New York: St. Martin's Griffin.

"A Voice for Those without." 2003. *Perspectives*, Autumn. http://www.artsci
.washington.edu/news/Autumn03/McGrath.htm.

Weitz, Mark. 2010. *The Sleepy Lagoon Murder Case: Race Discrimination and
Mexican-American Rights*. Lawrence: University Press of Kansas.

FIVE

The Riots

As CLASHES between servicemen and Mexican-American youngsters increased ominously in the spring of 1943, hostility between the groups grew more intense. Navy officials later claimed that from the beginning of the year, there had been over 50 confrontations between Zoot suiters and sailors.

As it had done throughout the Sleepy Lagoon trial, the Hearst Press dailies—the *Examiner* and *Herald Express*—along with other papers, continued a drumbeat of damaging character assassination against Mexican-American Zoot suiters. They were gangsters and hoodlums, and no-accounts who had spawned a crime wave that threatened the entire well-being of the city of Los Angeles. They were a menacing force that had to be put down.

In Venice, a beach resort town west of Los Angeles, local high school students had begun to complain that Zoot suit–wearing Mexican Americans had begun to take over the beachfront. On a day in the middle of May at Venice's Aragon Ballroom, a group of sailors, claiming that a serviceman had been stabbed, began to fight with Mexican Americans outside the facility. With an estimated crowd of 500 cheering on the sailors, the fighting continued until 2:00 A.M. When the police arrived, they simply arrested many of the Mexican Americans. A police officer later explained that "everybody was upset with jittery emotions wanting to let off steam . . . and the zoot suiters were the safety valve. You'll admit the only thing we could do to break it up was to arrest the Mexican kids . . . our actions are limited by what the public thinks" (Pagán 2003, 164).

On the evening of May 31, a group of sailors and soldiers approached some Mexican-American women on Main Street in Los Angeles. A group of young men wearing Zoot suits suddenly arrived on the scene. The ensuing battle between the two groups—with bottles and rocks as available

In the early days of the Zoot Suit Riots, most of the sailors who began their nightly quest to demean Zoot suit–wearing Mexican Americans (such as the ones pictured) chose sticks and clubs as their weapons of choice. The attacks represented a kind of ritualistic humiliation, not aimed to kill Latinos but to put them in their place both by beatings and destroying their uniform—the Zoot suit. The attacks were to demonstrate dominance of the Anglo soldiers over the alien foreigners who challenged that dominance. (Library of Congress)

weapons—left Seaman Second Class Joe Dacy Coleman unconscious with a serious head injury. The sailors carried Coleman back to the naval armory. He had a broken jaw. Over the next two days, as the stories about Coleman spread among the sailors, they decided that once and for all they would put an end to the menace of the Zoot suiters.

Day 1—Thursday, June 3

On Thursday night, June 3, at the Central Police Station on First Street, a group of about 35 Mexican-American youngsters from the Alpine area of the city assembled with a number of police officials to discuss the problems of juvenile delinquency. Some of the boys wore Zoot suits; others did not. But the meeting seemed to signal a willingness of city officials to try to recognize the atmosphere of growing up in the poor immigrant neighborhoods of the east side of the city and to encourage mutual understanding.

The meeting was soon interrupted by rumors that a large contingent of sailors was in Alpine looking for Zoot suiters. Nevertheless, the meeting continued.

Meanwhile, about 50 sailors carrying sticks, clubs, and heavy belts were indeed in the Mexican-American neighborhood. At the Carmen Theater, sailors walked up and down the aisles looking for anyone wearing a Zoot suit. After dragging many young men from their seats, they tore the suits off the boys, beat them with clubs and fists, and then set their clothes on fire. In some cases, the sailors looked for the nearest trash cans and dumped the Zoot suiters in them.

Rudy Sánchez, one of the boys who had been at the Central Police Station and arrived to see the bloodied teenagers, later wrote: "This is supposed to be a free country. We don't go around beating up people just because we don't like the clothes they wear. . . . On who's side is the Navy on anyway, Uncle Sam or Hitler?" (Pagán 2003, 171).

This was organized, premeditated violence. This was the beginning of the Zoot Suit Riots.

Day 2—Friday, June 4

In the early hours of Friday evening, some Mexican-American Zoot suiters drove cars back and forth in front of the armory, taunting sailors and guards. They did not realize the force that was about to be employed against them. The servicemen had planned a coordinated assault. It involved taxicabs.

At the Naval Reserve Armory, the officer of the day reported to his commanding officer:

At about 2120 June 4, 1943, I received a phone call from the Yellow Cab Co., asking who had called for twenty (20) cabs, and why they were all congregating in one section of the City. My answer was that no official call had gone from this station for any cabs that evening, and that I did not know who the men in the cabs were, or what their destination was. (Officer of the Day)

This would not be warfare in the usual sense. Although servicemen had planned an organized attack, they were not carrying guns. They were not out to kill. After all, killing the Zoot suiters would be of such an extreme criminal nature that the murderers would surely be punished and their own lives ruined. Instead, they gathered pipes, tire irons, knives, barbells, clubs, and other assorted instruments. They invaded Mexican-American communities with the intent to humiliate and degrade. As in the first few encounters on the previous night, they would inflict beatings, tear off the clothes of Zoot suiters, set the clothes on fire, and cut their hair. This was a kind of ritualistic attack, a demeaning act of force to cause ridicule and shame—an act showing the Mexicans just who they were dealing with when they insulted or challenged the power of white American soldiers. Theirs was a mission to assert superior identity and to demoralize those who would dare mock it.

About 200 sailors formed a caravan of about 20 cars and taxis to hunt Mexican-American youth dressed in Zoot suits. But this time, the attack was coordinated to strike within the neighborhoods of Mexican Americans. No longer was this neutral ground. The servicemen were going on an offensive mission into the enemy's home turf. Through downtown Los Angeles and out to the east side as far as Boyle Heights and Belvedere Gardens they rode in a kind of search-and-destroy operation looking for those in enemy clothes. Sailors moved through the barrio, breaking into bars and stores. They stopped streetcars and pulled out Mexican Americans from their seats onto the street.

Inside a drugstore at First and Rowan in Belvedere, two 17-year-old boys and an 18-year-old were assaulted by several sailors carrying corded ropes with pieces of metal attached to the ends. According to the report of the sheriff's office, the boys said that one of sailors tried to coax the three out onto the street. When they refused, "several more sailors—10 or 15 in number—. . . proceeded to beat up victims with the weapons named." At the General Hospital, one of victims was treated for a severe cut on the back of the head and the other for a fractured nose ("Sheriff's Office, First Report," June 4, 1943).

Los Angeles police did not take serious steps to prevent the roving bands of sailors. Indeed, some of the police began a unique kind of mop-up process. They would follow the soldiers, wait until the servicemen beat and stripped the Zoot suiters, and then swoop in and arrest many of the Mexican Americans on grounds of disturbing the peace. When asked why the injured and beaten became the criminals, one policeman simply said he and others in the force were not going to pick on servicemen.

Day 3—Saturday, June 5

On Saturday morning, after two nights of attacks, Commander Martin Dickinson of the Naval Training School told the servicemen under his command that the U.S. Navy did not condone attacks on civilians. He said that he was ordering a night patrol along the streets leading to the armory to protect those sailors heading out and returning from liberty.

Commander Dickinson's words and actions did nothing to deter day three of the attacks. Although a number of Zoot suiters attempted to launch counterattacks, they were, on most occasions, woefully outnumbered. Long caravans of cabs and private cars now toured the Mexican sections of Los Angeles. Every movie house, nightclub, bar, or other business establishment they encountered became a target to search. On one occasion, the servicemen broke the jaw of a 12-year-old boy. In the hospital, the boy said, "So our guys wear tight bottoms on their pants and those bums wear wide bottoms. Who the hell they fighting, Japs or us?" ("Zoot-Suit War" 1943, 18).

Soldiers, sailors, and marines now marched four abreast in parts of downtown and in Mexican-American barrios. One squad of sailors burst into a dance hall sorting out Zoot suiters, dragged them to the street, and stripped off their clothes. The brigades of servicemen were now aided by squads of police who cruised through Mexican-American neighborhoods and rounded up 44 youths. Police records began to show the cost of the first day of action—over 100 hospitalized with serious injuries; over 100 bookings at Central Jail; another 400 arrested and held without charges until the easing of tensions. Newspaper cameramen swarmed the jail snapping shots of black-haired youngsters behind bars for the next day's news consumption.

An African-American college student was walking with three Mexican Americans when a cab filled with four marines stopped: "Let's give those 4-F zoot suiters some combat training," one of the marines barked out. A fight ensued. When the police arrived, he, along with the three Mexican Americans, was taken into custody. He later recalled, "My guilt as a zoot-suiter was determined by a careful measurement of my trousers. My trousers proved me innocent. However, one of the officers phoned my mother and warned her that I should not be seen in public with Mexicans who apparently were zoot-suiters" (Peiss 2011, 122).

A Mexican American named Ralph Estrada later recalled:

A buddy of mine and I were in downtown Los Angeles when three sailors beat us up. They didn't do too well, but when three more joined them, we ran like rabbits . . . sailors would come into my neighborhood. Who were they fighting? We were already enlisted in the service. They were fighting little kids . . . I know because I was one of them. (Rasmussen 2007, 2B)

Day 4—Sunday, June 6

It was on June 6 that the hunt for the Zoot suiters reached a new point of idiocy. How can you tell a Zoot suiter when he or she is not wearing a Zoot suit? When Santa Monica lifeguards received a warning that Zoot suiters were on the beach, Captain George Watkins, chief of the Santa Monica lifeguards, made a search. Clearly frustrated, Captain Watkins reported on the bathers: "Some of them had long hair, which curled up at the back like a drake's tail, but their bathing togs weren't any different from those of the others so we were unable to tell just how many, if any, were gang members" ("Lifeguards" 1943).

Many Mexican-American youths attempted to exact revenge for the attacks. One Zoot suiter revealed that his friends tried to set traps for the sailors, using individual decoys to lure their attackers into a position of vulnerability. "And they let out a cry," the youngster said later, "There they are! There they are! And they came in. As they came in, once they got all the way in, we all came out. I, myself, had a bat. And I used it" ("Zoot Suit Riots" 2002).

Nevertheless, it was mostly the Mexican Americans who not only were getting the worst of the fighting but who were also getting arrested. Sailors in six cars stopped at Brooklyn Avenue and Ramona Boulevard and beat up eight youngsters. They raided a bar on Indiana Street, damaging much of the property. Yet, on Carmelita Street, six Zoot suiters beaten up by the sailors were arrested and taken into custody.

The lead story in the *Los Angeles Times* gloated about the turn of events:

> Those gamin dandies, the zoot suiters, having learned a great moral lesson from servicemen, mostly sailors, who took over their instruction three days ago, are staying home nights. With the exception of 61 youths locked up in County Jail on misdemeanor charges, wearers of the garish costume that has become a hallmark of juvenile delinquency are apparently "unfrocked." ("Zoot Suiters Learn" 1943)

Day 5—Monday, June 7

On June 7, the Naval Armory decided to confine enlisted men to the post and to cancel their leave. Nevertheless, even without the men from the armory, other U.S. Army enlisted men, accompanied by marines and sailors from as far away as San Diego, gathered for another assault on the downtown haunts of Mexican Americans and the barrios. With the number of the invading force estimated at about 1,000 by federal officials in Los Angeles, the servicemen went on a marauding rampage, overwhelming theaters, bars, and dance halls, looking for more elusive Zoot suiters.

In the theaters, the servicemen ordered management to turn on house lights. They then sorted through the patrons aisle by aisle, dragging any dark-skinned individual they could find from the seats. Many were then shoved up to the theater stage, stripped, and beaten.

Down Main Street, the servicemen marched, carrying on the rituals of humiliation. Throughout the night, Mexican-American families attempted to find the whereabouts of their children, checking with the Central Jail and other substations. The *Daily News* seemed particularly pleased with the evening's proceedings: "Meanwhile the drape shape, the reat [*sic*] pleat and the stuff cuff lay soiled and torn in the gutters of Main St. . . . while the characters who affected them as a uniform of their hoodlum careers anguished unhappily" ("6 Zoot Suiters" 1943).

Carey McWilliams, who was on the scene trying to figure ways to stem the violence and, at the same time, get his message through articles out to the general public, later remembered Mexican-American boys coming into the police station saying, "'Charge me with vagrancy or anything, but don't send me out there!' pointing to the streets where other boys, as young as twelve and thirteen years of age, were being beaten and stripped of their clothes." McWilliams had nothing but scorn for the newspapers that featured "huge half-page photographs, showing Mexican boys stripped of their clothes, cowering on the pavements, often bleeding profusely, surrounded by jeering mobs of men and women" (McWilliams 1990, 225).

Meanwhile, most Los Angeles dailies continued to frame the street chaos in terms of the forces of good dressed in military attire and the gangs of hoodlums and anti-Americans sporting the dreaded drapes. The *Daily News*, with especially fulsome prose, pictured Zoot suiters marauding through neighborhoods armed with pipes, broken bottles, and knives terrorizing law-abiding citizens and destroying private property. No effort

should be spared, the paper declared, to clean up the scum in the most ef-
ficient manner and in the shortest time.

And the papers rejoiced in the success. Large photographs of beaten
youngsters, surrounded by smiling and jeering civilians, accompanied the
sensationalist stories.

From the beginning of the riots, the federal office of the Coordinator
of Inter-American Affairs in Los Angles, headed by Churchill Murray, had
worked with military and civilian officials in an attempt to mitigate the violence. It was at the suggestion of Murray that leaves of all sailors stationed
at the armory were cancelled on June 7 and Los Angeles was declared off
limits for military personnel.

Yet, an estimated 1,000 servicemen once again rampaged through the
Mexican district, storming into bars, penny arcades, theaters, streetcars,
stores, and dance halls, again with relative impunity. A number of taxi drivers joined the fun, offering free rides to servicemen and civilians to the
riot areas. With large numbers of civilians now joining in the mayhem and
others milling about, the scene in downtown Los Angeles was increasingly
ominous. Local police were now joined by reserves of military police to
attempt finally to break up a massive downtown mob that some estimated
as high as 5,000 people.

Traffic was hopelessly snarled on parts of S. Main Street and Broadway. Servicemen tore at least 50 Zoot suits off Mexican-American youths
and beat them with unusual ferocity. The thousands of civilians crowding
around to take in the action firsthand cheered on the servicemen and even,
in some cases, joined in the attacks. After all, one Los Angeles paper had
printed a guide on how to "de-zoot" a Zoot suiter. The instructions were
simple. Just grab a Zoot wearer, rip off his clothes, and burn them.

At 10:30 P.M., Chief of Police C.B. Horrall, fearing that the masses on
the street were creating an exceedingly dangerous situation, declared a
general riot alarm. He called to duty every policeman on the force. Navy
shore patrolmen and military police, along with police plain-clothes men,
charged from one area to another as clashes broke out.

As the rampage reached Central Avenue, in the heart of the African-
American community, Loren Miller, a black lawyer and journalist for
the *Los Angeles Sentinel*, called Mayor Fletcher Bowron at City Hall
warning that the beginning incursions heading toward 12th Street would
be met with fierce resistance. "We were going to raise hell," Miller said
later, "and see that anybody that came over in the Negro community
looking around for any trouble was going to find plenty of trouble.
[I] told them that if anybody came up to 12th and Central, somebody

was going to get killed, and I didn't think it was going to be Negroes" (Smith 2006, 17).

Soon, scores of Mexican-American Zoot suiters, many of them young girls, headed to the action to join in a counterattack. "The Battle of 12 Street," as some later called it, was thus joined. Almena Lomas, publisher of the black newspaper the *Los Angeles Tribune*, gained a vantage point from the seat of a soda fountain and watched the clashes almost with disbelief. She especially recalled the fury of some of the Mexican-American girls as they lashed back at servicemen who swarmed the neighborhood.

Another Mexican American later remembered that blacks loaned them cars to bring in additional reinforcements from the barrios. At one point, the servicemen's charge through the streets was turned back. Then, busloads of police arrived and gradually moved amid the slashing broken bottles, baseball bats, tire irons, and other improvised weapons to separate the combatants. They sorted the dark skins from the whites and hauled away Mexican Americans and African Americans to jail.

Rudy Leyvas, the brother of Henry Leyvas, later remembered the fight: "All day we were just transferring guys from the neighborhoods into the city. The black people loaned us their cars to use. We called 'em neighborhoods, not gangs. There was 38th Street, Adams, Clanton, Jug Town, Watts, Jardine. We rounded up at least 500 guys" (Overend 1978, G1).

Thus, the attacks by U.S. servicemen in Los Angeles in June 1943 united for a time groups of Mexican Americans and African Americans in defense against a common enemy—U.S. servicemen in Los Angeles. In the so-called Battle of 12 Street, black and brown kids had come together in mutual defense.

The usual police roundup, which had followed each of the successive nights of street chaos, this time netted more than 200 youngsters, bloodied and "de-frocked," who were booked at the Georgia Street Juvenile Bureau on suspicion of inciting a riot. Although hundreds of servicemen were briefly detained, they were turned over to military authorities and sent back to their bases.

Beatrice Griffith, a social worker and author of books on Mexican-American youth and culture, later wrote about the storm trooper atmosphere pervading downtown Los Angeles: "It was like the whole of Los Angeles had burst out with riots—Central, Watts, Dogtown, Flats, Happy Valley Clanton, Hazard, Mariana, Pecan—all different territories had fights at once. Those sailors and soldiers sure got around in the Mexican streets. . . . All up and down the streets people were standing behind their fences crying and cursing . . . looking past the running sailors, soldiers, and civilians who were hunting their sons and brothers." Griffith quoted one woman who recalled, "One little guy, drunk and yelling names burst into the door, called out, 'Any zoot suiters live here' When he saw us guys and the girls in the room, he stopped a minute, then he yelled, 'Here's a mess of them. Come on guys, come and get 'em.' The fights was on. From the door in the kitchen my mother called them in English, 'you disgrace your uniform'" (Griffith 1948, 11–12).

Al Waxman, editor of the *Eastside Journal,* a Jewish newspaper, had been on the streets in the first days of the riots and was determined to do whatever he could to help stop further violence. He sent out word in the barrios for youngsters to meet with him at the corner of Brooklyn and Indiana. Over 200 showed up and Waxman pleaded with them to resist attempting to fight the servicemen and to go back to their homes. He told them that he had talked to Navy intelligence officers who had assured him that the sailors who had been attacking Zoot suiters would be punished.

Unfortunately, during the meeting, word came that sailors and soldiers were assaulting Mexican Americans on Central Avenue. Waxman again spoke forcefully, imploring the youngsters to stay away from the violence. Most did what he said. But others opted for revenge and headed for battle.

Waxman later described what he saw at Central and 12th. "It was," he said,

> a scene that will long live in my memory. Police were swinging clubs and servicemen were fighting with civilians. . . . Four boys came out of a pool hall. They were wearing the zoot-suits that have become the symbol of a fighting flag. Police ordered them into arrest cars. One refused. He asked: "Why am I being arrested?" The police officer answered with three swift blows of the night-stick across the boy's head and he went down. As he sprawled, he was kicked in the face. Police had difficulty loading his body into the vehicle because he was one-legged and wore a wooden limb. (Waxman 1943)

At another corner Waxman came across a Mexican-American mother crying out, "'Don't take my boy, he did nothing. He's only fifteen years old. Don't take him.' She was struck across the jaw with a night-stick and almost dropped the two and a half year old baby that was clinging in her arms" (Waxman 1943).

While Waxman was holding his meeting, other outbreaks of attacks broke out nearby. By the end of the evening about 35 juvenile Mexican

Americans had been booked at the Georgia police station on suspicion of unlawful assembly and carrying deadly weapons.

At 12th Street and Central, sailors and marines started a bonfire of the Zoot suits, which they had torn off youngsters. The young men made their way home in their underwear.

Day 6—Tuesday, June 8

On June 8, Commander Clarence Fogg, a senior patrol officer in Los Angeles sent a message to his superiors: "Continued Disorder . . . Hundreds of servicemen prowling downtown Los Angeles mostly on foot—disorderly—apparently on prowl for Mexicans. . . . Groups vary in size from 10 to 150 men and scatter immediately when shore patrol approaches. Men found carrying hammock clues, belts, knives" (Mazón 1984, 73).

The message is revealing in two particulars. In the first place, Commander Fogg's use of the word "prowling" is describing the actions of the servicemen. Second, from the substance of the memo, it was clear that the U.S. Navy in this instance had lost control of the men under its command.

As the street violence continued, naval authorities decided to take additional concerted action to defuse the chaos. They did so after a 20-year-old seaman had suffered serious injuries, including a deep cut across the abdomen. The 11th Naval District not only now barred all sailors from taking liberty in the city, but it also decided to place large forces of military police on duty, especially in the area along Main Street where much of the violence had recently centered.

In addition, General Maxwell Murray, Major General, U.S. Army Commanding, finally realizing the full magnitude of the disturbances, called out all reserves of military police and declared Main Street and other areas that had been scenes of violence out of bounds for military personnel.

But the marauding continued and some of the press seemed to take special delight. The *Los Angeles Daily News* tried a bit of jocularity. "Zoot suit panty gangs of hoodlums," it reported, "continued to lose their trousers to servicemen, and in many cases nearly lost what was in 'em" ("Near Martial Law" 1943).

The *Daily News* even took the day's reports of the Los Angeles street violence a step further. Breathlessly, it announced that it had evidence that agents of Adolph Hitler had fomented the violence from the beginning. The whole affair, the paper suggested, was a plot by Axis forces to undermine democracy. Hitler agents had convinced the Mexican-American youth to form Zoot suit gangs and terrorize the community. Hitler agents were also working to convince African Americans and even Anglo-Saxon populations to do likewise. The city was now closer to martial law, claimed the paper, than it had been since John C. Fremont captured California during the Mexican-American War in the 1840s. It was, to say the least, not only a dubious analogy but also an entirely bogus claim.

As the street chaos continued, the place of the Zoot suit itself in the entire dynamic of the riots seemed as elusive as ever. From journalists to sociologists, the debate wore on. Was the Zoot suit merely an adolescent dress fad that would take its place in a long history of adolescent dress

For generations after the Zoot Suit Riots, photographs such as this one of two beaten teenagers on a Los Angeles street surrounded by gawking onlookers would be shocking reminders of the subjugated cultural position in U.S. society that Mexican Americans would have to overcome. Boys such as these, victims of the violence and not their attackers, most often found themselves arrested by police authorities during the riots. Such outrages would help provide reformers and activists with increasing zeal to attempt to provoke social change. (AP Photo)

fads and then disappear? Was it a deep-seated expression of rebellion and rejection of the social and cultural mores of the dominant culture among a group that threatened law and order? One police spokesman had concluded that it had special meaning in Los Angeles. Elsewhere, he said, the Zoot suit was merely a garment "affected by jive-bitten adolescents." In Los Angeles, he insisted, it had become "in the last few months a uniform for roving gangs of Mexican-Americans and Negroes from 16 to 25 years old" (Peiss 2011, 135).

Amid all of the concern, anger, and assignment of blame for the near state of anarchy of their city, the Los Angeles Board of Supervisors announced a decision to stem the unrest: board members decided to close to Mexican-American youths one of the most notorious battlegrounds of juvenile delinquency—Sleepy Lagoon Reservoir. The infamous body of water and its environs were now to be converted into "paid recreation, swimming, bathing, fishing, and picnic area operated by private concern." The board of supervisors assured the public that the area would no longer be a playground for hoodlum troublemaking but would be a fenced area patrolled by guards ("City, Navy" 1943).

Day 7—Wednesday, June 9

The Los Angeles City Council finally decided that the Zoot suit menace could be wiped away by banning the wearing of the offending uniform. It passed a resolution prohibiting the wearing of a Zoot suit—"ankle choker pants" and knee-length coats. The vote on the measure was unanimous—8–0. Asked about the action, one member of the council explained that the city prohibits nudism by ordinance. If the city can prevent people from wearing no clothes, it can prohibit people from wearing too many clothes.

At the same time the city council was taking its unprecedented move on the population's apparel, the Governor of California, Earl Warren was into more serious business. After conferring with California State attorney general Robert Kenney, Warren created a Citizen's Committee of five members to investigate the riots, determine the causes, and suggest ameliorative steps to prevent further unrest. In announcing the investigation, Governor Warren declared, "Without regard to the basic cause of these riots, they promote disunity, race hatred and create an unwholesome relationship between of men in arms and the citizenry. They create doubts of our solidarity in our minds and bring joy to the hearts of our enemies" ("Los Angeles' Zoot Suit War" 1943).

On June 7, the fifth day of the Zoot Suit Riots, servicemen, egged on by jeering civilians, marched through Los Angeles city streets. From theaters, stores, and trolley cars, such as this one stopped on Main Street and 3rd, they dragged out people who appeared to be of Mexican descent, beat them, and ripped and tore their clothes. An estimated 1,000 servicemen stormed through the Mexican district with relative impunity. A number of taxi drivers even joined the fun, offering free rides to servicemen and civilians to the riot areas. Finally, at 10:30 P.M., the Los Angeles police chief declared a general riot alarm. Nevertheless, the violence continued well into the night. (AP Photo)

Governor Warren asked Bishop Joseph McGucken, auxiliary bishop of the Archdiocese of Los Angeles, a man who had special ties with the Mexican-American community, to head the special committee. Included among the membership was actor Leo Carrillo; Dr Willsie Martin, pastor of the Wilshire Methodist Church; Karl Holton, member of the Youth Correction Authority of Chief County Probations Officer; and Walter Gordon, African-American attorney.

The chaos in the streets still flared. Bands of servicemen determined to ferret out every Zoot suiter still sporting the look often found it difficult to determine the prey. One African-American young man on a streetcar returned from a pilot training program and watched as several servicemen hunters boarded, picked out a Mexican-looking worker wearing a helmet and work clothes, and dragged him into the street. They tore off his clothes and gave him a whipping. The clothes looked nothing like Zoot suit attire. The man, nevertheless, was a Mexican American. The African American who had witnessed the scene later said that one of the servicemen got back on the streetcar and approached him: "One guy said, 'you one of them zoot suiters too?' I said no and pointed to my clothes, ordinary street clothes. I said I was in the Air Corps Reserve and they said they didn't care a damn what I was. The attackers then pulled him off the streetcar but left quickly after a police car pulled up" (Peiss 2011, 121).

It was not until June 9, nearly a week after sporadic attacks by servicemen against Mexican Americans had thrown parts of downtown Los Angeles into chaos and rioting, that Mayor Fletcher Bowron addressed the city.

Mayor Bowron had recently received much public notoriety for his outspoken support of the wartime mass eviction and incarceration of Japanese Americans. Now, he faced in his city another crisis involving an immigrant population.

Accompanied by two officials of the city's police department, Bowron said in his broadcast, aired at 7:45 P.M.:

> Unfortunate happenings in this city during the past few days and nights have set a considerable portion of the people to talking about zoot suits and pachucos, hoodlums, mobs, attacks upon service men, retaliation, racial discrimination, prejudice against minority groups, and about the safety of our entire civilian population, especially women who use the city streets in certain sections of the city. The situation is serious but not as serious as many are led to believe. There is no reason for fear or hysteria. . . . Now let us keep our heads and keep loose. Precipitate action of the wrong sort will do infinitely more harm than good. (Bowron 1943)

The mayor assured city residents as well as concerned diplomatic officials and Mexican officials that no actions perpetrated by the bands of servicemen, by military authorities, or by civic leaders had been caused in any manner by racial discrimination against Mexican Americans or others of "colored blood" (Bowron 1943).

Rafael de la Colina, minister-counselor of the Mexican Embassy in Washington, expressed biting indignation about the unfolding saga on the streets of Los Angeles. He told an interviewer that he had received reports that a number of innocent Mexican nationals, passersby to the attacks on Zoot suiters, had themselves been assaulted. He warned that if substantial evidence of such mistreatment was credible, the Mexican government might present a formal protest to the U.S. government. This conflict in Los Angeles, he charged, this "mob violence," against those in the barrios was deplorable.

Concerned about the escalating attacks, Mexican consul Alfredo Calles sent messages to the Mexican Embassy in Washington and the Foreign Office in Mexico City. In addition, he personally distributed circulars advising Mexican nationals to stay off the streets after dark.

Meanwhile, County Supervisor Roger Jessup saw events moving in the right direction. The servicemen were doing the city of Los Angeles and the American people a great service. All that was needed to end the Zoot suit menace, he said, "is more of the same kind of action that is being exercised by servicemen. . . . If this continues, zooters will be as scarce as hen's teeth" (Jones 1969, 34).

There was one city official in Los Angeles who did publicly speak out against the "Halloween violence" meted out by the U.S. military. Los Angeles County district attorney Fred Howser bristled that there was no place for this kind of vigilante brutality. Howser asked the county grand jury to conduct an investigation.

Meanwhile, as news of the Zoot suit battles in Los Angeles spread nationwide, isolated incidents drew attention as far away as Philadelphia. After a concert by the celebrated orchestra of drummer Gene Krupa, two of the band members, a pianist and sax player, were assaulted by sailors, apparently inspired by the events in Los Angeles. The band members were attired in band uniforms of blue gabardine jackets, dark trousers, and bow ties. One of the victims of the beating remembered being cursed by the servicemen as a Zoot suiter.

Day 8, Thursday, June 10

Over a week after the riots had begun, Lieutenant Glen A. Litten of the 11th Naval District reported to his superiors about the causes of disturbances. Litten interviewed hundreds of sailors and carefully detailed instances in which they claimed to have been verbally or physically attacked. As expected, Litten clearly laid the blame for the chaos gripping the city to the cumulative indignities and physical assaults suffered by servicemen and even their wives and girlfriends at the hands of "Zoot Suiters." His conclusions included the charges that numerous attacks and verbal insults had been made by "Zoot Suiters" and their wives and friends in the weeks and months leading up to the riots; that insults had been

directed by the Zoot suiters at the naval uniform; that "there are indications of anti-American sympathies"; and "that the Zoot Suiters have used
dangerous and deadly weapons upon naval personnel" (Report of Glen
Litten 1943).

Yet, police statistics told another story. For the five weeks from May 1,
1943, to June 6, 1943, there had been seven major violent incidents reported to the police department involving U.S. servicemen in the Los Angeles
area that resulted in death, either of a sailor or the victim of a sailor. In
not a single one of the seven deaths was a Zoot suit Mexican American
involved.

Yet, Los Angeles papers focused not on the attacks by servicemen but
on pachucos. Photographs of three "notorious" gang leaders appeared—
Lewis English, 23 years old, an African American charged with carrying a
butcher knife; Frank Tellez, 22 years old, charged with vagrancy; and Luis
"The Chief" Verdusco, 27 years old, allegedly one of the central figures in
all of the city's pachuco warring culture. Articles on these arrests seemed
to confirm everything that the Los Angeles press had said for weeks—that
Zoot suit gang members were old enough to be serving in the military and
were avoiding conscription, and that the clothes, especially in the case of
Tellez, who sported a pancake-shaped hat with a feather, were expensive
and could only have been purchased with monies gained by theft or other
nefarious means. Tellez's drape coat, according to one story, was "part of a
$75 suit" and a pair of pegged trousers "very full at the knees and narrow at
the cuffs" (Cosgrove 1984).

On June 10, Murray Churchill, a representative of Nelson Rockefeller,
coordinator of Inter-American Affairs, reported to Washington that disturbances had begun to subside with increased military and civilian police
intervention. Churchill saw evidence of attacks from both sides in the violence but made an important point about the reaction of Mexican Americans to the riots. Churchill said that:

> Mexican resentment is not against arrest of Pachucos by law enforce-
> ment agencies but against service men and Anglo-Saxon hoodlums
> who have attempted to take law into their own hands, invading Mexi-
> can district, entering theaters, restaurants, even homes. They have
> retaliated not against Pachucos who committed assaults but indis-
> criminately against juvenile members of same race. (Churchill 1943)

Churchill called such action by the servicemen and citizens who abetted
them as "terroristic." The obvious point was also that such terrorism had

racial overtones, a point that local authorities continued to deny over and over again (Churchill 1943).

South of Los Angeles, a report reached San Diego police that carloads and truckloads of the undesirable wearers of the long coats were heading to the city's naval and marine bases. But, once again, the victims of subsequent confrontations were Zoot suiters. When 12 Zoot suit Mexican Americans were mobbed by 50 sailors and marines and then taken to jail by San Diego police during the evening, somehow by the next morning all of them had lost their ducktail haircuts. According to police officials, it just so happened that there had been a barber present in the jail in the middle of the night and that he had quite a workout.

The *San Diego Union* reported that groups of servicemen, some as large as several hundred, had protected the city's streets south of Broadway, ridding the area of Zoot suiters who had supposedly migrated from Los Angeles—a claim both farfetched and disingenuous. San Diego had its own population of Mexican Americans who wore Zoot suits. Other reports placed about 300 servicemen at Third Avenue and East Street, where city and military police dispersed the crowd.

Mexican consul Alfredo Calles feared that an explosion was brewing similar to the one taking place in Los Angeles. He sought out labor leader and social activist Luisa Moreno, who had many connections in labor circles and progressive groups.

Born Blanca Rosa López Rodríguez into a wealthy family in Guatemala, Moreno moved with her husband to New York in 1928 and worked briefly as a seamstress during the Great Depression. In 1935, she became an organizer for the American Federation of Labor (AFL). In Florida, she organized African-American and Latino workers. In San Diego, she helped organize "El Congreso del Pueblo de Habla Española" ("The Congress of Spanish-Speaking Peoples").

Moreno befriended Carey McWilliams and helped organize the Sleepy Lagoon Defense Committee (SLDC), especially in trying to disabuse the public of the notion, made by the mainstream press and public officials, that the accused young men were thugs and criminals. Moreno was quick to realize that the violence against Zoot suiters in Los Angeles was quickly spreading to San Diego and she feverishly began to use her considerable energy and passion to try to stop it.

Calles and Moreno enlisted in their alliance City Councilman Charles Dail, a politician who shared their sympathetic views toward the Mexican-American community. Moreno and Dail relentlessly threw themselves into efforts to try to stop the conflict in San Diego that portended a riot similar to the one still smoldering in Los Angeles. Moreno sought the help of her considerable number of allies of labor organizers and left-wing activists and she and Dail met with numerous community and political leaders asking for peaceful resolution and the lessening of tensions.

As the group began to investigate numerous reports of violence instigated by servicemen in the city, Moreno and Dail implored Admiral David Bagley, commandant of the 11th Naval District, to take appropriate action against the offending sailors in San Diego. They reminded Bagley that the violence directed toward Mexican Americans by servicemen was an attack against civilians. Councilman Dail warned Bagley that the actions of the military against the Zoot suiters could lead to violence more severe than the kind of ritual humiliation being carried out in Los Angeles. Those young men in service uniforms were certainly ignorant of the cultural and racial ramifications of their actions and the kind of lives the young men in the strange suits had lived.

The leadership of these servicemen must understand, Dail said, that they cannot allow such uncontrolled hysteria to thrive and grow: "Every civilian," Dail said, "no matter what type of clothing he is wearing, should be safe on the streets, and it is certainly the belief of the writer that the superior officers of servicemen should vigorously discourage any adverse attitude that they may have to civilians, cautioning the personnel that every civilian is not a 'draft dodger' and a 'slacker.'" In other words, Dali charged that the military needed to not only improve the education of its men but also exercise greater control over them (Mazón 1984, 90).

And yet Dail surely knew the general attitude of the Anglo public, much less the military, about the Mexican-American population. Admiral Bagley himself once joked about Mexican labor that was so vital to California agribusiness. He said: "Mexicans came cheap by the dozen and could be bought for ten cents each," and, if "the Japs bombed Mexico City, it would cost fifty cents to replace it" (Larralde and Griswold del Castillo 1997).

Not surprisingly, when challenged on the issue of racism and discrimination by the military, Bagley quickly issued a rejoinder. The violence in the street, he insisted, had resulted from continuing attacks against servicemen by bands of hoodlums; the military, he argued, was acting in self-defense. Bagley did say that he and his fellow officers would never condone or encourage racist behavior or attitudes on behalf of the troops under their command.

In the end, the violence in San Diego never did reach the levels of that in Los Angeles. Nevertheless, Moreno was convinced that there were numerous cases of unreported violence against Mexicans. She said: "We will never know much about the San Diego civilian casualties. The Navy and the local newspaper ignored the violence since most of the victims were Mexicans." She noted that they would be the last ones to complain to the authorities: "These Mexicans lived an extremely hard life. They were poorly educated and attempted to better themselves through menial jobs. They avoided trouble and refused to complain. When confronted with discrimination, they swallowed their anger and sorrow" (Larralde and Griswold del Castillo 1997).

***

It had been over a week now since the beginnings of Zoot suit hysteria in Los Angeles. The streets quieted. De-Zoot suiting and de-frocking and "commando raids," as some papers called them, came to end. As the physical violence in downtown Los Angeles and in the barrios ceased, an uneasy quiet hung over the city. Throughout the chaotic days, law enforcement officials, state government leaders, and federal investigators all were united in claiming that the riots had nothing to do with race.

These declarations were meant not only for local residents and for other U.S. citizens but also for the Mexican government. In a time of war, the country desperately wished to retain the support of its ally to the South. Yet, no matter how the argument was framed, those who insisted that the Zoot Suit Riots had nothing to do with race kept running into numerous cases that told a different story. For example, sailors stumbled across a group of Mexican musicians who had just left the Aztec Recording Company after a musical session. They were adults, not teenagers. They were not wearing Zoot suits. They posed no threat of any kind to the servicemen; yet, they were also ruthlessly attacked.

Bob Rodriguez, a young Mexican American caught up in the street battles, later remembered that sailors and soldiers were grabbing any dark-skinned individual they could find: "But first they used to check you over to see if you had any drapes on," he remembered, "and it got to the point where they couldn't find too many of those guys anymore. They were hanging around the neighborhoods, in case we came their way. So, anybody that's Mexican they dragged their ass out there and take your pants off in the middle of Broadway" (Alvarez 2009, 172).

Outside of Los Angeles, many clearly recognized the riots for what they were. An editorial in the *Chicago Daily Tribune* blasted Los Angeles officials and others for attempting to explain away the week-long battles in the streets as "roughhousing" or other euphemisms. "In fact," the editorial charged, Los Angeles has experienced a series of nasty little race riots between Americans in uniform and embittered Mexican bravos and toughs . . . under Hollywood's nose an ugly race conflict, damaging to this country's foreign relations, was allowed to develop for lack of human decency and civic responsibility. ("The Zoot Suit Riots" 1943)

As the Zoot Suit Riots played themselves out, groups of citizens, government officials, sociologists, reporters, activists, and others would now try to make sense of it all.

References

Alvarez, Luis. 2009. *The Power of the Zoot: Youth Culture and Resistance during World War II*. Berkeley: University of California Press.

Bowron, Fletcher Radio Address. June 9, 1943. Of 4512 Coordinator of Inter-American Affairs: Los Angeles "Zoot Suit" Situation 1943, FDR-FDRPOF: President's Official Files, 1933–1945, Franklin D. Roosevelt Library, Hyde Park, New York.

"City, Navy Clamp Lid on Zoot-Suit Warfare." 1943. *Los Angeles Times*, June 9, 8.

Cosgrove, Stuart. 1984 (Autumn). "The Zoot-Suit and Style Warfare." *History Workshop Journal*, 85. http://invention.smithsonian.org/centerpieces/whole_cloth/u7sf/u7materials/cosgrove.html.

Griffith, Beatrice. 1948. *America Me*. Boston: Houghton Mifflin Company.

Jones, Solomon. 1973. *The Government Riots of Los Angeles 1943*. Thesis. University of California, Los Angeles, 1969. Reprinted by R and E Research Associates, San Francisco.

Larralde, Carlos, and Richard Griswold del Castillo. 1997 (Summer). "Luisa Moreno and the Beginnings of the Mexican American Civil Rights Movement in San Diego," *The Journal of San Diego History*. http://www.sandiegohistory.org/journal/97summer/moreno.htm

"Lifeguards Can't Tell 'Zoot Suit' Bathers." 1943. *Los Angeles Times*, June 7, 1.

"Los Angeles' Zoot Suit War an International Incident." 1943. *The Washington Daily News*, June 10, 2.

Mazón, Mauricio. 1984. *The Zoot-Suit Riots: The Psychology of Symbolic Annihilation*. Austin: University of Texas Press.

McWilliams, Carey. 1990. *North from Mexico: The Spanish-Speaking People of the United States*. New York: Praeger.

Murray, Churchill to Victor Borella. June 10, 1943. Of 4512: Coordinator of Inter-American Affairs: Los Angeles "Zoot Suit" Situation 1943, FDR-FDRPOF: President's Official Files, 1933–1945, Franklin D. Roosevelt Library, Hyde Park, New York.

"Near Martial Law in L.A." 1943. *Los Angeles Daily News*, June 9, 1.

Officer of the Day to Commanding Officer. June 5, 1943. 11th Naval District, Commandant's Office, Attachment to Report of Glen Litten. (June 10, 1943. 11th Naval District, Commandant's Office, RG 181, Naval Districts and Shore Establishments, Central Subject Files, 1924–1958, National Archives and Records Administration, National Archives at Riverside, California.

Overend, William. 1978. "The'43 Zoot Suit Riots Remembered." *Los Angeles Times*, May 9, G1.

Pagán, Edwardo Obregón.2003. *Murder at the Sleepy Lagoon: Zoot Suits, Race, and Riot in Wartime L.A.* Chapel Hill: The University of North Carolina Press.

Peiss, Kathy. 2011. *Zoot Suit: The Enigmatic Career of an Extreme Style.* Philadelphia: University of Pennsylvania Press.

Rasmussen, C. 2007. "L.A. Then and Nows; World War II Brought Fear—And Opportunity." *Los Angeles Times*, September 9, B2.

Report of Glen Litten. June 10, 1943. 11th Naval District, Commandant's Office, RG 181, Naval Districts and Shore Establishments, Central Subject Files, 1924–1958, National Archives and Records Administration, National Archives at Riverside, California.

"Sheriff's Office, First Report." June 4, 1943. Of 4512: Coordinator of Inter-American Affairs: Los Angeles "Zoot Suit" Situation 1943, FDR-FDRPOF: President's Official Files, 1933–1945, Franklin D. Roosevelt Library, Hyde Park, New York.

"6 Zoot Suiters Sent to Hospital by Servicemen."1943. Los Angeles *Daily News* (June 8), 1.

Smith, R.J. 2006. "Zoot Suits against the World." *Los Angeles Times*, June 19, B17.

Waxman, Al. 1943. In McWilliams, Carey. 1990. *North from Mexico: The Spanish-Speaking People of the United States.* New York: Praeger.

"Zoot Suiters Learn Lesson in Fights with Servicemen." 1943. *Los Angeles Times*, June 7, A1.

"The Zoot Suit Riots." 1943. *Chicago Daily Tribune*, June 10, 14.

"Zoot Suit Riots." 2002. PBS American Experience. http://www.pbs.org/wgbh/amex/zoot/eng_peopleevents/e_murder.html.

"Zoot-Suit War." 1943. *Time*, June 21, 18–19.

SIX

The Aftermath

ON JUNE 11, 1943, the *Los Angeles Times*, in an editorial on its front page titled "Time for Sanity," charged headlong into an issue that had put the city and its political and civic leadership on its heels during the Zoot Suit Riots—the issue of race. The scenes of U.S. servicemen wielding clubs and bats and charging into Mexican-American neighborhoods to beat, strip, and humiliate youngsters wearing the "drape" look appeared to many observers, especially outside the city itself, that the war on the streets might have as a principal cause the cultural and racial ethnicity of those on the receiving end of the attacks. The *Los Angeles Times* was out to dispel any such notions. No, the police had not stood by idly while the servicemen went on a rampage. No, this was not a vigilante operation but one that emanated from the crimes of grotesque gangs preying on members of the armed services and their wives and girlfriends. The issue was one of law and order and the control of juvenile delinquency, not one of race persecution.

Backing up the assertions of the city's most notable newspaper, Los Angeles mayor Fletcher Bowron blamed the riots almost entirely on Mexican juvenile delinquents. Any suggestion that race had anything to do with the outbreak of violence, Bowron insisted, was caused "by citizens in this community . . . who raise a hue and cry of racial discrimination or prejudice every time the police make arrests of members of gangs or groups working in unison." It was unfortunate, he said, if Mexican boys were involved in riotous behavior but he stood by the police in enforcing the law. "If young men of Mexican parentage or if colored boys are involved, it is regrettable, but no one has immunity and whoever are the disturbers are going to be sternly dealt with" ("Issue Not Race" 1943, 4).

Chief of Police C. B. Horrall, added his own perspective. The Los Angeles Police Department, said Chief Horrall, had been thoroughly trained to act in all cases of law enforcement without regard to race, color, or creed. His

Los Angeles mayor Fletcher Bowron celebra-
tes his re-election in 1941. A strong proponent
of Japanese relocation at the beginning of U.S.
involvement in World War II, Bowron would
also be at the center of another racial and cultural clash affecting Los Angeles—the Sleepy
Lagoon Murder trial and the Zoot Suit Riots.
(AP Photo)

officers, he went on, had been especially advised to protect fully the rights
of Mexican Americans. Horrall said that he had concluded that those who
insisted that the riots were a racial affair that had international implications had either done so out of ignorance or from some ulterior motive.

Perhaps the most prominent of those citizens in the community who
raised the "hue and cry" of which Bowron and Horrall scorned was Carey
McWilliams. In the wake of the riots, McWilliams talked about the profound "residue of resentment and hatred in the minds and hearts of thousands of young Mexican-Americans in Los Angeles." The issue of race,
McWilliams insisted, was at the center of the riots. He spoke about the
second-generation of Mexicans who had grown up on the east side of
Los Angeles keenly aware of the second-class citizenship surrounding

their lives, especially the exclusion from many of the excitements of city life available to the dominant Anglo population. It was this generation, McWilliams said, that gradually encroached from its segregated territory into increasing view of that dominant class. When he first came to Los Angeles, McWilliams recalled, he rarely saw a Mexican American in the downtown section of the city. Now, as the second generation began to assert itself—began to become more visible to the larger society—race-consciousness, stereotypes, and ugly tensions took firm hold.

McWilliams mentioned particularly the callous and outrageous attack that one newspaper had made on young Mexican-American women, the *cholitas* or *pachucas*, inferring that they were drug-snorting, venereal disease-carrying prostitutes. Eighteen young Mexican-American women replied in a letter that the mainstream press refused to publish. In the letter, the women declared, "The girls in this meeting room consist of young girls who are now working in defense plants because we want to help win the war, and of girls who have brothers, cousins, relatives, and sweethearts in all branches of the American armed forces. We have not been able to have our side of the story told." Another group of girls who wore Zoot suits even offered to be examined by physicians to prove they were virgins. McWilliams later remembered seeing Mexican-American boys carrying clippings of the slanderous stories in their wallets and showing them to others with great indignation. It was this kind of stereotype, this racial profiling, that burned deeply (McWilliams 1990, 231).

The riots sparked heated rhetoric on the floor of the U.S. House of Representatives. Congressman John Rankin of Mississippi, displaying his segregationist passions with special gusto, declared that Zoot suit "savage brutes" had thankfully been tamed by patriotic servicemen. He praised the military men "for the manhood and courage they have displayed in stripping the masks, as well as the zoot suits, from these loathsome criminals and protecting innocent American girls from their beastly attacks" (Peiss 2011, 132).

On the other hand, some of the national media took another view. *Time* magazine, describing the violence, talked about a "Panzer" division of the "cab-and-car attack" rolling down Mexican-American side streets. The article scoffed at the meager attempts of both the military and local law enforcement to stop the mayhem. It excoriated the Los Angeles press for inflaming the violence. It concluded: "And Los Angeles, apparently unaware that it was spawning the ugliest brand of mob action since the coolie race riots of the 1870s, gave its tacit approval" ("Zoot Suit War" 1943, 19).

The African-American press also reacted sharply. George Schuyler, influential writer and editor of the *Pittsburgh Courier*, wrote about letters he had received from Los Angeles that "confirm our previous suspicions that the so-called zoot-riots were actually race riots." He wrote about Mexican Americans and other minorities subjected to "kicking and clubbing" by bands of servicemen outnumbering the victims by overwhelming odds (Schuyler 1943, 1).

Governor Warren's Citizen's Committee Report

When California governor Earl Warren appointed a citizen's committee on June 9, 1943, to investigate the causes of the disturbances and to recommend long-term actions to help deter any such future outbreaks, its members, led by Joseph T. McGucken, auxiliary bishop of Los Angeles, quickly went to work. Its first report, issued immediately after the end of the street violence, was a stinging rebuke to the sensationalist attacks on Mexican Americans in the press and the insistence of local authorities that race prejudice had nothing to do with the riots. The report went far beyond the usual demands for greater punishment for juvenile delinquents.

The citizen's committee's report found much blame to go around. It unequivocally stated that no group had the right to take the law into its own hands. It attacked the press for inflaming the situation. It found significance in the fact that almost all of the individuals who sustained injuries from the riots were of Mexican-American descent or African Americans. It said that any solutions to the problems inciting the violence must be designed to "combat race prejudice in all its forms." And the report encouraged aggressive measures to improve the living conditions and social well-being among immigrant communities in the city.

"There are approximately 250,000 persons of Mexican descent in Los Angeles County," the report stated. "Living conditions among the majority of these people are far below the general level of the community. Housing is inadequate; sanitation is bad and is made worse by congestion. Recreational facilities for children are very poor; and there is insufficient supervision of the playgrounds, swimming pools, and other youth centers. Such conditions are breeding places for juvenile delinquency." Such conditions, the report argued, lead to contempt, hostility, and denigration of entire groups of society.

Mass arrests, dragnet raids, and other wholesale classifications of groups of people are based on false premises and tend merely to aggravate the situation. Any American citizen suspected of crime is entitled to be treated as an individual, to be indicted as such, and to be tried, both at law and in the forum of public opinion, on his merits or errors, regardless of race, color, creed, or the kind of clothes he wears. . . . Group accusations foster race prejudice, the entire group accused want revenge and vindication. The public is led to believe that every person in the accused group is guilty of crime. . . . In undertaking to deal with the cause of these outbreaks, the existence of race prejudice cannot be ignored. . . . (Governor's Citizen's Committee Report 1943)

The report called for various reforms. It asked for an increase in youth recreational facilities in minority neighborhoods, an end to discrimination in public facilities, and special training for police officers assigned to multiracial communities. It called for a relaxation of the polarizing and vicious assaults by the local press in characterizing Mexican-American youth. It urged additional programs by the religious community to help assimilate minority youth into the larger Los Angeles community. It also encouraged community leaders to work with those in the legal profession to find ways to provide adequate representation for youths arrested in connection with gang activity.

The McGucken report challenged the basic assumption that Mexican-American youths and the Mexican-American community generally were somehow a threat to national security during wartime, much like the Japanese who had been removed from the general population. In fact, many Mexican Americans were serving ably in various war zones. An estimated 350,000 Mexican Americans served in the U.S. military in various capacities during World War II. In addition, Mexican Americans filled thousands of positions in military-related industries.

A Zoot suiter and self-proclaimed pachuco named Dan Acosta wrote a letter shortly after the riots defiantly challenging the contradictions of Mexican Americans being assaulted in the streets at the same time that thousands were on battlefields fighting for their country. "We are hoping, praying and fighting for a beautiful FREE world minus Nazism, fascism, aggression, and most of all discrimination," he wrote. So-called Zoot suiters, he said, were answering the call to duty but "the actions of the servicemen and police who tacitly encouraged the riot gave Mexican-Americans and zoot suiters reason to pause" (Pagán 2003, 182).

First Lady Speaks Out

First Lady Eleanor Roosevelt commented on the Los Angeles riots in a press conference on June 16. The question was much deeper than just

Zoot suits, Mrs. Roosevelt charged. "For a long time I've worried about the attitude toward Mexicans in California and the States along the border," she said. There had been long-term discrimination practiced against the Mexican-American community, she charged, and "we must begin to face it" ("First Lady" 1943, 4).

The *Los Angeles Times* went after the First Lady with particular ferocity. She was ignorant. She did not know the facts. She should have listened to the military and civic officials and the newspapers who told the truth. She parroted the line of the Communists who had been trying to make the Zoot Suit Riots a race issue. She had fueled international misunderstanding. After all, the *Times*, continued, "We like Mexicans and we think they like us." Californians bragged about their historic religious missions, the editorial went on. They had a proud Mexican American citizen as one of its sheriffs; they loved fiestas and their music; they maintained an old street in Los Angeles to honor its Mexican heritage; they loved fraternizing with Mexicans; they helped them in times of depression; and they were "ostentatiously" proud of the Spanish and Mexican civilizations (Mrs. Roosevelt 1943, A4).

Preston Hotchkiss, president of the California State Chamber of Commerce, joined in the chorus of denunciation against the First Lady. The riots, he insisted, had nothing at all to do with racial discrimination. The sailors and soldiers who chased down Zoot suiters were acting only on behalf of their wives and girlfriends who had been assaulted by youth gangs. As far as the victims of the riots being mostly of Mexican heritage, there was no connection. Mexican Americans, the head of the Chamber insisted, had always been treated with the utmost consideration. Indeed, some of them were prominent and useful community members.

Meanwhile, as the McGucken Committee issued its report on the Zoot Suit Riots in Los Angeles and as the First Lady commented on the tragedy, ominous signs from other cities began to make headlines.

Reports of skirmishes involving Zoot suiters came from other towns and cities in California, including San Jose and Santa Cruz. In Baltimore, Maryland, police arrested three members of the so-called Brimstone Gang on charges of disorderly conduct and carrying concealed weapons and issued warnings about the potential for Zoot suit gang depredations.

In Philadelphia, on June 12, four African-American young men wearing drapes and pancake hats were set on by a large gang of about 25 young white boys, who ripped their clothing and beat them fiercely. When police arrived, the patrolmen arrested the two African Americans for breaching the peace. Later, one of the patrolmen said that the arrests were for the protection of the boys. As the two Zoot suiters were sent to the hospital for treatment, the police ignored the fleeing assailants. The scene was nearly a mirror image of those that had plagued Los Angeles for over a week, except the attackers were not servicemen.

At about the same time, at the Thomas M. Cooley High School in northwest Detroit, Michigan, a similar incident of whites attacking blacks wearing Zoot suits was also eerily reminiscent of the violence in Los Angeles. To some observers, the race discord portended serious trouble.

Race Riots in Detroit and Other Cities

In Detroit, on June 20, 1943, at a beach and amusement park known as Belle Isle in the middle of the Detroit River, a series of clashes between white and black teenagers ignited a three-day race riot that brought tragic death and destruction. As in Los Angeles, sailors from a nearby naval armory aligned themselves against minority youth. Rumors of atrocities fueled the anger of citizens—stories about whites throwing a black woman and her baby over the bridge at Belle Isle; stories about black men raping white women; stories about a black man slitting the throat of a white sailor; and stories about other numerous senseless acts of terror and horror.

The violence spread into the city—mobs of both races stoning cars, stabbing, assaulting, and looting. Besieged by uncontrolled chaos, the police, as they had done in Los Angeles, resorted mostly to arresting and beating young minorities—in this case, African Americans. So fierce was the violence that Mayor Edward Jeffries called for help from the federal government. More than 6,000 U.S. Army soldiers soon occupied Detroit.

By the time the streets quieted, 25 African Americans and 9 whites had been killed. Approximately 700 individuals had been seriously injured. Property estimated at the time at $2 million had been destroyed. Of the arrests made by police, 85 percent were African American.

The *New York Times* tied the race riots in Detroit directly to the Zoot Suit Riots in Los Angeles: "Detroit needs to listen to its enlightened citizens of both races who have worked together and separately to educate their own people and to understand other people." Detroit and other cities have lessons to be learned, the editorial proclaimed, and "so has Los Angeles, where many innocent Mexicans and some equally innocent Negroes suffered in the 'zoot suit' riots. Keeping peace and good-will among all sorts and conditions of people at home is an indispensable part of the war effort. Those who hamper this work, whatever their race or creed, are not good Americans" ("Tragedy" 1943, 18).

In Detroit, Michigan, on June 20, 1943, two weeks after the violence in the streets of Los Angeles, clashes between white and African-American teenagers at a beach resort ignited a three-day race riot that brought tragic death and destruction. As in Los Angeles, sailors from a nearby naval armory aligned themselves against the minority youth and the violence spread into the city, as seen in this photo taken on June 22—mobs of both races stoning cars, stabbing, assaulting, and looting. So fierce was the violence that Mayor Edward Jeffries called for help from the federal government. More than 6,000 U.S. Army soldiers soon occupied Detroit. By the time the streets quieted, 25 African Americans and 9 whites had been killed. Many observers linked the riots in Detroit to the stories of mob violence coming from Los Angeles. (Library of Congress)

The *Washington Post* nearly matched the *Times* editorial word for word. What happened in Detroit, the *Post* declared, was no isolated incident:

> It is a piece with the rioting experienced last week . . . the "zoot suit" disorders which disgraced Los Angeles. We are in a dangerous state which can find its remedy only in wise and firm leadership at the community as well as the national level. . . . Anyone who seeks to stir

enmity between the races is an enemy of the United States. ("Detroit Tragedy" 1943, 8)

In many parts of the United States, especially the South, the explanations for the Zoot Suit Riots and the Detroit riots drew very different explanations. The Jackson, Mississippi *Daily News*, still bristling over the remarks of the First Lady concerning the Zoot suit disturbances, blamed the talk of equality for the riot. "It is blood upon your hands, Mrs. Roosevelt," declared the editorial. "You have been . . . proclaiming and practicing social equality. . . . In Detroit, a city noted for the growing impudence and insolence of its Negro population, an attempt was made to put your preachments into practice" ("Detroit Race Riots" 2000).

Race riots in the United States, in 1943 would not end in Detroit. On August 1, in the Harlem section of New York City, where nearly half a million African Americans, plagued by discrimination and poverty, were crowded in inferior housing conditions, a confrontation between a police officer and a black U.S. soldier ignited the kind of brutal street violence that had plagued Detroit weeks earlier. As in Detroit, various rumors fueled the violence. By the end of the rioting, six black residents were dead, nearly 500 individuals were sent to local hospitals, and over 500 were arrested, mostly blacks.

The *New York Times*, in a series of articles reflecting on the violence, noted the blatant discrimination confronting the black community, the lack of recreational facilities for its youth, and the dreary economic opportunities available for its people. The *Times* unequivocally pointed to injustices of racism that had to be addressed in New York, as in other major cities across the United States.

The Tenney Committee

In the summer of 1943, California senator Jack Tenney, an avid hunter of communists whose work in the state presaged by a decade the infamous, national witch hunt crusade of U.S. senator Joseph McCarthy of Minnesota, joined the fray. Chairman of the California Committee on Un-American Activities Committee (CUAC), Tenney was not one to place credence on the findings of the Governor's Citizen's Committee headed by Bishop McGucken. To Tenney, the Sleepy Lagoon defendants and the Mexican-Americans Zoot suiters who were pummeled by sailors on the streets of Los Angeles were not victims; they and those that formed citizen's committees to advance their rights were likely part of the larger Communist menace.

class distinction liable to be found in any country, and particularly in Mexico where class distinction exists. I feel that if the truth were known, persons of the "peon" type have been used as test cases by Mexican societies acting in connection with the Consulate to prove racial discrimination; in other words, they have stepped down in the lower strata of their people who are themselves underprivileged in Mexico as far as class distinction is concerned in attempting to force acceptance of these people upon the higher intellectual element in communities in the United States. (Blocker 1943)

As the Debate Raged On

And so, in the weeks and months following the Zoot Suit Riots, the war of analysis and blame continued. Aside from the competing charges of foreign involvement and conspiracy, the basic question remained—whether race discrimination against Mexican Americans, African Americans, and others was a root cause of the disturbances or was the chaos mainly a manifestation of growing juvenile delinquency? Despite the report of the McGucken Committee, government officials, the media, law enforcement, American diplomats, and the Anglo population generally denied with much certainty and vigor that Los Angeles had a race problem and that it had anything to do with the actions of the servicemen who carried on their de-zoot-suiting mission.

The grand jury of Los Angeles County, for example, issued a report following a month of investigation that further reinforced the prevailing views among the dominant powers within the community. The grand jury found, among other things, that the wartime exigencies had reduced the size of the local police force and its ability to cope with a large influx of both Mexicans and African Americans involved in the war effort. It decried the poverty under which the minority populations lived, lamented the lack of discipline administered by parents, and pointed to inadequate education levels that the new arrivals possessed when they moved to Los Angeles. Detention and rehabilitation facilities were inadequate to handle the level of juvenile delinquency spreading in the county, the report added, and steps must be made to increase the number and efficiency of such institutions.

Thus, the grand jury attributed the Zoot Suit Riots almost entirely to increasing juvenile delinquency:

There has been a disposition to attribute the outrages committed by these zoot suit gangs (composed mostly of Mexicans, although occasionally we find white and Negro boys participating in their activities) to the dislike or hatred created in the minds of the Mexican youth by repressive and discriminatory treatment inflicted upon them by the Anglo-Americans. The Grand Jury found no evidence to substantiate any such belief. They found no evidence that these activities were in any sense due to or incited by race prejudice or anti-Mexican feeling. ("Findings and Recommendations of the Grand Jury of Los Angeles County" 1943)

A number of sociologists and psychologists, however, saw the riots differently. George I. Sanchez, a professor of Latin American Education at the University of Texas, reacted sharply to the violence in Los Angeles. He mocked the actions of the Los Angeles City Council in outlawing Zoot suits as its only answer "to the deep-rooted negligence of public service agencies." He charged that the word Mexican has become a term of opprobrium and that those who fell under its definition were often denied service in restaurants, barber shops, public parks, and swimming pools; segregated in separate schools; and paid discriminatory wages. In all ways, he wrote, the aim was to

keep the Mexican in his place. . . . The vicious practices referred to above do harm to the "Mexican," yes. However, infinitely more harm is done to the group which perpetrates or tolerates the practices. The pachuco is a symbol not of the guilt of an oppressed "Mexican" minority but of a cancerous growth within the majority group which is gnawing at the vitals of democracy and the American way of life. The pachuco and his feminine counterpart, the "cholita," are spawn of a neglectful society—not the products of a humble minority people who are defenseless before their enforced humiliation. (Sanchez 1943)

The analysis of Sanchez and others echoed a simple explanation offered by journalist Lawrence Lamar writing for the African-American paper the *Amsterdam News* on June 19. In an article titled "Mexicans, Negroes Victimized," Lamar concluded that the attacks by the white servicemen in Los Angeles and the tacit support given by local authorities, especially the police, were a way of "keeping the Mexicans and Negroes in their places" (Alvarez 2008, 235).

Over 30 years after the event, a notable public servant of the city of Los Angeles reflected on the events of 1943. Thomas Bradley, raised in the black Los Angeles community on Central Avenue, attended UCLA and then joined the police department in 1941. Bradley would eventually leave law enforcement, earn a law degree, and venture into politics. In 1973, he made history, becoming the first African-American mayor of a major city with a white majority—Los Angeles.

But in 1943, Bradley was part of the police force that faced the Zoot Suit Riots. "It was a rather unsettling experience because of the racial hostility that existed," he remembered. "It was directed primarily at Mexican-Americans, but it was not limited to them, because blacks also came in for some rather vicious treatment. In fact, some of the police officers were involved in what I thought was improper conduct. Their treatment of anyone who happened to be black or Mexican-American who happened to be wearing the clothes, the style—it was called the zoot suit, the narrow cuffs and the big knees—that was all that was necessary for that person to be the subject of rather vicious police handling." Bradley even remembered that some of his fellow African-American officers in their off-duty time were subjected to rough treatment: "So it wasn't a matter of fiction or a matter of false allegation by the general public who happened to be targets of that kind of police abuse; I got it first hand from some of my fellow black officers. So it was a very ugly period both for the community and, as far as I was concerned, for law enforcement" (Bradley 1978).

Meanwhile, from inside San Quentin prison in 1943 came yet another and unique analysis. It was from Manuel Reyes, serving his sentence along with other Mexican-American youths convicted in the Sleepy Lagoon murder trial. Reyes wrote to Alice Greenfield, the main contact between the defendants and the SLDC now assiduously working to gain support for the appeal. Reyes told Greenfield that he had been listening to the radio and reading about the riots: I read . . . how the police beat up two of my friends. I seen their pictures in the paper, the one with the wooden leg and other, I know them both. It sure is terrible what's going on in L.A. I never dream that things like that would happen in the U.S.A., a land of freedom. I thought it only happens in Germany and Japan. (Alvarez 2009, 197)

References

Alvarez, Luis. 2009. *The Power of the Zoot: Youth Culture and Resistance during World War II*. Berkeley: University of California Press.

Blocker, William Blocker to Secretary of State. August 3, 1943. Dispatch # 1855, Zoot Suit Disturbances at Los Angeles, California, National Archives and Records Administration, RG 59 General Records of the Department of State, Decimal File, #811.4016/651.

Bradley, Thomas. August 11, 1978. "The Impossible Dream." Oral Interview, University of California, Los Angeles, Calisphere, University of California Digital Library. http://content.cdlib.org/view?docId=hb4c6009nh;NAAN=13030&doc .view=frames&chunk.id=div00013&toc.depth=1&toc.id=&brand=calisphere& query="Zoot Suit Riots".

"Detroit Race Riots." 2000. PBS, American Experience: Eleanor Roosevelt. http:// www.pbs.org/wgbh/americanexperience/features/general-article/eleanor-riots/.

"Detroit Tragedy." 1943. *The Washington Post*, June 23, 8.

"Findings and Recommendations of the Grand Jury of Los Angeles County." August 3, 1943. Enclosure in Dispatch # 1855, Zoot Suit Disturbances at Los Angeles, California, National Archives and Records Administration, RG 59 General Records of the Department of State, Decimal File, #811.4016/651.

"First Lady Traces Zoot Riots to Discrimination." 1943. *Los Angeles Times*, June 17, 4.

Governor's Citizen's Committee Report on Los Angeles Riots. 1943. "The Zoot Suit Riots, Digital History ID 606." http://www.digitalhistory.uh.edu/disp_textbook .cfm?smtID=3&psid=606.

"Issue Not Race." 1943. *Los Angeles Times*, June 10, 4.

McWilliams, Carey. 1990. *North from Mexico: The Spanish-Speaking People of the United States*. New York: Praeger.

"Mrs. Roosevelt Blindly Stirs Race Discord." 1943. *Los Angeles Times*, June 18, A4.

Pagán, Edwardo Obregón. 2003. *Murder at the Sleepy Lagoon: Zoot Suits, Race, and Riot in Wartime L.A.* Chapel Hill: The University of North Carolina Press.

Peiss, Kathy. 2011. *Zoot Suit: The Enigmatic Career of an Extreme Style*. Philadelphia: University of Pennsylvania Press.

Sanchez, George I. Sanchez. 1943. "Pachucos in the Making." *Common Ground*, Autumn 13–20. http://historymatters.gmu.edu/d/5155/.

Schuyler, George. 1943. "World Today." *The Pittsburgh Courier*, June 26, 1.

"Tragedy in Detroit." 1943. *New York Times*, June 22, 18.

"Zoot-Suit War." 1943. *Time*, June 21, 18–19.

SEVEN

The Appeal

For Carey McWilliams, the violence in the streets of Los Angeles, in June 1943, was further evidence of what he and others seeking the release of those convicted in the Sleepy Lagoon murder case had been saying all along about the racial environment in the city. He wrote that the Zoot Suit Riots had exposed the flimsy "Paper-maché façade" of goodwill that existed among Anglos and Mexican Americans. For McWilliams, the Sleepy Lagoon case reeked of prejudice and led to the ugly courtroom scenes and ultimate convictions of innocent young men. And now, he said, "During the riots, the press, the police, the officialdom, and the dominance control groups of Los Angeles were caught with the bombs of prejudice in their hands . . . the riots were not an unexpected rupture of Anglo-Hispano relations but the logical end-product of . . . years of neglect and discrimination" (McWilliams 1990, 231).

With the riots now a recent backdrop, McWilliams and others of the Sleepy Lagoon Defense Committee (SLDC) would press for an appellate court to overturn the injustice of the trial. The time was right, he declared, for Mexican Americans in Los Angeles and their supporters to fight back with all the power they could muster.

In mid-June 1945, just as the violence in Los Angeles city streets ebbed, the SLDC issued a pamphlet titled *The Sleepy Lagoon Case*. McWilliams, who, a few years later, traced the cultural heritage of Mexican immigrants in his book *North from Mexico*, insisted that wearing of Zoot suits by Mexican-American youths and the emergence of the pachuco generation had nothing to do with the outrageous pronouncements made by Edward Duran Ayres of the Los Angeles Sheriff's Office that Spanish people had inherent blood and racial tendencies toward excessive violence. The pamphlet stressed heavily the theme that the trial had been the product of the same kind of noxious racial attitudes set forth by people such as Ayres and that had marked the Zoot Suit Riots.

It also forcefully asserted that the Sleepy Lagoon trial was affirmation that the press, city officials, and law enforcement in the city all had, in a sense, become representative and captive of a general fascist conspiracy by the Axis powers to engender race hatred and disunity in the United States and abroad during the war. After all, the racial rhetoric espoused by

Latino youths Noe Vasquez (left) and Joe Vasquez were photographed at the Los Angeles Police Department after being attacked by a group of sailors during the Zoot Suit Riots. With their pegged trousers slashed, the two had been "dezooted," to use a term that became popular during the riots with both servicemen and the Los Angeles press. (AP Photo)

Mr Ayres before the Los Angeles grand jury paralleled the ideas of racial superiority and purity so notably advanced by Adolph Hitler.

The pamphlet not only carefully laid out the injustices surrounding the arrest and conviction of the Sleepy Lagoon trial defendants, but it also aggressively attempted to blunt the guilty verdicts in the Sleepy Lagoon trial and the anti-Mexican hysteria gripping the city of Los Angeles as a betrayal of the principles of liberty and justice for which Americans were so gallantly fighting in the wars in Europe and the Pacific. It charged that those forces of intolerance and racial hatred, so epitomized by the Axis enemies, must be turned back, not only in foreign lands but in United States as well. "WE ARE AT WAR," the pamphlet thundered:

> We are at war not only with the armies of the Axis powers, but with the poison-gas of their doctrine, with the "biological basis" of Hitler and with his theories of race supremacy. The unity of all races, creeds and colors has been sealed in blood, in the blood of our heroes of Bataan and Corregidor, Stalingrad, Tunis and Bizerte, in the vast expanses of China, in the African desert and the mountain passes of the Caucasus. Our coming victory on the continent of Europe will be won by "men of the same stamp" though different races, and it will be the victory of all—Indians, Malays, Chinese, Negroes, Russians, Slavs, French, English, Americans, yes, and of Germans, Italians and Japanese. The rivers of blood will wash away the fascist creed of "Aryan supremacy." And with it will go the last vestiges of discrimination in the United States, the Jim-Crow cars in the south, the signs in Los Angeles that still say "Mexicans and Negroes not allowed here." ("The Sleepy Lagoon Case" 1943)

Garnering Support

McWilliams and others vigorously sought support to pay legal fees for the appeal and to shape public opinion and community awareness around the injustice of the trial. The SLDC approached African-American reformers, left-wing activists and organizations, and progressive newspaper reporters. They approached the heads of a number of labor unions, many of which responded with contributions and lent their names to petitions and advertising materials—unions such as the Brotherhood of Sleeping Car Porters, the United Auto Workers, the International Longshore and Warehouse Union, and a number of affiliates of the Congress of Industrial Organizations.

They gained active support from a number of family members of the boys. Lupe Leyvas, the younger sister of Hank Leyvas, was especially eager to help as was Margaret Telles, the mother of Bobby Telles. They appeared at fund-raising events and worked hard to help inform the Mexican-American community of the issues involved in the Sleepy Lagoon case.

The SLDC also cultivated association with editors of several major Spanish-language press publications such as *El Pueblo* and *La Opinión* in Los Angeles and *Pueblos Hispanos* in New York. This would be a special effort to marshal Spanish-speaking supporters to the cause. It would challenge a people plagued by a history of and constant threat of deportations, discriminatory law enforcement, and racial prejudice to stand firmly against a judicial case that was demeaning to their culture. It would challenge the "Mexican Community" to fight back.

Some responded with much dedication. Manuel Ruiz, who with Eduardo Quevedo had recently founded the Coordinating Council for Latin American Youth (CCLAY), heartily joined in the defense effort. The CCLAY was an organization consisting of youth groups that helped Latino teenagers gain a footing in Anglo society and worked with police and others to try to help prevent juvenile delinquency. A strong supporter of SLDC, Ruiz had been a tireless figure during the riots, attempting to quell the violence. And now, he fought to right the injustice of the trial.

Josefina Fierro de Bright, whose husband John Bright was a Hollywood screenwriter, played an important role in helping to bring to the cause numerous Hollywood and artistic luminaries such as actress Rita Hayworth, actor Anthony Quinn, singer Nat King Cole, and writers John Steinbeck, Lillian Hellman and Robert Lowell.

In November 1942, Orson Welles, acclaimed actor, director, writer, and producer in theater, radio, and film, a man who often lent his voice to progressive political causes, had earlier chaired an invitational forum of individuals in the Hollywood motion picture industry to raise funds for the defense of the 22 Sleepy Lagoon defendants. And now, after the conviction and imprisonment of 17 of the individuals, Welles continued to fight for their release.

Welles wrote an introduction to the SLDC pamphlet and later sent a letter of support to the parole board at San Quentin. "After a very careful examination of the records and facts of the trial," he said,

> I am convinced that the boys in the Sleepy Lagoon case were not given a fair trial, and that their conviction could only have been influenced by anti-Mexican prejudice. I am convinced, also, that the causes leading up to this case, as well as its outcome, are of great importance to the Mexican minority in this community. That is to say, the case has

importance aside from the boys incriminated—the whole community is undermined. Any attempt at good relations is impaired—as is the importance of unity in the furtherance of the war effort. To allow an injustice like this to stand is to impede the progress of unity. (Welles 1944)

Guy Endore

Among the Hollywood insiders that rallied to the SLDC cause was novelist and screenwriter Guy Endore. Displaying his gifted prose, Endore authored a pamphlet titled *The Sleepy Lagoon Mystery*, a scathing attack against yellow journalism as practiced by William Randolph Hearst and other Los Angeles publishers that accused them of fomenting racial strife that benefited the Axis powers in the war.

Born Samuel Goldstein in 1900 in New York and educated at Columbia University, Endore was best known for a number of horror thrillers, including his 1933 novel *The Werewolf of Paris*, a work that became over the years something of a cult classic. He also wrote an array of novels and screenplays unrelated to the horror genre, many of them that reflected a left-wing political bias. His membership with the American Communist Party later led to his blacklisting during the years of political witch hunts in the late 1940s and 1950s.

A committed political activist, Endore eagerly worked with the SLDC. His pamphlet outlined in vivid prose the disgraceful and unjust proceedings that led to the convictions of the 17 youths. He blasted the actions of the Hearst Press and the *Los Angeles Times* of journalism that, even if unwitting, aided the cause of America's enemies and the Sinarquista Fascist forces active not only in Mexico but also in the United States.

Endore spoke vigorously on radio and in meetings about the trial. The pamphlet sold over 50,000 copies, was widely circulated, and became a principal weapon of the SLDC in its campaign to free the young Mexican Americans.

"The Sleepy Lagoon case has become a symbol of the struggle of the Mexican minority to free itself from a pattern of racial ostracism and discrimination which has too long prevailed in Southern California," the pamphlet began. It spoke of larger issues than just the fate of the individuals now locked up for the murder of José Díaz. The effort of the SLDC, he declared, was the "first well-organized and widely-supported effort in Southern California to bring the case of the Mexican or the citizen of Mexican descent, to the attention of all the peoples of the area." In fighting for justice in this case, the effort sought to help bring about "a correction of those stereotyped attitudes which have long resulted in more than one type of discrimination against the Mexican. We are seeking to correct a social as well as a case of individual injustice" (Endore 1944a, 3).

A shipyard worker named Eliseo Hernandez walked into the office of the SLDC one day in July and said that he had read *The Sleepy Lagoon Mystery* and figured that he could sell copies. In a short time, he had sold 140 copies. When he returned with the money he had collected and asked for more copies to peddle, those in the office were astonished. Where had he sold them? "Mostly I've been selling them to Mexican people," he said. "They are very glad to get it. A lot of them are learning for the first time what the Sleepy Lagoon case means to them. They are learning the real meaning of the newspaper lies and of the riots" (Barajas 2006, 49).

Manuel Reyes, serving a sentence of from five years to life imprisonment, wrote from San Quentin: "glad to know they are letting people know that there is prejudice against the Mexicans, and how the police treated us when we were arrested. We were treated like if we were German spies or Japs. They didn't figure we are Americans just like everybody else that is born in this country" (Greenfield 1943).

Even former president of Mexico Lazaro Cardenas, after reading *The Sleepy Lagoon Mystery*, wrote to McWilliams lauding the work of the SLDC: "I have read this booklet with great interest and wish to congratulate you and all members of your committee for your great spirit of justice which has led you to enter into a campaign in defense of the seventeen boys of Mexican extraction" (Barajas 2006, 48).

Alice Greenfield: A Lifeline

Only a few years older than the imprisoned young men of the Sleepy Lagoon case, attractive, and bristling with enthusiasm for their cause, Alice Greenfield became something of a lifeline for their hopes of being released. She regularly sent them notes and letters enclosing the SLDC's press releases, bulletins, and pamphlets. She visited each one in jail about every six weeks, telling them of the active movement on their behalf, of the genuine concern of people not only in Los Angeles but also across the country—many of them famous people—to see the injustice against them overturned. She told them that each day more individuals were rallying to their cause.

A number of them were at first wary of her intentions and somewhat suspicious of this young Jewish woman who had seemingly come from nowhere to be their most ardent champion. But most of them quickly realized the depth of her concern and the spirit of her commitment to make things right in this case of gross injustice.

After her fourth visit to San Quentin, Greenfield wrote:

> We talk about a lot of different things—the activities of the Defense Committee first, then what kind of work they are doing in prison, what sports they are going out for; and sometimes they just reminisce. The outside seems terribly far away and long ago. They tell little anecdotes—nothing important, but it's good to talk and think about things that happened out there. When they were convicted they were stunned and bewildered. It didn't make sense. It was a terribly shocking thing—a personal tragedy for each one, but without much connection to the rest of the world. The DA and the judge were the villains of the piece. It was liable to happen that way if you were a Mexican. Now they understand. They put it in its most simple terms. Maybe this case will keep the same sort of thing from happening to other American citizens of Mexican extraction. (Greenfield 1943 or 1944)

The letters from the prisoners to Greenfield became increasingly warm, even tender. Those who, at first, had doubted her motives or sincerity now saw her as a friend, comforter, and fierce combatant on their behalf. They looked forward to her visits and her messages. To some she remained "Miss Greenfield"; to others it was "Darling Grandmother" or "Honey."

Greenfield gained confidence as a public speaker. "I started out very nervous, with trembling hands," she says. "But I kept doing it, and a year later I spoke to 1,000 longshoremen in San Francisco. I was passionate and articulate and they gave us $1,000" ("A Voice for Those without" 2003). Given her personal acquaintance with each of the inmates, she was able to bring a unique perspective to those public appearances before a variety of audiences.

Greenfield even helped enlist the support of Vicente Peralta, consul-general of Mexico in Los Angeles. Impressed with her knowledge of the case and her determination to help Mexican Americans unjustly convicted, Peralta used his extensive contacts with influential members of the Latino community to arrange meetings and speaking engagements. Through Greenfield and her close communication with the young men in prison, a growing number of Mexican Americans began to learn details about the boys, the trial, and the injustices that seemed clearly aimed not only at

those individuals convicted in the trial but also at their own cultural and
racial identity. To many of them, the Zoot Suit Riots now made more sense.

In one of the SLDC press releases, Greenfield mocked the prosecution
who

> can proudly claim that it secured the conviction of more defendants
> for a single death than has ever been obtained in the history of Cali-
> fornia. To this claim can be added the facts: first, that 12 boys so con-
> victed averaged about 17 or 18 years of age; second, that the boys,
> with one exception, were all of Mexican origin; third, that there is no
> direct proof that any one of the boys ever touched the boy whom they
> were charged with murdering; and fourth, it is clear that most of the
> boys were not at or near the spot where the killing allegedly occurred.
> (Sleepy Lagoon Defense Committee 1944)

In this press release as in others to follow, Greenfield and the SLDC
emphasized that it was not just the particular boys who had been denied injustice and railroaded but the Mexican people in Los Angeles. In the press,
in the dragnet in which hundreds of citizens were subjected to violent interrogation, in the grand jury room, in statements by law enforcement and
government officials—in all of these instances the myths of pachucos and
Zoot suiters as criminals and thugs had been driven nail by nail into the
public consciousness. It was an outrage to common justice and humanity.

Ben Margolis and the Appeal

Although still only in his early 30s, Ben Margolis had sat next to men
and women accused of crimes long enough to gain a reputation as an able,
cagey, and ardent defense attorney. As he continued to sift through the
original voluminous trial transcript that exceeded 6,000 pages and as he
met with witnesses, the entire Sleepy Lagoon case increasingly appeared
to him as one of most egregious judicial outrages he had ever come across.
His ire and disgust with the entire proceeding grew as he put together the
pieces of the appeal brief. So breathtaking were the instances of judicial
misconduct, Margolis believed, that he did not regard the challenge of preparing a convincing brief especially daunting.

Nevertheless, as he delved deeper and deeper into the proceedings,
Margolis became increasingly emotional, struck by the lengths to which
this group of people marked only by their racial and cultural background
had been castigated in the press, herded like cattle by the police and then

sorted out, leaving over 20 youths subjected to charges of murder with no evidence to back up those charges. Margolis had seen much injustice in his decade as a lawyer but the Sleepy Lagoon trial itself brought him even greater disgust toward the American judiciary in regard to race.

In characterizing Judge Fricke's handling of the trial, Margolis said later in an interview:

> I have never in my whole life seen a case in which there was so much bias and so many errors. . . . His open expressions of race bias are of a character that no judge would today say the same things. They might believe it, they might feel it, but no one would say the things he did. No one would make the kind of orders that he made, today, unless he was crazy. And yet in those days, while he was probably extraordinarily bad, there were other judges who would run him a close second. (Margolis 1984)

As Margolis began to assemble the brief for the appeal, the document grew to over 500 pages. It asked for reversal of the convictions on many grounds of misconduct of the trial itself and Judge Fricke in particular. It charged that the defendants had been deprived of their constitutional rights to confer with their attorneys during the trial. It claimed that not one of the convicted young men had been tied to the murder at the Sleepy Lagoon and that the prosecution had, for lack of evidence, resorted to the charge of conspiracy, a charge that also lacked any evidence whatsoever. It pointed to numerous incidents of misconduct by Judge Fricke, from his treatment of the defendants' attorneys to his allowing in trial masses of evidence that should have been inadmissible. It claimed that the community temper of hatred against Zoot suiters stirred by law enforcement, government officials, and the press had made a fair trial impossible. It charged that the state, in denying the accused a change of clothing and haircuts, engaged in an outrageous prosecutorial stunt further prejudicing the case, in effect attempting to display the boys as live exhibits of a criminal type. On and on the brief continued citing one glaring injudicious action after another.

On October 21, 1943, Margolis delivered the brief to the Second District Court of Appeals. He later reflected:

> Here, you had a group of fourteen: *all* convicted of murder. . . . So that it was a case that had a combination of qualities that most individual cases did not have, in many different ways. So, it was unusual

because of that. . . . These were people without money. They could take appeals and have a lawyer appointed, and they'd do a half-ass job. You know there wasn't a great deal—It was sort of accepted to a very large extent. And the courts didn't bother much with this kind of appeal. The important thing in this case was to get the attention of the court. It was a wonderful case in which to do it, because it was all there. Everything that you wanted to argue was there. All spelled out. So it was an opportunity to do something that wasn't easy to do in those days. (Margolis 1984)

When Alice Greenfield showed copies of the brief to the convicted young men, they were excited and impressed at the devastating challenge to the judicial circus that had landed them in prison. Greenfield watched as they intently leafed through the pages, shaking their heads in approval. "Man! this is it," she remembered one exclaiming. As the SLDC waited for the appellate court proceeding, its supporters continued with its fund-raising and community outreach activities. Coming on the heels of the disgraceful riots in June 1943, the efforts of the SLDC to gain support among the Mexican-American community to release the Sleepy Lagoon prisoners intensified. Margolis clearly saw the evidence of a heightened outrage in the community that could be marshaled into action. "The most important of the activities in my opinion," Margolis said, "were the activities in the Latino community . . . that the community began to organize itself around this case and laid a basis for the future. Also, the victory in the case created the concept that you can win some of them; you don't lose all of them" (Margolis 1984).

Along with Greenfield, Margolis visited the prisoners in San Quentin several times. He particularly remembered Henry Leyvas, the oldest of the young men, and the lawyer came to believe that under different circumstances that had marked Leyvas's life he could have been a natural leader. Passionate, articulate, Leyvas understood, Margolis said, that his own experiences were part of a larger fight for social justice for those of his fellow Mexican Americans in Los Angeles. The Sleepy Lagoon trial in which he was so wrongfully imprisoned, the Zoot Suit Riots, the everyday instances of bigotry and scorn—all of it rocked in him a deep sense of outrage.

"But most important was," Margolis said,

that of all of them, he had the greatest sense that he was a member of a group that was being walked on, being discriminated against, and that he was going to fight against it. He never really established the idea that he would be able to come out in a normal—any acceptable manner to carry on the fight. But he was going to carry on the fight wherever he was. *Nobody* was going to walk on Henry Leyvas. . . . [H]e understood what was going on in a very fundamental sense: what was going on, and how the people were being affected. I think they all understood it to some extent, but not really at that kind of a fundamental understanding that I think Leyvas had. (Margolis, 1984)

People v. Zammora *Appellate Trial*

On May 15, 1944, Attorney Ben Margolis delivered oral arguments as the appellate trial in the Sleepy Lagoon case began in the Second District Court of Appeals. According to many observers, Margolis was brilliant. Cogent and impassioned, he demolished the Sleepy Lagoon case verdict piece by piece, from its lack of evidence and prejudicial actions by the prosecution and the judge to the copious amount of the so-called evidence that should have, under any normal courtroom proceeding, been deemed inadmissible. But Margolis dared to go further. He talked about the humiliation of the defendants and how the court's behavior exemplified the ways in which society dealt with its minority populations. His emotional argument held the courtroom in rapt attention.

Soon, in June 1944, the SLDC received extraordinarily welcome news that the Board of Prison Terms and Paroles had acted on parole applications submitted earlier on behalf of the prisoners. Based on the good behavior of the Mexican-American youths imprisoned in the Sleepy Lagoon case and on many of the same claims that Margolis had made in his brief and oral arguments about the injustice of the trial, the board acted favorably for a number of the prisoners convicted of second-degree murder. Beginning with the release of Manuel Delgado on August 18, the board scheduled releases for three others in September, three more for December, and others in 1945. The action by the board was the cause for increased confidence that the appellate challenge could be successful.

Although much buoyed by the action of the board, Carey McWilliams implored the SLDC members to vigorously continue their advocacy efforts. Even the boys who were to be paroled would still suffer greatly, McWilliams said, if the appellate court did not act favorably. "They will have lost their citizenship rights, they will be stigmatized for life, with problems of employment, and always suspect" (Weitz 2010, 160). And for the three young men convicted for first-degree murder, there would be no parole eligibility for several years.

Manuel Delgado walked out of prison on August 18 as scheduled. He headed straight to the offices of the SLDC to help with the appeal. Less than two months later, he and all others who worked for the overturn of the case had a cause for celebration.

On October 4, 1944, the judicial fiasco of *People v. Zammora* that had resulted in the conviction and imprisonment of multiple defendants in the Sleepy Lagoon murder was finally reversed on appeal. The justices of the District Court of Appeal, in a 121-page decision written by Associate Justice Thomas P. White, voted unanimously to overturn the verdicts and set aside the sentences. The appellate decision would still have to be considered by the Los Angeles Superior Court for further action. The Superior Court could decide to retry the case or overturn the sentences and free the Sleepy Lagoon defendants.

The court affirmed that there was no basis for conspiracy charges, that the record of the trial did not in any way show that there had been a collective intent on the part of the group from 38th Street to commit murder. The court further stated that not one of the boys convicted on the charge of murder or second-degree murder had been tied to the whereabouts of the victim, José Díaz, or were in any way connected by the evidence in his assault. It condemned the actions of Judge Fricke as being prejudicial to the defense "by his insulting remarks to defense counsel, by (unwarranted) rebukes, and by failing to make provisions for consultation between defendants and their counsel."

The court concluded:

It is greatly to be desired for the safety of the public that the guilty be apprehended and punished for their crimes. But, as a stabilizing influence looking toward the permanence of our institutions, it is of equal or greater importance that the guaranty of a fair trial in accordance with the meaning and intent of the Constitution and statutes should be assured and that such a trial be made a certainty so far as possible within the bounds of average human ability, attended by its unavoidable imperfections and frailties. (*People v. Zammora* 1944)

The court did not go as far as Ben Margolis had wanted but likely had not expected. Although the court overturned the original decision, it refuted the notion that the actions of law enforcement, the trial judge, and everything else involved in the case were products of indigenous racism.

Guy Endore, on behalf of the SLDC, wrote:

The case soon swelled into the broadest kind of democratic movement. Unions, large and small collected dimes and dollars in their shops, Motion picture people contributed their talents and their money. Los Angeles business men sent in their checks. The newsboys at one of their union meetings voted to push the sales of the SLEEPY LAGOON MYSTERY. Lawyers gave generously of their time and their experience. Good wives baked cakes and made sandwiches for pay-parties to help the boys. Girls gave up their afternoons to address envelopes. From all over the country came letters of inquiry and approval. Wires of encouragement came from high officials in Latin America, and in particular from ex-President Lazaro Cardenas of Mexico. All these people rejoice now in a victory for American democracy and for American love of justice. (Endore 1944b)

Looking back later, Carey McWilliams effusively praised Margolis's work in preparing the case. It was a first-rate argument, he said,

quite conclusive, quite interesting; and they, of course, unanimously reversed the conviction. Not only did they reverse it; they gave Judge Fricke quite a working over for obvious bias and prejudicial rulings and outrageous comments about the defendants, and all the rest of it. So it was a terrific victory for the defendants and for the community. . . . [I]t was the first major victory in the courts of this kind that the Mexican-American community had ever won. ("Conviction Overturned" 1944)

The Superior Court action on the appellate decision came less than three weeks later. Alice Greenfield could not sleep in the early morning of October 23, 1944. She later wrote to Guy Endore:

After five on Monday there wasn't any sleep left. For the next two and a half hours disjointed thoughts went crashing around and around in my brain. The one thing that came back and again was 'This is the day. This is it. This is what we have been waiting for and working for for two years. This is the day. This is the day.' I tried to imagine how Mrs. Leyvas and Mrs. Telles and Mrs. Ruiz felt. (Greenfield 1944)

The courtroom was packed with members of the friends and families of the Sleepy Lagoon defendants, along with many individuals, such as Ben Margolis and George Shibley, who had doggedly fought through the two years and through the days of the Zoot Suit Riots to overturn the original verdict.

The direction the court was going to take was clear from the beginning. Deputy District Attorney John Barnes asked Judge Clement D. Nye to dismiss the case. Nye agreed, officially wiping away the guilty verdicts of all individuals caught up in the Sleepy Lagoon murder trial fiasco. The defendants were ordered released and their records cleared.

Alice Greenfield told of what followed: "A blur of embracing and kissing. Crying. Mrs. Leyvas says over and over 'My hijo. Mi hijo. Mi hijo. . . .' Everybody, kisses everybody. When they kiss me they say 'thank you, thank you, thank you, gracias, gracias'" (Greenfield 1944).

The judicial evils inflicted on the young Mexican Americans had now been, to some degree, eased. They were now free. The scars, however, would remain. Gus Zamora's family, for example, never forgave their son for somehow besmirching the Zamora name. A number of the boys would return to prison for various offenses. Some, nevertheless, would go on to be successful members of the Los Angeles community.

But the Sleepy Lagoon trial, so inextricably linked to the Zoot Suit Riots in time and tenor, would not be forgotten. They would be remembered by activists and organizations and by the Mexican-American community as something of a watershed, a moment in time when the drive for basic rights, cultural identity, and the need to strive for political and economic power was so clearly evident.

References

Barajas, Frank. 2006. "The Defense Committees of Sleepy Lagoon: A Convergent Struggle against Fascism, 1942–1944." *Aztlán: A Journal of Chicano Studies* (Spring). http://history.msu.edu/hst327/files/2009/05/Defense-Committees-of-Sleepy-Lagoon.pdf.

"Conviction Overturned." 1944. "The Sleepy Lagoon Case: Constitutional Rights and the Struggle for Democracy." University of California, Los Angeles. http://unit proj.library.ucla.edu/special/sleepylagoon/slexoverturned.htm.

Endore, Guy. 1944a. "The Sleepy Lagoon Mystery." S. Guy Endore Papers, UCLA, Special Collections, Charles E. Young Research Library. http://content.cdlib.org/ark:/13030/hb7779p50c/?order=5&brand=calisphere.

Endore, Guy. 1944b. "Sleepy Lagoon . . . Victory for Democracy." October 4. http://content.cdlib.org/ark:/13030/hb8c6011nb/?query=sleepy lagoon case&brand= calisphere.

Greenfield, Alice. 1943 or 1944. "Hard times for the boys up at San Quentin." UCLA, Special Collections, Charles E. Young Research Library; Sleepy Lagoon Defense Committee Records, 1942–1945, Online Archive of California. http://content. cdlib.org/view?docId=hb596nb648&brand=calisphere&doc.view=entire_text.

Greenfield, Alice. October 14, 1943. "On October 21 the First Brief Will Be Filled with the Appellate Court in the Sleepy Lagoon Case." UCLA, Special Collections, Charles E. Young Research Library; Sleepy Lagoon Defense Committee Records, 1942–1945, Online Archive of California. http://www.oac.cdlib.org/ark:/13030/hb4m3nb6b1/?brand=oac4.

Greenfield, Alice to Guy Endore. October 25 1944. "The Sleepy Lagoon Case: Constitutional Rights and the Struggle for Democracy." University of California, Los Angeles. http://unitproj.library.ucla.edu/special/sleepylagoon/slexoverturned.htm.

Margolis, Ben. July 9 1984. Margolis Interviewed by Michael S. Balter Department of Special Collections. University of California, Los Angeles, Tape Number V, Side Two. http://content.cdlib.org/view?docId=hb6c6010vb;NAAN=13030&doc.view=frames&chunk.id=div00028&toc.depth=1&toc.id=&brand=calisphere.

McWilliams, Carey. 1990. *North from Mexico: The Spanish-Speaking People of the United States.* New York: Praeger.

People v. Zammora. 66 Cal. App. 2d 166 [Crim. 3719, Second Dist, Div. One, Oct., 4, 1944]. http://online.ceb.com/calcases/CA2/66CA2d166.htm.

"The Sleepy Lagoon Case: Prepared by the Sleepy Lagoon Defense Committee." 1943. UCLA, Special Collections, Charles E. Young Research Library; Sleepy Lagoon Defense Committee Records, 1942–1945, Online Archive of California. http://www.oac.cdlib.org/ark:/13030/hb7779p4zc/?brand=oac4.

Sleepy Lagoon Defense Committee. 1944. "News Release: Reasons for the Convictions in the Sleepy Lagoon Case." UCLA, Special Collections, Charles E. Young Research Library; Sleepy Lagoon Defense Committee Records, 1942–1945, Online Archive of California. http://www.oac.cdlib.org/view?docId=hb6t1nb7s5&brand=oac4&doc.view=entire_text.

"A Voice for Those without." 2003. *Perspectives*, Autumn. http://www.artsci.washington.edu/news/Autumn03/McGrath.htm.

Weitz, Mark. 2010. *The Sleepy Lagoon Murder Case: Race Discrimination and Mexican-American Rights.* Lawrence: University Press of Kansas.

Welles, Orson to Parole Board, San Quentin. March 1, 1944. UCLA, Special Collections, Charles E. Young Research Library, Sleepy Lagoon Defense Committee Records, 1942–1945, Online Archive of California. http://www.oac.cdlib.org/view?docId=hb3m3nb5sz&brand=oac4&chunk.id=meta.

EIGHT

Continuing the Fight

LOOKING BACK YEARS LATER on the tumultuous times of the Zoot Suit Riots and the Sleepy Lagoon murder case, Carey McWilliams and others saw the events as milestones. So outrageous had been the treatment accorded to Mexican-American citizens in Los Angeles during wartime that activists, reformers, and the immigrant community itself began to fight back, to make demands, and seek ways to come together to force change against the kind of systemic prejudice and dehumanization so evident in the trial and the riots.

The ordeal of the Sleepy Lagoon defendants and the publicity surrounding the judicial fiasco of the trial and subsequent overturn of the decision had made national news. Even more sensational had been reports in popular magazines and newspapers across the country about the violence on the streets of Los Angeles, violence that the First Lady of the United States had defined as rooted in racial hostility against Mexican Americans.

Most government officials and even the court decision that freed the imprisoned Sleepy Lagoon defendants denied that racism was involved. After all, such an admission, especially during the war, would have compromised the image of American democracy. Nevertheless, the scenes from the riots and the blatantly injudicious courtroom drama belied the claims that Mexican-American immigrants were being accorded equal treatment under U.S. law and a fair place in society. And those segregated schools, theaters, and public facilities, those low-paying jobs, and the daily humiliation of seeing signs excluding Mexican Americans from patronizing various business establishments did not exemplify the ideals of freedom and equality.

Life was tough in the barrios. And now, when thousands of Mexican Americans returned from serving their country in the war once again to take their place in U.S. society, the stories and images of Mexican-American youngsters being unjustly imprisoned and others being beaten in the streets by white servicemen seemed to many surreal. Was this treatment what those Mexican-American troops had been fighting for in Europe and Asia? It seemed a cruel irony. For many in the Mexican-American community and for other groups and activists, it now became a rallying call for reform.

Various investigations in the aftermath of the Zoot Suit Riots recognized the lack of educational opportunities and social and recreational programs available to help Mexican-American youth. The Citizen's Committee chaired by Joseph McGucken, auxiliary bishop of Los Angeles, for example, had called on city leaders not only to provide such youth services but also to strive to provide improved housing and employment opportunities and other measures to help equip the immigrant population in Los Angeles. The recommendations did lead to a number of youth projects that began to address the growing problems.

They even led to the creation of the Los Angeles County Commission on Human Relations, a group organized to foster better relations between the Mexican-American community and the Los Angeles Police Department. The Commission was crafted with the explicit goal of creating a mutual atmosphere of understanding that would ward off any future riots involving the police and the city's minority populations.

But the Sleepy Lagoon trial and the riots had an impact that resonated far beyond the hysteria of wartime Los Angeles. Those men and women— both Anglo and Mexican American—who established the Sleepy Lagoon Defense Committee (SLDC) and others who banded together in grassroots groups to try to ameliorate the conditions that led to the Zoot Suit Riots gave hope that the powerless could gain power and that change could really happen through coordinated and cooperative efforts.

Organizing

Mendez v. Westminster, 1947

One of the most profound early victories for Mexican-American reformers after the Zoot Suit Riots was a case called *Mendez v. Westminster* in which a federal court ruled that segregation of Mexican Americans in public schools was illegal. A resounding victory for the Mexican-American community, the case set a precedent that helped the eminent African-American lawyer Thurgood Marshall and the National Association for the Advancement of Colored People(NAACP) prevail in the landmark 1954 U.S. Supreme Court decision of *Brown v. Board of Education* declaring unconstitutional state laws establishing separate public schools based on race.

In 2007, the U.S. Postal Service issued a commemorative stamp honoring the 1947 case of *Mendez v. Westminster* in which a federal court ruled that segregation of Mexican Americans in public schools was illegal. A resounding victory for the Mexican-American community, the case set a precedent that helped African-American lawyer Thurgood Marshall and the National Association for the Advancement of Colored People (NAACP) prevail in the landmark 1954 U.S. Supreme Court decision of *Brown v. Board of Education*. The case also marked the beginnings of strong organizing efforts by Latinos to fight against injustices illustrated vividly by the Sleepy Lagoon murder case and the Zoot Suit Riots. (AP Photo/USPS)

The *Mendez v. Westminster* case was filed in 1944 in the U.S. District Court in Los Angeles by five Mexican-American parents whose children had been denied entrance to public schools in the Westminster School District of Orange County and forced to attend "schools for Mexicans."

They formed a small advocacy group and began going to local Board of Education meetings. They joined an organization called the League of United Latin-American Citizens, a Hispanic civil rights group that had been formed in Texas in 1930. And they attracted to their cause a young Anglo organizer named Fred Ross.

Born in 1910 in San Francisco, a graduate of the University of Southern California, Ross took a job as a case worker for the state relief administration and later for the U.S. Farm Security Administration (FSA). In 1939, he became the director of the Arvin Migratory Labor Camp near Bakersfield, California, that famed author John Steinbeck used as a setting in *The Grapes of Wrath*. Working with farm workers and other migrants, Ross sought ways to help those workers fight for their rights through grassroots organizing.

When the federal government imprisoned Japanese Americans in concentration camps amid the anti-Japanese hysteria, Ross worked with the War Relocation Authority, helping thousands of residents get jobs and housing. Following the Zoot Suit Riots, Ross joined a group called the American Council for Race Relations, an organization based in Chicago that had been formed to ameliorate racial tensions. In San Bernardino, he began to organize Latinos into "Councils for Civic Unity."

But soon, Ross moved once again to another project. He began to work with the famed community organizer Saul Alinsky and the Industrial Areas Foundation (IAF), an organization established to help enable oppressed people in American society gain a measure of power in shaping their lives and communities. In Los Angeles, Ross worked to help African Americans and Mexican Americans fight against unfair housing ordinances, school segregation, and police brutality.

When he heard of the lawsuit in Orange County challenging segregation of Mexican Americans in public schools, he offered to serve as an advisor. Ross helped the plaintiffs in the *Mendez* case to mobilize support in the community. In early 1946, the court ruled that segregated "Mexican schools" were unconstitutional. In a later appellate decision, the Federal District Court of Appeals in San Francisco upheld the ruling.

Hector Tarango, a Mexican-American civic leader who helped with the case, said later that the verdict was something of a vindication, a welcome victory for the Mexican-American community. "We had actually set the first precedent of anti-segregation in schools in the country at that time," Tarango said. "Right here in Orange County. Mendez versus Westminster . . . was the pilot case we had for the whole group. Several families were involved. . . . We did a lot of things that opened the door for others." (Tarango 2005).

Community Service Organization

Shortly after the *Mendez v. Westminster* decision, Bishop McGucken, who remained an ardent supporter and friend of the Mexican-American community, welcomed the advent of a major organization to promote an unprecedented organizing effort in the Latino community. It would be called the Community Service Organization (CSO).

Seventy years after the humiliations of Zoot suiters on the city streets and in the barrios of Los Angeles, Olga Guiterrez, who was five years old at that time, vividly remembered the gross violation of their own home. Two pachucos who were friends of her uncle, she said, came to the front door and anxiously asked if they could pass through to the back entrance. Shortly afterward, they were followed by two sailors who barged through the front door. She remembered the screams of her family. "We were the most square family in East Los Angeles," Gutierrez said. "And, until then, my dad did not like the pachucos. But after that day, he changed his mind. At least they were polite enough to ask for permission to come in. The sailors scared us, all of us little kids. After that, those two pachucos were OK to my dad" (Baeder 2013).

Bishop McGucken knew well these types of families. He knew that attitudes had changed among many in the community because of the riots and the degrading treatment of fellow citizens in the barrios and their exclusion from mainstream Los Angeles. He was excited by this new group that would focus on mobilizing these citizens.

CSO was formed in 1947 by Fred Ross, acting under the auspices of and with financial support from the IAF, Edward Roybal, an executive with the Los Angeles Tuberculosis and Health Association and an aspiring political figure, and Antonio Rios of the Steelworkers' Union.

It was designed to be a civic action group dedicated to promote community improvement, awareness of citizenship rights and responsibilities, and to fight against human and civil rights abuses. The grassroots organization would help fight discrimination in housing, employment, and education; promote political involvement; and establish self-help programs. Ross taught various organizing techniques including so-called house meetings. From such simple concepts, organizers were able to not only gain the confidence of workers wary of joining an organization but were also able to engender a sense of community and camaraderie that drew them together.

In less than two years, thousands joined the organization and established chapters across California. Its members worked together to gain new footholds that before seemed merely fanciful. Thousands of men and women in CSO held house meetings, conducted voter registration drives, protested police and courtroom treatment, and began citizenship classes for families of immigrant working men and women.

Ed Roybal and Election Success, 1949

Born in Albuquerque, New Mexico, in 1916 to a Hispanic family that traced its roots for many generations in Bernalillo County, Ed Roybal moved with his parents to Boyle Heights, a working class neighborhood east of downtown Los Angeles, when he was six years old. After graduating from Roosevelt High School, he joined the Civilian Conservation Corps (CCC) and subsequently attended the University of California at Los Angeles. He had seen the scars of the Zoot Suit Riots in East Los Angeles up close and knew many families who had been affected. He bore the same kind of determination that many others had that such an outrage should never happen again.

After helping found the CSO, Roybal worked hard as its president to enlist broad-based support among the community—organized labor, church groups of various denominations, and activists in the Democratic Party. But he began to see his own personal future in politics.

In late January 1949 at a meeting of the CSO, Roybal officially declared his candidacy for the ninth district city council seat of Los Angeles. Roybal had tried two years earlier to win the seat but had fared poorly with little organization. But this time, with Roybal using to great advantage his support not only from the CSO but also from unions and church groups and with Fred Ross leading a voter registration drive and pushing CSO members in the district to get to the polls, the race seemed winnable. Most important, it became in the eyes of many Mexican Americans something more than a seat on the city council. Six years after the degrading riots against Zoot suit wearing youngsters in East Los Angeles, Roybal, a man who had roots in the community, was challenging the entrenched interests on behalf of his fellow Mexican-American citizens. And now he had an organization to back him up. He was acutely aware of not only the political reverberations of his possible victory but also the symbolic meaning of his candidacy.

In May 1949, Roybal, in a historic, landslide win, became the first Mexican American in the 20th century to win a seat on the Los Angeles City Council. He served as a council member until 1962 when he celebrated another victory. He won a seat in the U.S. House of Representatives and began a long and distinguished career in Washington.

Bloody Christmas, 1951

On December 25, 1951, at the Central Station of the Los Angeles Police Department on First Street, law and order and the protection of the public, for which the department had pledged its resolve and fidelity, became, instead, egregious disorder and mayhem.

At a boisterous Christmas night gathering at the Showboat Bar northeast of downtown Los Angeles on Riverside Drive, police arrived after complaints that merriment had gotten out of hand and that minors were drinking. Officers removed seven young men, all over the drinking age, and a scuffle broke out in the street and two officers suffered minor injuries. Although no arrests were made at the time, all seven were later rounded up at their homes. One of them who resisted arrest, Danny Rodela, a meter reader for the local gas company, was beaten up so badly in front of his family that he was taken to the hospital with a punctured kidney and broken cheekbone. Doctors later said that he had been near death when admitted and required a series of blood transfusions in order to survive. The others were hauled into Central Station.

By the time the six other young men arrived at the station, a false rumor had circulated among police that one of the officers at the scene outside the bar had lost an eye in the fight. The six who had been booked were in for a terrifying ordeal. For over 90 minutes blows and kicks rained on the six and blood began to cover the floor. One of the victims of the beatings suffered for months from the effects of a ruptured bladder. Others were injured almost as seriously. These were echoes of June 1943 and the week of beatings on the streets of Los Angeles.

The gruesome brutality was initially covered up from public scrutiny. But, by late February, the details began to emerge as the victims told their stories. And this time, Mexican-American resistance to such police violence, especially through the CSO, became increasingly determined and vocal. That determination was fueled further by yet another incident in which Anthony Rios, a high-ranking official of the CSO, was also involved in a street altercation with police. The CSO began documenting other cases of police violence and made them public through the press.

In March 1952, at the trial of six of the seven men accused of starting the fight outside the bar on Christmas night, the judge allowed them to describe the beatings they endured at the station. The testimony infuriated the judge who called for an independent investigation.

In a subsequent grand jury hearing of actions by the police, eight officers were indicted for assault. Five of the eight officers were convicted at trial, one receiving a sentence in prison for over a year. The Los Angeles Police Department transferred 54 officers and temporarily suspended 39 others without pay. Like the Zoot Suit Riots, "Bloody Christmas" would be long remembered in the Mexican-American community.

Also in the early 1950s, as Fred Ross was engaged in one of his many house meetings to convince Mexican Americans to join the CSO, he met a young farmworker who would be his most famous recruit. After meeting Ross, the farmworker said, "I didn't know what CSO was, or who this guy

Fred Ross was, but I knew about the bloody Christmas case, and so did everybody in that room. Five cops actually had been jailed for brutality. And that miracle was the result of CSO efforts" (Levy 2007, 98). That farmworker was named Cesar Chavez.

A Zoot Suiter Named Chavez

At the time of the Zoot Suit Riots, in 1943, Cesar Chavez was a young teenager living in Delano, California, in the center of the crop-rich San Joaquin Valley about 150 miles northwest of Los Angeles. He was a migrant worker, who, with his family, followed the harvests, picking a variety of fruits and vegetables.

Chavez also became infatuated with the pachuco lifestyle. He began wearing the pegged pants and long coats and listened to the music of Duke Ellington and Billy Eckstine. Later, he remembered hearing and reading about the riots of 1943. "The rioters were not Mexicans," he said. "They were soldiers, marines, and sailors who raided the barrios attacking the pachucos. I saw clippings of the Los Angeles papers with pictures of pachuco kids with pants torn to the thighs and their long hair clipped." But it was not in the nature of the young Chavez to be intimidated by the stories from Los Angeles. "We needed guts to wear those pants," he said, "and we had to be rebellious to do it, because the police and a few of the older people would harass us. But then it was the style, and I wasn't going to be a square" (Levy 2007, 81–82). In 1944, he was arrested in a segregated Delano movie theater for sitting in the "whites only" section and held in custody by the police for a brief time.

After a stint in the navy, Chavez returned to Delano, resumed his work in the fields, and got married. In 1952, he moved to a barrio outside San Jose named Sal Si Puedes ("Get Out if You Can") to work in a lumber mill. And it was there that he met Fred Ross. At first, Chavez ignored Ross, thinking he was just another white social worker or sociologist curious about barrio residents' habits. But he finally agreed to meet the organizer and Ross impressed the young Chavez mightily with his talk of how change was possible, about how, through community organizing, they could take on the corrupt and powerful. Later that night, Ross wrote in his journal "I think I've found the guy I've been looking for" (Levy 2007, 102).

As one of Ross's protégés, Chavez traveled the state helping develop CSO chapters. He employed the various methods taught by Ross—house meetings that led to new converts that subsequently led to local collaboration and political participation. He convinced people that they could make a difference. From Madera to Bakersfield to Hanford, he signed up hundreds of individuals for the CSO. Meanwhile, the CSO organization became an increasingly potent force in promoting a variety of services from medical care and job referral to political organization and civil rights litigation.

Ross also recruited for the CSO a young, dynamic former school teacher named Dolores Huerta to run the Stockton chapter. Attractive and gregarious, Huerta would be an especially effective representative for CSO in face-to-face meetings with local government leaders and with potential donors. She also lobbied members of the California legislature on issues such as disability assistance to agricultural workers. During her years with the CSO, Huerta crossed paths with Chavez and begin a friendship and working relationship that would last a lifetime.

Chavez read about the nonviolent tactics of reform advanced by Mohandas Gandhi in India. He also learned from the work of Martin Luther King and other civil rights leaders in taking on the entrenched power of racial segregation. Through the examples of these leaders and through his own indefatigable energy and belief in organizing and fighting for the rights of migrant laborers, Chavez decided on another course.

A Union of Farmworkers

In 1962, Chavez decided to leave the CSO and take on a seemingly quixotic quest—to establish a union of farmworkers. Largely illiterate, extremely poor, and divided culturally from mainstream America, farm laborers usually lived mostly in crude shacks constructed by the farms and purchased most of their living supplies from makeshift stores owned by the farmers. This was the underside of the American Dream where unscrupulous labor contractors skimmed off portions of the workers' wages. This was the time of the short-handled hoe in the lettuce fields where workers filed along the lines of crops stooped over in painful contortion, hours on end—painstaking labor that led to many physical ailments and afflictions. Chavez asked Dolores Huerta to join him in this effort to organize this group of workers long deprived of fair wages and working conditions and even human dignity. She agreed.

On Sunday, September 30, 1962, in an abandoned theater in Fresno, California, approximately 200 workers gathered to show their solidarity. They called the new organization the National Farm Workers Association. Later, it would be called the United Farm Workers (UFW). They adopted a union motto: "Viva la causa!" or "Long Live the Cause!"

Chavez and his lieutenants struck away at defeatism and convinced large numbers of people that they could fight back. Not only for farmworkers but also for other Mexican Americans, the movement became an exciting struggle. People for the first time in their lives joined picket lines in front of grocery stores, passed out leaflets, registered others to vote, sang songs and chants of protest, and gained a new awareness that they could actually take on the powerful.

In September 1965, much of the membership of over 500 farmworkers gathered in a church in Delano. Chavez had sent out word through local disk jockeys on Spanish radio and in the Union's paper that something big was in the works. Chavez and the union leadership had decided to join Filipino grape workers in a strike against Delano growers. They would demand higher wages, better living conditions, and fair hiring practices. It would later be called "the Great Delano Grape Strike" and it would be the beginning of many strikes, boycotts, political power struggles, and legislative achievements for the UFW.

Although the UFW never ultimately achieved great lasting gains as measured by traditional labor unions, it did, for a time, attract much international recognition for its struggle against agribusiness interests to win union contracts. It helped win the first state law in the country granting agricultural workers the right to organize. It taught organizational techniques and led many Latino voter registration drives and other actions to gain empowerment.

Two months after the Delano strike began, Chavez was joined by an old acquaintance. His name was Luis Valdez.

Luis Valdez

When he was a boy growing up in Delano in the early 1940s, Valdez had an older cousin, Billy Miranda, who used to come around the house with a friend named they called CC. The two young men, Valdez later recalled, were pachucos and they made a big impression on the little boy. They became like heroes to him, Valdez said later. CC was Cesar Chavez.

Luis was the second of 10 children of farmworkers, both of whom were from Arizona and had roots in the Yaqui Indian culture of Mexico. Like most children who worked as farmworkers, his schooling was sporadic. Nevertheless, the precocious boy always impressed his teachers and developed an unusual skill—the art of puppetry. He appeared as a ventriloquist on local television shows. After attending high school in San Jose, he earned a scholarship to attend San Jose State College and turned his energy to studying the theater.

After graduating from San Jose State in 1964, Valdez joined the San Francisco Mime Troupe. He began to learn the techniques of agitprop (agitation and propaganda) theater, plays designed to infuse the spirit in political and social change movements. Valdez received an offer from Brandeis University to enroll in a Master of Arts program and an offer from an off-Broadway producer interested in producing Valdez's work. In the end, he chose to remain in California. Looking back later, Valdez wrote: "So I knew that there was a possibility, a road, going in one direction. The other road that showed up in the summer of 1965 was that there was a grape strike in the town where I was born called Delano. And as it turns out it was being led by this old pachuco that I had known back when I was six years old" (Bruns 2008, Vol. 2, 504).

Chavez greeted his old acquaintance from Delano with welcoming arms. Valdez, Chavez knew, could bring another, vital dimension to the farmworkers movement. It would be a theater company of actor-laborers who, by staging plays, could raise enthusiasm on the picket lines and publicize the farmworker strike. The talents and imagination of Valdez would soon turn the effort into something much greater—a grassroots theatrical movement. He called it El Teatro Campesino (the Farmworkers' Theater).

Combining Mexican comedic folk theater and mime, the company offered skits about workers, scabs, bosses, and others in the world of the farmworker. The actors themselves were campesinos. The company created short skits that they performed not only at union meetings but also on flatbed trucks at strike sites. Using a few props such a pans or wine bottles to make points, the actors would often hang signs around their necks indicating the portrayed characters.

Chavez also saw in Valdez the makings of a public speaker and sent him out on the campaign trail to make speeches about the grape boycott. "But he saw the value of the arts," Valdez said of Chavez. "He saw the value of music and the Teatro and integrated those early and gave us a lot of leeway to develop our techniques" (Keefer 2013).

By 1967, the UFW was well established. Valdez decided to take El Teatro Campesino to a wider audience. He left the unionizing efforts and of the UFW and in Del Rey, California, established the Centro Campesino Cultural, a cultural center, where he would work to expand El Teatro's reach. He took his plays on the road and was sometimes overwhelmed by the response from workers. Valdez would later be known by many as the "Father of Chicano Theater."

Chicano

Throughout the 1960s and early 1970s, the so-called Chicano Movement produced a new generation of activists and leaders who brought to national attention a variety of issues vital to the Mexican-American community and sought to remedy the ills of discrimination and powerlessness through direct political action. Most scholars trace the derivation of the word "Chicano" to the early 1900s when it was associated with poor, unskilled, uneducated, backward immigrants from Mexico. But in the 1960s, a time of social unrest with the Civil Rights Movement and the Vietnam War, the word took on a totally different meaning for Latinos. It was now a word of cultural and ethnic pride and determination to secure rights, liberties, and equal opportunity in American society.

In New Mexico, in 1963, Reies Lopez Tijerina founded the Alianza Federal de Mercedes Libres, a group dedicated to an improbable fight to reclaim Spanish and Mexican land grants held by Mexicans and Indians before the U.S.–Mexican War. His militant organization led marches and started a newspaper.

In Denver, Colorado, in the mid-1960s, Rodolfo (Corky) Gonzales, an ex-prizefighter, founded a civil rights and cultural movement called the Crusade for Justice and organized an annual Chicano Youth Liberation Conference, which brought together large numbers of Chicano youth from throughout the United States and provided them with opportunities to express their views on self-determination. It was at a 1969 conference that the group produced a so-called Plan de Aztlan. The plan set out the vision of the recovery of Aztlan, the mythical original homeland of the Aztecs. The dream was fanciful; the fighting spirit of protest was strong.

In 1967, in San Antonio, Texas, José Angel Gutiérrez co-founded the Mexican American Youth Organization (MAYO), an activist group that attacked discrimination in the schools and in local and state governments and developed a political agenda. In 1970, Gutiérrez and other MAYO members organized a political drive in Crystal City, Texas, and nearby towns that successfully ran candidates in local elections. They christened a political party called La Raza Unida (the United People) that two years later convened more than 1,000 delegates at a national convention.

In 1966, in East Los Angeles, David Sanchez and other Chicanos founded the Young Citizens for Community Action(YCCA). As its members began donning brown berets, the organization became popularly known by their hats. The Brown Berets were established as a group whose main function was to address social problems such as police brutality and the lack of social programs for activities among Latinos. By September, the group had opened chapters in cities across the country. Mexican-American youngsters now talked about justice and liberation. The slogans were "Chicano Power" and "Brown Is Beautiful."

At a cafe on Whittier Boulevard in Los Angeles, where a number of marches were held in the late 1960s and early 1970s protesting the Vietnam War and the treatment of Chicanos, Brown Berets befriended an individual who gave them historical perspective on their cause. The cafe was called "Hank's" and its owner was Henry Leyvas, the central figure in the Sleepy Lagoon Murder case.

It had been a struggle for Leyvas after his release from prison in 1944. He had spent additional prison time for drug dealing. But by the late 1960s he had straightened out his life and opened his business. He would tell the Brown Berets who gathered in his place about Sleepy Lagoon, about the Zoot Suit Riots, and about the injustices and discrimination that had burned him so deeply. He encouraged them to keep organizing and to keep up the fight.

It was in the neighborhood very close to "Hank's" in late August 1970 that Mexican-American journalist Ruben Salazar, news director for the Spanish language television station KMEX, was killed by a projectile fired by Los Angeles County Sheriff's deputies during a rally protesting the disproportionate number of Latinos killed in the Vietnam War. Although a coroner's inquest ruled the shooting a homicide, no member of the police department was prosecuted. Many in the Mexican-American community believed that Salazar's killing was a premeditated assassination of a very vocal advocate of social change.

Unfortunately Hank Leyvas's tragic life ended a year later after a heart attack. He was only 48 years old.

Cesar Chavez often said that the UFW and his crusade on behalf of farmworkers was not, as such, part of the Chicano movement. But the UFW's fight, steeped in Mexican-American culture, symbolized by the Aztec eagle on its flag, spoke about the power of unity. For most Chicanos, Chavez and the UFW stood as symbols of rebellion and gave a deep measure of pride in being a Mexican American.

In 1978, a play, written and directed by a notable Chicano, debuted on Broadway. It brought to the fore once again those events in wartime Los Angeles that had seared the Mexican-American community—the Sleepy Lagoon murder trial and the Zoot Suit Riots. Its creator was Chavez's old friend—Luis Valdez.

Zoot Suit, *1978*

After leaving the UFW to explore his career in the arts, Valdez led El Teatro Campesino to increasing international acclaim, authoring and directing many successful plays such as La *Virgen de Tepeyac*, 1971; *La*

Carpa de los Rasquachis, 1974; and *El Fin del Mundo*, 1976. He inaugurated a grassroots Chicano artistic movement, created new theater forms, brought to life the history, music, and folklore of his cultural past, and set the stage for the further development of Chicano theater that would continue well into the 21st century.

In 1968, David Sanchez, the founder of the Brown Berets, saw Valdez at a club in Los Angeles called the Ash Grove on Melrose Avenue that had become a center for folk and rock musicians and a gathering place for progressive writers and activists. Sanchez gave Valdez a pamphlet about the Sleepy Lagoon case. Valdez tucked it away but kept in mind the possibility of producing a theatrical production based on the events of the case and the riots.

In 1978, it all came together in a play he called *Zoot Suit*. For Valdez, the historical and cultural clashes of decades earlier were bountiful themes for exploration and he set out to give perspective, through the stories of the trial and the riots, to the continuing tensions still raw, still calling for reform. He was determined that the historical facts not be lost in the drama. He studied books and articles and traveled to New York to interview Cary McWilliams, now editor of the *Nation*, at his apartment near Columbia University.

McWilliams said later, "Luis Valdez came to see me in New York . . . and wanted to talk about the case. We spent an evening talking about it. I put him in touch . . . with Alice (he didn't know about Alice) and also with Ben Margolis. And I was very much impressed with him as a person" ("Honorable in All Things: Oral History Transcript: The Memoirs of Carey McWilliams" 1982).

From Alice (Greenfield) McGrath, Valdez got much of the inside story and was able to contact a number of individuals who were active in the SLDC and the trial. She gave him firsthand impressions of the riots and he visited a number of individuals who had been on the frontlines. Throughout Valdez's work on the script, Alice became a valuable helpmate. She also inspired one of the characters in the play—Alice Bloomfield.

In late February 1978, Valdez sent a note to Alice outlining the substance of the play. He said that the character of Alice symbolized "a real progressive social consciousness taking root in America during World War II; a deep awareness of racial equality that preceded the Civil Rights Movement by a decade" (Valdez to McGrath 1978).

Opening at the Mark Taper Forum in Los Angeles, *Zoot Suit* ran successfully for two years and, because of record, sold-out performances, it was moved to the larger Aquarius Theater. The play eventually won the

Los Angeles Critics Circle Award for "Distinguished Productions" and eight Drama-Logue Awards for "Outstanding Achievement in Theater."

Valdez then took the play to New York and the Winter Garden Theater in 1979. It was the first play written and produced by a Mexican American ever to reach Broadway. Valdez later wrote and directed the 1981 movie version of the play. The film was nominated for a Golden Globe Award.

Impressionistic, with much vitality, the play featured memorable characters and musical interpretation breathing life in the racial conflict from the 1940s that still seethed in Valdez's own time and in his own feelings. He told a reporter that he wanted the play to reach much further than the barrio. "I wrote 'Zoot Suit' for an American audience," he said. "The Anglos have to face reality, but I didn't want to offend the Anglo community. I want the pachuco life to be part of the American experience, not just the Chicano experience" (Breaking Down the Barrios" 1978, 85).

Valdez talked about how the experiences with the farmworkers' struggle and the development of El Teatro Campesino had made the production of *Zoot Suit* possible. "I know that our work reaches into the streets," he said. "We attract young people, people who are confronted with rather stark realities. They have to hope for something, man. If they don't have the arts telling them about the essence and meaning of life, offering some kind of exploration of the positive and negative aspects of life, then there is no hope. I was a very angry young man not too many years ago, and I was able to channel that anger into the arts" (Heyward 1985).

The play revolved around three central characters. The mythical figure of El Pachuco, a kind of devilish master of ceremonies who interacts with the audience, who can change scenes and direction with a snap of his fingers, and who translates the events of the early 1940s into a cultural reference to ancient times and culture; Henry Reyna, modeled after the real-life Henry Leyvas; and Alice. "She was the heart line of my story," Valdez said. "She maintained contact with 'her boys,' as she called them. She was a selfless person, with compassion and humor" (Roosevelt 2009).

Valdez saw much cultural symbolism in the riots as servicemen stripped Mexican Americans of their clothes. "That is to me someone wanting to strip away your identity," he said. His own family had come from Sonora, Mexico, over 100 years ago, he went on, and his parents were born in Arizona. Yet, he always felt that his own identity and citizenship had been in question and had been thought of by Anglos as invalid. In his work in the theater, especially in the writing and directing of *Zoot Suit*, he wanted to make a cultural statement, not only for Anglos but for young Chicanos. "I have always focused in on the issue of cultural fusion, that the progress

Playwright Luis Valdez (center), author of *Zoot Suit*, poses in New York in 1979 with young actors Edward James Olmos (left) who starred in the play as the character El Pachuco, and Valdez's brother Daniel who performed as Henry Reyna, a character based on Henry Leyvas, the central figure in the Sleepy Lagoon murder trial. The first play written and produced on Broadway by a Mexican American, *Zoot Suit*, which was also made into a movie in 1981, brought to life the real-life struggles and social injustices faced by Latinos during World War II to audiences nearly 40 years later now familiar with the Chicano movement. (Stephanie Maze/Corbis)

of America has been to blend the cultures of the world. . . . [U]nfortunately there are people that don't see it that way, that resent any new group that comes in and adapts the American culture to its own lifestyle ("Transcripts" 2004).

Valdez also stressed that the emphasis on racial prejudice was in no way exaggerated in the play. In the early 1940s, he said, "There were signs in downtown Los Angeles that read, 'No Mexicans or dogs allowed.' As ugly and exaggerated as it may seem to some people, I can only say that it's true" (Gussow 1979, III, 13).

Zoot Suit was an affirmation of empowerment. El Pachuco, Valdez explained, represented the superego, the power within every individual that can overcome any human barrier. El Pachuco cries out that it will take more than the U.S. Navy to beat him down. He mocks the treatment accorded to Mexican Americans at the same time many young men from the barrio are fighting and dying overseas. "Rommel is kicking ass in Egypt," El Pachuco declared, "but the Mayor of L.A. has declared all-out war on Chicanos. On you! . . . Forget the war overseas. . . . Your war is on the home front" (Pizzato 1998).

The play featured exact courtroom transcriptions of testimonies and quotes from the press that covered the historical events. Valdez also incorporated music of the time, especially the works of Lalo Guerrero, who, along with other artists, helped preserve contemporary pachuco slang.

Over three decades after its debut, *Zoot Suit* stills stirs passions. In 2012, the San Diego Repertory Theatre and the San Diego School of Creative and Performing Arts collaborated in another fresh and vibrant production that brought the lives of Hank and Alice and El Pachuco to new audiences. The Sleepy Lagoon trial and the Zoot Suit Riots remain a constant historical marker in the Mexican-American drive toward equal rights.

The Bending Arc

The eminent civil rights leader Martin Luther King, Jr., on a number of occasions, echoed the words of the 19th-century Unitarian minister and abolitionist Theodore Parker: "The arc of the moral universe is long but it bends toward justice" ("Theodore Parker and the Moral Universe" 2010).

The battles continue. In 1994, the State of California passed a ballot measure—Proposition 187—that sought, among other things, to require police, healthcare professionals, and teachers to verify and report the immigration status of all individuals, including children. It was not until 1999 that court-approved mediation killed the measure, affirming that the state shall not deprive education or healthcare on the basis of an individual's place of birth and that the state cannot regulate immigration law, a function that the U.S. Constitution assigns to the federal government. Interviewed in 1997, Alice (Greenfield) McGrath described Proposition 187 in these terms that harkened back to the early 1940s: "It is the same spirit, the same mean-spiritedness," McGrath said, echoing her passion for social justice that had not diminished with the passing of years. "Besides being wicked, it's ignorant" (Tobar 1997).

The battles continue. In April 2010, the State of Arizona enacted the nation's toughest law on illegal immigration. It required citizens to carry immigration documents and gave police broad powers to detain anyone suspected of being an illegal alien. The obvious effects of the law in encouraging racial profiling and inviting harassment of Mexican Americans ignited a storm of protest. President Barack Obama declared that the law threatened "to undermine basic notions of fairness that we cherish as Americans" (Archibold 2010).

In the same year as Arizona passed its draconian immigration measure, over three decades after *Zoot Suit* premiered in Los Angeles, the play opened in a production by Mexico's National Theater Company in Mexico City. It was the first time the play had been performed in a major venue in Mexico. It featured an all-Mexican cast and was the first major production performed entirely in Spanish. It was directed once again by Luis Valdez.

In the final scene of *Zoot Suit*, a character remarks to Henry Reyna after they are released from prison: "Let's face it, Hank. There's no life for us in this city. I'm taking my family and I'm moving to Arizona" (Hernandez 2010).

Upon hearing that line, which was in the original script written by Valdez years before, Mexico City audiences invariably hooted and laughed at the irony. "This production maintains its permanence in light of recent events in Arizona," said the online magazine *Interescena*. " 'Zoot Suit' displays a permanent process in the United States, where the abuse of 'the other' never disappears" (Hernandez 2010, A5).

The battles, indeed, continue. Many challenges and struggles remain ahead. Fights over border security and immigration reforms in the U.S. Congress reveal continuing animus and racism that speak loudly about just how difficult and agonizing is the process of assimilation. Deportations still divide families. Strident rhetoric harkens back to earlier generations. But for the Mexican-American community in Los Angeles there are major contrasts from the years of the Zoot Suit Riots in East Los Angeles. There has been progress.

In 1992, Lucille Roybal-Allard, daughter of Congressman, Edward Roybal, became the first Mexican-American woman elected to the U.S. Congress. She remains as the Representative of the 34th Congressional District of California. It is in East Los Angeles.

In 2005, Los Angeles elected a mayor who would serve for eight years. His name was Antonio Ramón Villaraigosa and he was born to Mexican-American parents. They lived in a county east of Los Angeles.

On April 26, 2012, friends, relatives, and fellow activists gathered to celebrate the 82nd birthday of Dolores Huerta, still a dedicated activist, still involved in political battle, and still doing her best to help bend that arc toward justice. Hosted by the Dolores Huerta Foundation, the event was labeled a "zoot suit tardeada" and took place at La Plaza De Cultura y Artes in downtown Los Angeles. The celebration was not only for Huerta's birthday but also to acknowledge the 70th anniversary of the Sleepy Lagoon trial and the Zoot Suit Riots that occurred a year later. There was live music and dancing and impassioned remarks by several of Huerta's long-time warriors for Latino and women's rights, including Luis Valdez. The invitation read: "Zoot suit attire is strongly encouraged" ("Dolores Huerta's 82nd 'Zoot Suit' Themed Birthday" 2012).

References

Archibold, Randal. 2010. "Arizona Enacts Stringent Law on Immigration." *New York Times*, April 23. http://www.nytimes.com/2010/04/24/us/politics/24immig.html?_r=0.

Baeder, Ben. 2013. "Zoot Suit Riots: Remembering the WWII Era Los Angeles Race Riots on Its 70th anniversary." *SVG Tribune*, July 30. http://www.sgvtribune.com/news/ci_23356963/zoot-suit-riots-remembering-wwii-era-los-angeles.

"Breaking Down the Barrios." 1978. *Newsweek*, September 4, 85.

Bruns, Roger. 2008. *Icons of Latino America: Latino Contributions to American Culture.* Westport, CT: Greenwood Press.

"Dolores Huerta's 82nd 'Zoot Suit' Themed Birthday." April 29, 2012. https://www.facebook.com/events/321395264564396/.

Gussow, Mel. 1979. "Pachucos in Musical 'Zoot Suit.'" *New York Times*, February 15, III, 13.

Hernandez, Daniel. 2010. "'Zoot Suit' in Vogue Even After 30 Years." *Los Angeles Times*, July 1, A5. http://articles.latimes.com/2010/jul/01/news/la-mexico-zoot-suit-2010070.

Heyward, Carl. 1985. "El Teatro Campesino: An Interview with Luis Valdez." http://www.communityarts.net/readingroom/archivefiles/2002/09/el_teatro_campe.php.

"Honorable in All Things: Oral History Transcript: The Memoirs of Carey Mc Williams." 1982. Oral History Program, University of California, Los Angeles. http://con tent.cdlib.org/view?docId=ft2m3nb08v&brand=calisphere&doc.view=entire_text.

Keefer, Bob. May 25, 2013. "One Chicano Optimist: A Noted Playwright and Film-maker Will Discuss How He Never Lost Hope." *The Register-Guard.* http://projects .registerguard.com/web/entertainmentarts/27471542–41/valdez-theater-teatro-delano-mexican.html.csp.

Levy, Jacques. 2007. *Cesar Chavez: Autobiography of La Causa.* Minneapolis: University of Minnesota Press.

Pizzato, Mark. 1998. "Brechtian and Aztec violence in Valdez's 'Zoot Suit.'"*Jour-nal of Popular Film and Television,* June 22. http://www.clas.ufl.edu/users/jimenez/ spw4304teatro/B2%20Zoot%20suit.Brechtian%20and%20Aztec%20violence%20 in%20Valdez.htm.

Roosevelt, Margot. 2009. "Alice McGrath Dies at 92; Activist Backed Defendants in 1942 Sleepy Lagoon Trial." *Los Angeles Times,* November 29. http://articles .latimes.com/2009/nov/29/local/la-me-alice-mcgrath29–2009nov29.

Tarango, Hector. November 15, 2005. Interview, CSO Project, Oral Histories. http://www.csoproject.org/Histories.html.

"Theodore Parker and the Moral Universe." 2010. National Public Radio inter-view with Dr. Claiborne Carson, September 2. http://www.npr.org/templates/story/ story.php?storyId=129609461.

Tobar, Hector. 1997. "Sleepy Lagoon Victims Laud Their Champion; History: De-fendants in Sensational 1942 Murder Trial Gather to Celebrate Birthday of Woman Who Helped Organize Their Defense Committee." *Los Angeles Times,* April 20, 2.

"Transcripts." 2004. Interview of Luis Valdez and Helen McGrath. *Horizonte: Arizona through a Hispanic Lens,* September 23. http://www.azpbs.org/horizonte/ transcripts/2004/september/sept23_2004.html.

Valdez, Luis to Alice Greenfield McGrath. February 21, 1978. Papers of Alice McGrath, UCLA Department of Special Collections. http://unitproj.library.ucla.edu/ special/sleepylagoon/slzoot2.htm.

Biographies of Key Figures

José Díaz

(December 9, 1919–August 2, 1942)

On August 2, 1942, a young, 22-year-old Mexican-American farmworker named José Díaz was found murdered after a birthday party not far from an irrigation reservoir that was a favorite swimming and gathering spot for the immigrant poor in Los Angeles, a place the locals called "Sleepy Lagoon." His death and the subsequent sensationalist accounts in the press not only catapulted the name of the young man to national notice but also exacerbated growing racial and cultural tensions in Los Angeles involving Mexican-American youth gangs, especially those sporting so-called Zoot suit clothing. His death also led to one of the most disgraceful judicial proceedings in California state history in which 17 young men were imprisoned on the flimsiest of evidence.

Díaz was born on December 9, 1919, in Durango, Mexico. In the early 1920s, his family fled the violence and dislocation in the aftermath of the Mexican Revolution and headed north across the Texas border. In 1928, the family, along with other immigrants, settled in a bunkhouse on a ranch outside Los Angeles and began work laboring in the fields. After finishing the eighth grade, José left school, joined a brother and sister working at the Sunny Sally Packing Plant processing vegetables, and began to help support the Díaz family.

Nevertheless, as many other poor Mexican-American youths of his wartime generation, Díaz in the summer of 1942 decided to seize an opportunity to get ahead, a way to break away from the lower class, segregated life of the immigrant class. He decided to enlist in the U.S. Army. A few days before the fateful birthday party, he posed before a camera for his army induction photograph, neatly dressed, well-groomed, a young man ready for the next chapter of his life.

Lorena Rosalee Encinas

(September 4, 1922–January 5, 1991)

The murder of José Díaz near the Sleepy Lagoon reservoir, the subsequent trial, and the notorious Zoot Suit Riots that occurred in their wake provoked intense examination of the culture and norms of Mexican-American youth in wartime Los Angeles. That attention did not focus exclusively on young men. Nineteen-year-old Lorena Rosalee Encinas, and a number of other young Latino women, were also caught up in the maelstrom of sensationalist hysteria and reporting that swept through the city and beyond.

Born in 1922, in Nogales, Arizona, Lorena was the third child of her parents who had recently entered the United States from Mexico, later moving into the 38th Street neighborhood in South Central Los Angeles. Besides the unremitting challenges facing a poor immigrant family, Lorena, at the age of 13, faced additional emotional trauma—her father passed away from cancer. In addition, her younger brother Louis began a life of petty crime that would lead him to a number of incarcerations and later to suicide after a bank robbery.

On August 1, 1942, Lorena, now 20 years old and the mother of a child, was at the birthday party at the Williams ranch. When authorities questioned her during the murder investigation, she, along with a number of other young women, refused to say anything about what she saw or heard from others. They were taken into custody and, because of their defiance, placed in the Ventura School for Girls, a reformatory known among the Mexican-American community for its harsh punishment and mistreatment of those unfortunate enough to find themselves under its charge. Lorena was released on her 21st birthday. Years later, she told friends that one of the reasons she had remained silent was to protect her brother Louis whom she suspected might have been involved in the Sleepy Lagoon murder.

Guy Endore

(July 4, 1900–February 12, 1970)

In the wake of the conviction of 17 Mexican-American young men in the Sleepy Lagoon murder case, a number of prominent artists, writers, and movie producers joined in supporting a major effort to free the prisoners on appeal. One of those Hollywood figures was Guy Endore, novelist and screenwriter.

Endore, born Samuel Goldstein in 1900 in New York, educated at Columbia University, was best known for a number of horror thrillers, including his 1933 novel *The Werewolf of Paris*, a work that became over the years something of a cult classic. He also wrote an array of novels and screenplays unrelated to the horror genre, many of them that reflected a left-wing political bias. His membership with the American Communist Party later led to his blacklisting during the years of political witch hunts in the late 1940s and 1950s. He was nominated for an Oscar for the screenplay *Story of G.I. Joe* in 1945.

A committed political activist, Endore eagerly worked with the Sleepy Lagoon Defense Committee (SLDC). His pamphlet, titled *Sleepy Lagoon Mystery*, outlined in vivid prose the disgraceful and unjust proceedings that led to the convictions of the 17 youths. Endore spoke vigorously on radio and in meetings about the trial. The pamphlet was widely circulated and became a principal weapon of the committee in its successful campaign to free the young Mexican Americans.

Charles W. Fricke

(April 2, 1882–January 28, 1958)

Judge Charles W. Fricke, a noted jurist with a distinguished career on the bench as well as the author of a number of influential law treatises, quickly became an archenemy of the Mexican-American defendants who sat before him and his gavel at the Sleepy Lagoon murder trial. To many observers it seemed as if Fricke were on a mission to destroy the evils of the Zoot suit culture and that he had bought to the trial all of the racial and cultural stereotypes rampant in the press and prevalent in a predominant part of the Anglo community in Los Angeles. He conducted a trial notable in its lack of judicial restraint and fairness and one that sullied his reputation.

A native of Milwaukee, Wisconsin, Fricke was educated at New York University, served as a municipal judge in Wisconsin, and moved to Los Angeles where he steadily moved up in the judicial system to become a Superior Court judge known for his toughness and numerous harsh sentences.

In the 1942 trial, Fricke not only sided with the prosecution in almost every judicial challenge but he also made such outrageous demands on the defendants that the case, from its inception, seemed to cry for appeal. He forced the defendants to dress in the clothes they had worn when apprehended and did not allow them to cut their hair. He wanted them to be seen, he said, as the gang that they were. He severely limited the amount of time they could confer with their attorneys, in effect denying them the right to counsel. In addition, his contemptuous demeanor toward the defendants and their principal attorney, George Shibley, was on full display throughout the proceedings.

Although the prosecution's case was riddled with weak, hearsay evidence, 17 of the 22 defendants were found guilty, 12 of them with such severe sentences of first- and second-degree murder that they ended up in San Quentin Penitentiary. The verdicts were later overturned on appeal. The infamous case and its ruling were notable not only for its miscarriage of justice but it also effectively ended the practice in California in which large numbers of individuals were tried en masse.

Henry Leyvas

(April 24, 1923–July 6, 1971)

In the wake of the notorious "Sleepy Lagoon Murder," the dragnet instigated by Los Angeles police that rounded up hundreds of Mexican-American youths, and the subsequent trial of 22 suspects, the public face of youth gang violence portrayed by the police and the press was that of Henry "Hank" Leyvas. Although Leyvas certainly did not kill José Díaz on the fateful night of August 2, 1942, he became the central figure not only in the murder trial but also as the representative figure of all the dangers that lay ahead if society did not eradicate the threat of immigrant gangs.

Born in Tucson, Arizona, on April 24, 1923, Leyvas was the third of 10 children of his parents who had fled the violence of the revolution in Mexico. They married in Arizona in 1919 and later moved to Los Angeles. Hank had several confrontations with the police as a teenager. On one occasion, he had been arrested for assault and held for three months before being cleared. In late 1941, he and two friends were arrested on suspicion of armed robbery. He pleaded guilty to simple assault and was given three years of probation. There had been other run-ins with the authorities. Intelligent, with a defiant attitude, he stood his ground in a number of cases where he was falsely accused of minor offenses. On a number of occasions, he was beaten by the police. Leyvas decided to enlist in the Merchant Marines but the night of August 1, 1942, changed everything.

There is no question that Hank was at the party near Sleepy Lagoon and that he and his friends got into fisticuffs shortly after midnight. When police learned that Hank had been at the party, he became a logical target as a leader of a criminal element that had to be brought down. Indeed, during the trial, Clem Peoples, head of the Sheriff's Office, wrote an account of the murder titled "Baby Gangsters" that appeared in *Sensation* magazine, a pulp favorite. On the cover was a picture of Hank Leyvas with the words, "Ring Leader."

Along with two others, Leyvas was convicted of first-degree murder and sent to San Quentin and later to Folsom Prison. In 1944, the Second District Court of Appeals overturned the Sleepy Lagoon verdicts and Judge Clement Nye dismissed the case. Leyvas, along with others, had been incarcerated for nearly two years. Embittered, he turned to drugs and, finally, was imprisoned for drug distribution. Later, he turned his life around, opening a restaurant in East Los Angeles. He befriended members of the Brown Berets, a Chicano youth group that sought to fight against the kind of injustices that Leyvas had endured. In 1971, Hank Leyvas died of a heart attack. He was only 48 years old.

Ben Margolis

(April 23, 1910–January 27, 1999)

Shortly after the Sleepy Lagoon trial in Los Angeles had brought to national prominence the racial and cultural divide between the Anglo and Mexican-American communities, prominent and highly skilled lawyer Ben Margolis agreed to join the attempt to free the young Latino men convicted in the case. With deft precision, Margolis would slice the case against the men into the bits of sloppy police work, unsubstantiated rumors, judicial improprieties, and racism that put 17 young men behind bars.

The son of Russian immigrants, Margolis spent his early years on New York's East Side. His father, a house painter, was a member of the International Workers Order, a socialist organization. Margolis followed in the family's political bent, becoming a leading labor and civil rights attorney. With a law degree from Hastings School of Law, University of California, Margolis began to practice in San Francisco and was in the process of moving to Los Angeles when he was contacted by members of the SLDC.

Aggressive and committed to the defense of the imprisoned Mexican Americans, Margolis, after examining the transcripts of the original trial, said that in his entire career he had never seen such unremitting bias and persecution of defendants.

After the successful appeal of the Sleepy Lagoon case, Margolis became an increasingly notable attorney in major cases of national importance, including the defense of a group of Hollywood screenwriters and directors accused of being Communists before the powerful U.S. House Un-American Activities Committee.

Alice Greenfield McGrath

(April 5, 1917–November 27, 2009)

For a young, progressive reformer named Alice McGrath, the Sleepy Lagoon murder case represented everything that drove her passion for the underdog—an obvious witch hunt against poor, Mexican-American youngsters who had been vilified by the public, the press, and the police; a trial that reeked of injustice; and the incarceration of an extraordinarily large number of young men in a single trial for long prison sentences. She committed herself to their cause.

The daughter of Russian Jewish immigrants, she was born Alice Greenfield in Calgary, Canada, in 1917. In her early 20s she volunteered for the Congress of Industrial Organizations and met labor lawyer George Shibley. When Shibley took over the case of the Sleepy Lagoon defendants, he hired her as an assistant. After the conviction of 17 Mexican-American boys, McGrath joined the SLDC, founded by writer and activist Carey McWilliams and others, to work toward an appeal. She became the group's executive secretary, not only devoting endless hours helping the legal team and soliciting financial and other assistance but also personally interjecting herself toward the well-being of the imprisoned young men. She visited them in prison, exchanged correspondence, and tried to keep up their spirits as the team made progress toward the appellate proceeding

When the Second District Court of Appeals and Judge Clement Nye overturned the verdicts of the case, McGrath was the first to notify the boys of the appeal's success. With most of them, she made lasting friendships. For over half a century, McGrath continued to work for progressive causes until her death in 2009.

Carey McWilliams

(December 13, 1905–June 27, 1980)

One of the most notable muckraking progressive writers of the 20th century, Carey McWilliams wrote over 200 articles and nine influential books between 1939 and 1950 alone. His writings and activism on issues relating to labor, race, and ethnicity made him a celebrated nemesis to right-wing, conservative political leaders, and business interests, especially during the Sleepy Lagoon murder case and the Zoot Suit Riots.

Born in Steamboat Springs, Colorado, McWilliams earned a law degree in 1927 from the University of Southern California and began a legal career that introduced him to individuals and cases involving the rights of the powerless. From 1939 to 1942, he headed California's Commission of Immigration and Housing where he fought to increase inspections of labor camps and other reforms. Soon, McWilliams became the growers' most persistent critic. His research and work on California migratory labor, especially the books *Factories in the Field* and *North from Mexico,* influenced a young organizer named Cesar Chavez as he began his quest to form a union of farmworkers.

In Los Angeles, McWilliams was a fierce crusader in attempting to reverse the Sleepy Lagoon case, helping form the SLDC. The successful appeal in 1944 has been viewed by some historians as one of most important events in the emerging Chicano movement.

In 1943, when riots in Los Angeles between U.S. sailors and Latinos gained nationwide attention, McWilliams covered the story for several publications with an eye to the racial prejudice that surrounded the fights. His prominent voice helped convince Governor Earl Warren to call for a gubernatorial commission to investigate the racial divisions in the city.

Luis Valdez, friend of Chavez and creator of "El Teatro Campesino," the farmworkers theater, credited McWilliams's work in inspiring and informing his own artistic inspiration in creating the play *Zoot Suit.* For 20 years, beginning in 1955, McWilliams became the head editor of the influential progressive magazine the *Nation.*

Luisa Moreno

(August 30, 1907–November 4, 1992)

Civil rights activist Luisa Moreno was never one to back away from confrontation. During the Sleepy Lagoon Murder fiasco and the Zoot Suit Riots, a time when powerful civic and governmental forces combined to humiliate Mexican Americans in California, Moreno stood up against the persecution—joining a number of progressive groups to fight the injustice and even directly challenging U.S. military leaders to tell the truth about the violence that had engulfed Latino communities in 1943.

Born Blanca Rosa López Rodríguez into a wealthy family in Guatemala, Moreno moved with her husband to New York in 1928 and worked briefly as a seamstress during the Great Depression. In 1935, she became an organizer for the American Federation of Labor, a job that launched her efforts on behalf of workers and oppressed minorities. She helped organize African-American and Latino workers in Florida, became the editor of a Spanish-language newspaper for the United Cannery, Agricultural, Packing, and Allied Workers of America, and, from a home base in San Diego,

California, helped organize "El Congreso del Pueblo de Habla Española" ("The Congress of Spanish-Speaking Peoples").

In 1942, Moreno joined her friend Carey McWilliams in organizing the SLDC, especially in trying to disabuse the public of the notion, made by the mainstream press and public officials, that the accused young men were thugs and criminals. Following the Zoot Suit Riots, the following year, she worked with city council member Charles Dail in San Diego in investigating numerous reports of violence instigated by servicemen in that city. She pressed Admiral David Bagley, commandant of the 11th Naval District, to take appropriate action against the offending sailors. When he refused, she and McWilliams gathered evidence and made it public.

Moreno's aggressive work in defending the civil rights of Mexican Americans continued into the 1950s and she became a central target of California state senator Jack Tenney, whose Committee on Un-American Activities eagerly sought ways to deter the work of Communists or their sympathizers. Tenney detested Moreno and her work and took frequent salvos charging her with anti-American conspiracy. Unfortunately for Moreno, the witch hunt atmosphere of the early 1950s, epitomized by the national hearings headed by Minnesota senator Joseph McCarthy, aided Tenney in his drive to punish Moreno. He was able to persuade immigration officials that she was a dangerous alien, a threat to national safety. She was deported to her birthplace of Guatemala, never to return to the United States.

George Shibley

(May 6, 1910–July 4, 1989)

In this courtroom, at this time, faced with this judge, Defense Attorney George Shibley faced impossible obstacles. Nevertheless, although the defense lost the Sleepy Lagoon trial in 1942, Shibley left a record, through his tactics and legal challenges, upon which a later defense team could rally an appellate victory. Shibley, known as a lawyer for the powerless, had once again done laudable work.

Shibley was born in New York City, the son of Syrian immigrants. After graduating from Stanford University Law School in 1934, he began practicing law in Long Beach, California, a place that would remain his home. He quickly earned a reputation as a battler for those with little chance and most of whom had little money—African Americans and Mexican Americans fighting injustice, homosexuals, members of striking labor unions, and left-wing individuals and groups accused of anti-American and subversive activities.

As *People v. Zammora* began in October 1942, with 22 defendants in the courtroom, it was the largest mass trial in the history of California. Shibley realized from the beginning that winning the case outright would be nearly impossible, given the bizarre conditions, the obvious bias of Judge Charles Fricke, and the outrageous yellow journalism coverage in the press. His strategy was to challenge aggressively and put on the record every egregious judicial outrage displayed in the courtroom—the racist slurs, the demand by the judge that the defendants wear the same clothes they wore when arrested, the prohibition that the accused could not consult with their individual lawyers during the proceedings and many other defamatory actions against the young men.

On January 12, 1943, the jury handed down its convictions. Seventeen of the 22 boys were found guilty. Three of them were sentenced to life imprisonment. Nevertheless, Shibley had established a solid record upon which to build an appeal. But it would not be Shibley who would follow through on that appeal. He was soon drafted into the military. But the appeal, argued by Attorney Ben Margolis, Jr., was, indeed, successful in October 1944. The charges were erased for all those found guilty in the original tainted trial.

Through the years Shibley remained close to a number of the defendants in the Sleepy Lagoon case. When he died, a number of them joined the mourners at his funeral.

Jack Tenney

(April 1, 1898–November 4, 1970)

Jack Tenney was a red-baiting hunter of Communists whose work in California presaged by a decade the infamous, national witch hunt crusade of U.S. senator Joseph McCarthy of Minnesota. State senator Tenney was head of the California Committee on Un-American Activities Committee (CUAC). To Tenney, the Sleepy Lagoon defendants and the Zoot suit–wearing Mexican American who were pummelled by sailors on the streets of Los Angeles were not victims; they and those that formed citizen's committees to advance their rights were somehow all part of the larger Communist menace.

Tenney was born in St. Louis, Missouri, and moved to California in 1909. After serving in the army during World War I, he returned home and worked his way through law school and entered politics. In 1942, he won a seat in the California state senate as a Republican and became chairman of CUAC, a position from which he drew increasing power to investigate those he suspected of having Communist ties. From movie actors to labor leaders to progressive activists, Tenney brought before the committee a stream of individuals he believed harbored anti-American sympathies.

Among his targets were Luisa Moreno and Carey McWilliams, both of whom worked with much fervor on behalf of the Sleepy Lagoon defendants and who attempted to ward off some of the vituperative attacks and characterizations of Mexican Americans attacked in the Zoot Suit Riots. Tenney's continuing attacks against Moreno for her connections to Communist leaders and organizations helped lead to her eventual deportation.

But Tenney's wild ride of nationalistic fervor and obsessive hysteria about Communist infiltration finally played itself out after a decade of destructive hearings. He ended his career writing anti-Semitic books.

Luis Valdez

(June 26, 1940–   )

When the Zoot Suit Riots occurred in June 1943, Luis Valdez was two years old. In 1978, over three decades later, Valdez, now a recognized artistic director of Chicano theater, produced the play *Zoot Suit*. Re-creating the events on stage that occurred in the wartime years in Los Angeles, Valdez turned the story of that fateful night at Sleepy Lagoon and the judicial outrage against Mexican-American young men into a powerful cultural plea for justice and equality. The wartime saga lived on in another generation and in the continuing fight against prejudice and bigotry.

Valdez was born in Delano, California. After graduating from high school in San Jose, he earned a scholarship to attend San Jose State College where he studied theater. In 1964, he joined the San Francisco Mime Troupe, a company that performed open-air, free theater on political and social issues. It was there that he learned the techniques of agitprop (agitation and propaganda) theater. When he heard of the farmworkers strike back in his home town spearheaded by Cesar Chavez, he realized that he might be able to make a unique contribution. Chavez listened with much enthusiasm to the ideas of Valdez on how he could, through use of a traveling theatre, add additional richness and cultural pride to the efforts of the striking farmworkers. Thus, Valdez created "El Teatro Campesino" ("the Farmworkers' Theater").

In 1978, after Valdez had moved on with his career from the farmworkers' movement, he wrote, directed, and produced a play that marked his breakthrough into mainstream theater—*Zoot Suit*. He researched extensively the events of those days and sought to weave his own ethnic heritage and that of his fellow Latinos in a larger historical context. Opening at the Mark Taper Forum in Los Angeles, *Zoot Suit* ran successfully for two years and, because of record, sold-out performances, it was moved to the larger Aquarius Theater. The play won several awards. Valdez then took the play to New York and the Winter Garden in 1979. It was the first play written and produced by a Mexican American ever to reach Broadway. Two years later, *Zoot Suit* was made into a film by Universal Studios with Edward James Olmos playing "El Pachuco." The reason *Zoot Suit* was so successful, Valdez claimed, was because it spoke to a disenfranchised people and helped give a sense of their roots, religion, and culture.

Valdez continued a career so illustrious that he is widely known as "the Father of Chicano Theater."

Brief Sketches of Convicted Sleepy Lagoon Trial Defendants

Three of the 17 convicted defendants were handed first-degree murder sentences and two counts of assault, given life sentences, and sent to San Quentin Prison.

Nine were convicted of second-degree murder and two counts of assault, given sentences of five years to life, and sent to San Quentin.

Five were convicted of assault, given sentences ranging from six months to one year, and sent to the county jail.

Convicted of First-Degree Murder
Henry Leyvas—see Biography earlier
José "Chepe" Ruíz

At the time of his conviction, José "Chepe" Ruíz had a history of run-ins with the Los Angeles Police. An aspiring baseball player who won letters at Andrew Jackson High School, Ruíz, nevertheless, had a record of delinquency that worked against him in the Sleepy Lagoon trial. At age 15, he had been arrested for auto theft. On a number of occasions, he was charged with robbery and assault. On several occasions he was beaten by police, once with a pistol butt for a crime in which he was later acquitted. Convicted of first-degree murder for the death of José Díaz, he served time at San Quentin before his release in October 1944. He spent a long life in and out of prison.

Robert "Bobby" Telles

At the time of his arrest in the Sleepy Lagoon murder, Bobby Telles was working at the North American Aviation defense plant. He had dropped out of Jordan High School after his second year. During the skirmishes on the night of the Sleepy Lagoon murder, Telles suffered serious injuries, hit repeatedly with a beer bottle. Like Henry Leyvas and Chepe Ruíz, he found himself wrapped in a web of circumstantial evidence enough for a guilty verdict of first-degree murder. Telles had artistic skills and amused his codefendants at the trial by drawing caricatures of the judge, jury, and prosecutor. He died in his 40s.

Convicted of Second-Degree Murder
Manuel "Manny" Delgado

Unlike most of the other Sleepy Lagoon defendants, Manny Delgado, 18 years old, was married at the time of the *People v. Zammora* murder trial and his wife was expecting a child. A first-generation Mexican American, he was born to parents who had fled the revolution in Mexico. He left Jefferson High School after two years, worked at the Hammond Lumber Company, and intended to join the U.S. Army Air Corps. Although he had not amassed a record of confrontations with the police before the Sleepy Lagoon murder, he was friends with a number of young men who had made themselves known to authorities. Sentenced for second-degree murder to five years to life in San Quentin, Manny joined Chepe Ruíz on the prison baseball team. He was released on parole in August, 1944, five months before the appellate verdict freed his friends.

John Matuz

John Matuz, whose parents were of Hungarian descent, lived briefly in the 38th Street neighborhood. Although he did not speak Spanish well, he made close friends with several of the Mexican Americans. He went to both Jefferson and Van Nuys high schools for a time but took a job briefly in Alaska working for the U.S. Engineering Department as a waiter. After returning to Los Angeles, he ended up at the Williams ranch with his friends that fateful night in 1942. The timing could not have been worse. Matuz had no criminal record, no rough encounters with the police, no history to suggest violent tendencies—only his relationship with others that night. During the police roundup, one of the officers found $98 in his pocket. Convinced that he had stolen the money, they beat him unconscious trying to get a confession.

He was sentenced to San Quentin for five years to life. After the appellate decision freed him, he remained in Los Angeles to become a small business owner.

Jack Melendez

Jack Melendez, born to immigrant parents, attended Jefferson High School, and worked at several jobs. A few days before his arrest in the Sleepy Lagoon murder case, he was sworn in to the navy and was ready to report for duty. Before his arrest in the death of José Díaz, he had two brief altercations with the police, one at the scene of a fight and the other on suspicion of driving a stolen vehicle, a charge from which he had been exonerated. After he was convicted and sent to San Quentin, the navy announced his dishonorable discharge, an action he deeply regretted. He later began a small business in Los Angeles.

Angel Padilla

Angel Padilla was a first-generation Mexican American born in 1924 in Los Angeles to parents who came to the United States two years earlier. After attending both Jefferson and Fort Hill high schools for a time, he dropped out and took a variety of jobs. Padilla was one of the accused who had a number of recorded criminal charges, from car theft at age 15 to several incidents of fighting. He was sent to a work camp for five months for robbery and assault. When he was interrogated in the José Díaz death, the police roughed him up to such an extent that he spent a week recovering in bed. After being released in the Sleepy Lagoon appeal, Padilla later spent time in prison on other charges.

Ysmael "Smiles" Parra

Born in Superior, Arizona, in 1922, Ysmael moved with his parents to Los Angeles when he was three years old. During his high school years and after, he was in and out of trouble with the police, at one point serving 30 days in Lincoln Heights Jail for disturbing the peace. For a time, he worked at a Civilian Conservation Corps (CCC) camp. At the time of his arrest in the Sleepy Lagoon murder, he lived with his wife and their two-year-old daughter. He was sentenced to serve five years to life at San Quentin in the trial. He was later moved to Chino Honor Prison for good behavior. Following his release, he divorced and remarried, moved to Arizona, and, with his father, ran a rock and gem store selling Southwestern silver jewelry.

Manuel "Manny" Reyes

Manny Reyes was 17 years old when he was arrested in the Sleepy Lagoon murder dragnet. Born in Los Angeles, he had dropped out of high school in the 10th grade. He worked with his uncle on a garbage-collecting route, took a job as a clerk in a garment factory as a tailor, and decided to join the navy. He was scheduled for his physical examination a week after his arrest. Prior to the death of José Díaz, Reyes had never been in trouble with the police. After he was released from prison, he remained in Los Angeles and eventually opened El Taco Mexicano in south Los Angeles with his wife Maria. Like all of the innocent young men imprisoned in the Sleepy Lagoon case, Reyes was emotionally scarred. Even in his declining years, he could still recite his prison number: 69597.

Victor "Bobby Levine" Thompson

Victor Thompson, known to his friends as "Bobby Levine" (a surname of a stepfather), was one of the two young men convicted in the Sleepy Lagoon trial who was not Mexican American. His family, along with a number of other Anglo families, lived in the 38th Street Latino section of the city because the home prices were lower. Thompson left Jefferson High School after the 11th grade, worked at a CCC camp for a year, and also found other short-term jobs before being apprehended on the night of the killing of José Díaz. It was not the first time he had been arrested. In 1941, he was convicted of assault with a deadly weapon and given a one-year suspended sentence. During the Sleepy Lagoon trial, the prosecutor described Bobby as "bad" as the Mexicans because he ran in their crowd. After his stint in San Quentin, he left his friends and Los Angeles behind.

Henry "Hank" Joseph Ynostroza

When Henry Ynostroza was caught up in the mass arrest and convictions in the Sleepy Lagoon murder, he was 18 years old, married, and a father of a young girl. He had completed two years at Jacob Riis High School and worked for short periods of time to help support the family after his father had been deported to Mexico. He had once been arrested for stealing a car and, on another occasion, served over a week in jail for hopping a freight car. When officers picked him up near the Williams ranch, they beat him severely under questioning. He remained in Los Angeles after his release from San Quentin.

Gustavo "Gus" Zamora

Gustavo Zamora was born in Mexico 10 months before his family entered the United States. After completing two years at Jefferson High School, he began work in a furniture factory. Unlike many of his friends in the 38th Street neighborhood, he could not consider joining the military because he was not a U.S. citizen. On two separate occasions, he had been arrested by Los Angeles police on suspicion of theft. In the second instance, he was held for three months before pleading guilty and given probation. Sentenced to five years in San Quentin in the death of José Díaz, he was transferred to Chino Honor Prison before his release. His name (misspelled by a court recorder who chose his name among the larger group) would be forever linked to the famous trial: *People v. Zammora.*

Convicted of Lesser Charges
Andrew Acosta

Born in 1925, Andrew Acosta was the son of Mexican immigrants who entered the United States in 1915. At the time of his apprehension in the Sleepy Lagoon murder investigation, he had completed junior high school and was working as a laborer for a defense contractor. He hoped to be a mechanic. His only prior connection with the Los Angeles police was at the age of 13 when he was taken into custody with friends for auto theft. He spent one year in the county jail on a charge of assault during the violent fracas at the Williams ranch that led to the death of José Díaz.

Benny Alvarez (1923–2000)

Benney Alvarez was 18 years old at the time of his arrest in the Sleepy Lagoon police dragnet. The second of eight children born to parents who were native Californians, he dropped out of high school to work as a furniture maker for Union Steel Corporation, a defense contractor. He had been arrested for stealing a car on two occasions and held in custody for a number of weeks even though he was later exonerated. After his arrest near the Williams ranch, he was beaten with a pistol butt. In *People v. Zammora*, he was convicted of assault and served one year at a work camp.

Eugene Carpio

Eugene "Geney" Carpio and his older brother Joey were both caught up in the mayhem at the Williams ranch. Joey avoided conviction, but Geney did not. The youngster had started his junior year of high school and, along with his brother, had worked part time at the Sunny Sally Packing Plant. He hoped to join the marines after graduating. He spent one year in a work camp on assault charges and died early at the age of 45.

Victor Segobia

Victor Segobia was only16 years old at the time of his arrest in the Sleepy Lagoon murder. He had been learning auto mechanics and wanted to follow his older brother into the armed forces. He wanted to join the navy but was not yet old enough. Prior to this arrest, Victor had no police record. He was found guilty of assault and was sentenced to spend one year in the county jail.

Joseph Valenzuela

Joseph Valenzuela, 19 years old, was working at the Gillespie Furniture Company when he was arrested after the death of José Díaz. He had planned to join the navy or marines. On a number of occasions in his teenage years, he was rounded up with other Mexican-American youngsters after fights. He was once arrested for participating in a so-called riot and held for over three days. In fact, he had not even been near the scene of the fight. Found guilty of assault in the Sleepy Lagoon case, he spent one year at the county detention farm.

Primary Documents

EXTRACT OF REPORT OF ALAN CRANSTON ON GROWING RACIAL TENSIONS IN LOS ANGELES, NOVEMBER 1942

In November 1942, amid increasing unrest in Los Angeles between Anglos and Mexican Americans fueled by the Sleepy Lagoon murder case and its publicity, a young federal official arrived in California to try to ease tensions. Alan Cranston, born in Palo Alto, California, in 1914, graduated from Stanford University in 1936 and joined the International News Service for two years as a journalist covering England, Germany, Italy, and Ethiopia. After working as an editor and writer for the magazine Common Ground, *he took a job with the newly created Office of War Information (OWI), an agency designed to coordinate news releases favorable to U.S. interests during the war. Cranston would later serve several terms as a U.S. senator from California. In late 1942, the OWI, led by Elmer Davis, worried that open hostility toward Mexican Americans was being exploited by Axis propaganda attacking U.S. claims that it was a democratic nation free of the persecution of minorities and attacking American democracy as a sham. Cranston met managing editors and publishers of all four of the major newspapers in the city encouraging them to stop using the term "Mexican" to describe the so-called crime wave that they were trumpeting in the pages of their dailies. He also worked with city officials in preparing a plan to help ameliorate the conditions under which Mexican Americans were struggling in the city. It proposed a number of actions including an expansion of educational and recreational activities in Mexican-American communities, broader employment opportunities especially in defense projects, Spanish-speaking attorneys as public defenders and law enforcement officers, and numerous other actions. Cranston left Los Angeles encouraged by the response of local officials. A few months later, that confidence would be shattered.*

November 28th, 1942
To: Mr. Elmer Davis
From: Alan Cranston
Subject: Activities in Los Angeles

My first call in Los Angeles was upon Mayor Fletcher Bowron who was initially sympathetic to my mission, but who became more so when I made him understand that Axis propaganda was giving Los Angeles a black eye the world over by exploitation of the local Mexican situation.

The Mayor made appointments for me with the editors and publishers of all four Los Angeles daily newspapers. He then requested me to draw and present to him a program for local action on all fronts of the Mexican problem.

Managing Editor Jack Campbell of the Herald and Express, Managing Editor R.T. Van Ettisch of the Examiner, and Publisher Manchester Hoddy of the News all agreed that they would stop using the term "Mexican" in connection with the local disturbances, since Americans are really involved. They likewise agreed to carry positive stories of the war participation of Americans of Mexican extraction, and Publisher Norman Chandler of the Los Angeles Times agreed to do likewise—provided I would see if I could get him more gasoline for his reporters. All four papers have already run several extremely valuable stories of a positive nature, and the Los Angeles O.W.I. office is now busy digging up such stories for them.

In the process of getting to the roots of the local problem in order to draw up the program requested by Mayor Bowron, I talked with innumerable citizens of Los Angeles. . . . I then drew up a program for local action and presented it to a small group. . . . They approved it with only a few changes and I then selected a small group of local citizens to go with me to present it to the Mayor. We were also invited by the Los Angeles County Board of Supervisors to present it to them. . . .

An extremely well balanced group presented this program to the Mayor and the County Supervisors. Monsignor O'Dwyer actually led the delegation. The following people spoke in behalf of the program to the Mayor and the Supervisors:

Monsignor O'Dwyer, Manual Ruiz of the Coordinating Committee for Latin-American Youth, Chief County Probation Officer Holton, Rev. Willsie Martin of the Committee for Church and Community Cooperation, Mrs. Bigelow of the League of Women Voters, Mr. Cecil, representing Chairman Tibbets of the Los Angeles Chamber of Commerce, Burt Corono of the C.I.O., George Bradley of the A.F.L., Rev. Farnham of the Church Federation, and myself. I merely stated that it was not within my province, as a Federal officer, to comment in detail on this local program, but that I would say that this program would be bad news of Hitler and the Axis and good news for the United States and the United Nations. . . .

On my last day in Los Angeles, I visited District Attorney Dockweiler, whose subordinates are prosecuting the twenty-two youths of Mexican extraction. . . . [T]his is the first time in the history of Southern California that so many people have been charged with . . . murder for the death of one person. The prominent publicity given to the local Mexican situation in the Los Angeles dailies just prior to my visit to him had shown District Attorney Dockweiler that Los Angeles is really concerned over its Mexican problem. Thus he was easy to handle. I convinced him that the District Attorney and the O.W.I. would have a terrific problem on their hands is the trial was permitted to turn into a Sacco-Vanzetti case—as it will if many of the kids are given stiff sentences. He eagerly agreed, said that he was personally avoiding the courtroom to keep publicity of the trial to a minimum, and that he had decided to narrow the real case down to two of the youths. He said that before the case goes to the grand jury they might ask for a general reduction in the charges, and that in any case he would tell the Judge about the dangerous consequences of too stiff a verdict. I am convinced that this takes the trial out of the danger zone. . . .

The critical situation has been overcome completely. All that remains for the O.W.I. to do is for the Foreign Language Division to continue its present program of war information in the Spanish language to Mexicans in the United States. That this program must be carried on goes without saying, and there is room for considerable expansion of it via the media of posters and radio transcriptions.

Source: Record Group 208, Records of the Office of War Information, Records of the Office of the Director, File: Subversive Activities, 1942–1943, National Archives and Records Administration, College Park, Maryland.

<hr>

EXCERPTS OF RADIO BROADCAST BY LOS ANGELES CITY OFFICIALS, JUNE 9, 1943

On June 3, 1943, with tensions escalating between U.S. sailors stationed in Los Angeles and Mexican-American youths, many of whom donned Zoot suits, oversized draped clothing common among rebellious youth, approximately 50 sailors on shore leave ventured into Mexican-American neighborhoods armed with clubs and other weapons. Their mission, supposedly in retaliation for earlier attacks on servicemen, was simple—beat up and rip the clothing from any Zoot suiter they could find. For several days, sporadic attacks by servicemen against Mexican American threw parts of downtown Los Angeles into chaos and rioting. Mayor Fletcher Bowron, who had received much public notoriety for his outspoken support of the wartime mass eviction and incarceration of Japanese Americans, now faced in his city another crisis involving an immigrant population. On June 9, Bowron, accompanied by two officials of the city's police department, addressed the citizens of Los Angeles on a radio broadcast.

Broadcast by Mayor Fletcher Bowron . . . Wednesday, June 9, 1943, 7:45 P.M.

Citizens of Los Angeles:

Unfortunate happenings in this city during the past few days and nights have set a considerable portion of the people to talking about zoot suits and pachucos, hoodlums, mobs, attacks upon service men, retaliation, racial discrimination, prejudice against minority groups, and about the safety of our entire civilian population, especially women who use the city streets in certain sections of the city.

The situation is serious but not as serious as many are led to believe. There is no reason for fear or hysteria. No good can come from exaggeration or over-statement of the facts, and of course there are plenty who are ready to criticize without first having the advantage of knowing what they are talking about.

It is regrettable if anyone has gained the suspicion that the situation is beyond the control of the local authorities.

Now let us keep our heads and keep loose. Precipitate action of the wrong sort will do infinitely more harm than good. In the first place, we should know the facts. It is characteristic of the average American that he would like to believe the worst and plain facts are too often not very exciting. The people of Los Angeles are entitled to a report on the condition of the affairs of the city in this particular, and in order to do so adequately and properly I have brought with me the Chief of Police, C. B. Horrall, and Deputy Assistant Chief of Police E. W. Lesser. Time is all too short for such a big and important subject, but they will they will give you the background, the history, the facts of occurrences during the past week, and tell you what is being done for your protection.

First, let me give you the assurance that there has been no breakdown of local governmental authority, and order will be maintained. I would like to make a few more general observations as follows.

Nothing that has occurred can be construed in any manner as prompted by prejudice against Mexicans or racial discrimination against young men of Mexican or colored blood.

Neither is there a foundation for anyone to say that attacks or arrests have been directed towards members of minority groups. Police working with the FBI and other Federal agencies have not been able to uncover sufficient evidence to justify the statement that gangs of juveniles and young men roaming over parts of the city and county have been organized, controlled or directed by Nazi or other enemy agents. It is, however, significant that what we are having in Los Angeles is not peculiar to this section. The same kind of gangs and the same kind of disturbances have been reported in cities of Arizona and West Texas and in various other California cities.

Elsewhere, as here, there have been numerous instances of fights between tough young gangsters and soldiers and sailors. In other places, as in this city, service men have been beaten up, slugged and robbed, and in other places, as here, service men have retaliated and have in turn beaten up a number of boys and civilians who look like or bear resemblance to the gangsters who beat up their buddies.

The so-called zoot suit, an outlandish apparel that no good wholesome young American youth would wear, is not necessarily a uniform of gangsterism. Many of the young gangsters wear zoot suits, but not all of those who wear zoot suits are gangsters. Unfortunately, many Mexicans and quite a number of negro youth wear zoot suits. This probably led to the unfortunate attack upon Mexican and colored boys when young men from the armed forces, for all the world like college boys would act if some of their fellow students had been beaten up by students from a rival institution came piling into Los Angeles, looking for excitement and feeling that, if there was going to be a fight anyway, they wanted to get in on it.

The action of the service men was entirely understandable and largely excusable. It is unfortunate that Mexicans and negroes, whether they wore zoot suits or not, happened along the street at the wrong time.

The gangs of young men must be broken up. They are a menace to the community and are affording excellent training for young criminals. These young rascals and hoodlums must be sternly dealt with, lest they lose all semblance of respect for law.

Now, for the background of the gangs of juveniles and local young men, I will present Deputy Chief Ervis W. Lester, whom I consider one of the best informed men in the State of California on the subject of juvenile delinquency. For many years he was head of the Crime Prevention Bureau of the Los Angeles Police Department. He has worked with the various judges who have presided over the Juvenile Court, with social workers, and with

Federal agencies. He knows the facts and can analyze them as well as anyone I know.

Deputy Chief Lester.

(Deputy Chief Lester speaks for four minutes)

Deputy Chief Lester:

Our greatest current social problem centers around the activities of the zoot-suit gangs. It seems important that we carefully analyze this problem. When we examine the background of these gangs we find that they have been known to the police and social agencies for many years, contrary to the general belief of the public. Fifteen years ago there were a dozen or more neighborhood gangs well known to the police and courts. Five years ago there were half as many as exist today. Four years ago the depredations of one large neighborhood group brought much attention to the problem that the Coordinating Councils and social agencies formed committees to study the situation.

Nearly two years ago the "zoot suit" began to make its appearance among these groups. Up to that time the depredations of the gangs had consisted for the most part in the breaking up of each other's parties, dances and other social events, with seldom anything more serious than blackened eyes and bloody noses. About this time, however, some unfortunate clashes resulted in the deaths of two or three of the participants. Prior to this there had been little or no publicity attending the activities of these groups, but with the more violent crimes there came a great deal of publicity which seemed to stimulate the leaders to engage in even more aggressive sets of violence. These youths had at long last gained a desire that is fundamental in all human beings—the desire for recognition, and as these newer acts of violence were reported by the press a phenomenal recruiting program went on among the younger boys of the neighborhoods who were clamoring to belong to these organizations which were receiving so much public attention.

To understand all this, one has to realize that most of these youngsters come from over-crowded, colorless homes that offer no opportunities for leisure-time activities. It must be remembered that they are living in neighborhood where the standards of social conduct are poor, and where their own conduct does not deviate greatly from the norm. Under these conditions, the problem has become progressively worse during the past two years until it has reached proportions which demand intelligent and forthright action on the part of all who can be helpful in its solution.

It is definitely wrong to blame the law enforcement agencies for the present situation. Society as a whole may be properly charged with mishandling the problem. The state has failed in its responsibility to provide adequate facilities to deal with delinquents. In fact, we are struggling along with about the same treatment facilities that were available thirty years ago. The Juvenile Court has been forced to be over-lenient in returning children again and again to their own homes and neighborhoods, glaring examples of the fact that little or no corrective action could be expected.

On this basis, perhaps the recent clashes between service men and zoot-suited hoodlums are understandable. In fairness to all concerned it must be stated that violations of laws have not been confined to either side. One thing at least is clear—these outbreaks and the attendant publicity has brought into focus a serious problem of long standing, and it is to be expected that an aroused public will demand that the state, through its new crime control agency—the California Youth Authority—provide adequate facilities for effective control. It must be borne in mind that to be effective any law enforcement program must have the full support of the prosecuting agencies and the courts.

Mayor Bowron:

Thank you, Deputy Chief Lester, for that excellent report to the people of Los Angeles. And now, to give you a brief review of the facts relative to the recent disturbances and to tell you what the police are doing to cope with the situation, I give you Chief of Police, C. B. Horrall.

(Chief Horrall speaks for five minutes)

Chief Horrall:

Several days ago clashes occurred between members of the military and youths of this city garbed in "Zoot" suits. It resulted in injury to some of the men in uniform.

We all know the fighting spirit of our men in the Armed Forces and when those in the various camps and stations in this vicinity heard of these occurrences, thru the publicity that was given them, they took it upon themselves to retaliate. This is the spirit that has always been exhibited by young Americans, and has been noticeable in our High School and College students through the years, so it is natural to expect that those boys who are now in the Service would continue to have this feeling.

The "Zoot Suiters" retaliated in turn and while many arrests were made by the Police Department, the clashes were brought to a climax with the occurrences on Monday night. On that night, many Service men were in the City, and attracted by the publicity many citizens of Los Angeles appeared on the street in the hope of seeing some excitement. The number of persons on the street was so great that despite the fact the crowds were continually broken up by the police, they would again congregate, especially if a youth in a zoot suit could be found.

Police reserves were utilized to the fullest and the amount of damage done and the injuries received was slight. And while those crowds were large and contained many Service men, the spirit was one of fun rather than an attitude of belligerency.

The Police Department, reinforced by all available reserves, took definite action of an unbiased and impartial nature, resulting in the arrests of "Zoot Suiters," civilians, and Service men. These arrests occurred whenever persons responsible for any disturbances or unlawful act could possibly be identified, regardless of their race, creed, color or occupation.

The Los Angeles Police Department will continue to operate in this manner, and wishes to assure the public that we can and will fully control this situation.

We have been severely handicapped by those sightseers who insist upon driving their cars up and down the streets or congregating in crowds on the sidewalks, in the hope that they may be able to observe some excitement. These persons, in hampering the operations of the Police Department, are also committing offenses and action will be taken to see that this practice is discontinued.

Every available policeman will be continually used in the sections of the city where occurrences may be anticipated, until the situation is entirely cleared. We realize the seriousness of the problem and accept the responsibility for its control. We wish to inform those sight-seers, who insist on blocking traffic, sidewalks, and being present at unlawful assemblies, that they will be subject to arrest the same as all persons participating in disturbances and assaults, and we will make as many arrests as necessary in all cases.

May I again say to all law-abiding citizens of Los Angeles, that the Police Department can and will control this situation and in doing so will act in an impartial and unbiased manner.

Mayor Bowron:

Thank you, Chief Horrall, and I am sure that the big majority of the people of Los Angeles thank you, too. I am glad to have this opportunity to bring local citizens a little closer to their Police Department, in order that they may understand the good work that is being done. . . .

The Police Department is using effective, vigorous methods to meet the present situation. They are going to do the job, and I am going to back up the Police Department despite the criticism that are bound to come from those citizens who just can't bear the thought that juveniles or persons who happen to be members of so-called minority groups can do anything so wrong that they must be arrested and punished. Racketeers and gamblers and vice barons don't like Chief Horrall's methods either. . . .

Source: Of 4512 Coordinator of Inter-American Affairs: Los Angeles "Zoot Suit" Situation 1943, FDR-FDRPOF: President's Official Files, 1933–1945, Franklin D. Roosevelt Library, Hyde Park, New York.

EXCERPTS OF "LITTON REPORT," 11TH NAVAL DISTRICT, COMMANDANT'S OFFICE, JUNE 19, 1943

On June 5, 1943, two days after sailors began their assaults against Zoot suit–wearing youngsters on the streets of Los Angeles, Lieutenant Glen A. Litten of the 11th Naval District was ordered to prepare a report detailing recent attacks against naval personnel stationed in Los Angeles by hoodlums. Litten and others dutifully interviewed hundreds of sailors who detailed various assaults they had suffered when venturing into the Mexican-American areas of the city. In a letter forwarding his report to his superiors, Litten clearly lays the blame for the chaos now gripping the city to the cumulative indignities and physical assaults suffered by servicemen at the hands of Zoot suiters.

From: Lieutenant Glen A. LITTEN, C-V (S), USNR
To: The Commanding Officer. . . .

On the afternoon of June 5, 1943, the Commanding Officer of this station gave orders to post a night patrol along the main arteries leading to this station from the streetcar stops and through the sections habituated by so-called "Zoot-Suiters." This order was carried out and twenty-two (22) men and two (2) Chief Petty Officers per watch were assigned this duty and posted as a protection and precaution against possible offenses against men from this station. This patrol was maintained Saturday and Sunday nights, June 5 and June 6, 1943. The patrol experienced a considerable amount of annoyance and received many insults from Zoot-Suiters. . . .

Liberty was suspended on Monday, June 7, 1943, by order of the Commanding Officer, as a precautionary measure against possible conflict. . . .

On Tuesday, June 8, 1943, by order of the Commandant, liberty was suspended indefinitely. . . .

According to the statements taken, the following information is revealed:

(a) That numerous attacks have been made by "Zoot-Suiters" upon naval personnel attached to this activity.

(b) That the naval personnel and the wives and friends of naval personnel have on many occasions been insulted by the so-called "Zoot-Suiters."

(c) That in some instances wives of naval personnel have been attacked by "Zoot-Suiters."

(d) That particular insult has been directed by the "Zoot-Suiters" at the naval uniform.

(e) That there are indications of anti-American sympathies.
(f) That the "Zoot-Suiters" have used dangerous and deadly weapons upon attacks of naval personnel.
(g) That in many cases such attacks were not previously reported to proper authorities.
(h) That such attacks have been made on naval personnel over a considerable period of time.

The cause of the outbreak between "Zoot-Suiters" and servicemen which occurred on Thursday night, June 3, 1943, and which has continued up until the present time is undetermined. The information . . . above indicates a history of animosity by "Zoot-Suiters" toward servicemen, extending over a period of many months, which animosity has grown in intensity and violence and extended to wives, families, and friends of servicemen. . . .

It is believed that every reasonable precaution has been taken at this activity to safeguard its personnel.

GLEN A. LITTEN

Source: Lieutenant Glen A. Litten to Commanding Officer, 11th Naval District, Commandant's Office, RG 181, Naval Districts and Shore Establishments, Central Subject Files, 1924–1958, National Archives and Records Administration, National Archives at Riverside, California.

JOSEPH T. McGUCKEN, AUXILIARY BISHOP OF LOS ANGELES, TO EARL WARREN, GOVERNOR OF CALIFORNIA, JUNE 21, 1943

On June 9, 1943, as rioting continued in Los Angeles, Governor Earl Warren appointed a citizen's committee to investigate the causes of the disturbances and to recommend long-term ameliorative actions that would help deter any such future outbreaks. To chair the committee, Governor Warren asked Joseph T. McGucken, auxiliary bishop of Los Angeles, an individual who was familiar with the social and cultural challenges facing Mexican-American communities in the city. Working closely with California state attorney general Robert Kenny, McGucken and his committee, made up of a cross-section of judicial, law enforcement, social service, and religious groups, heard from a variety of witnesses and issued an eight-page report. Unlike the sensationalist press accounts, the citizen's committee's report found much blame to go around. It unequivocally stated that no group had the right to take the law into its own hands. It attacked the press for inflaming the situation. It found significance in the fact that almost all of the individuals who sustained injuries from the riots were of Mexican-American descent or African Americans. It said that race prejudice could not be ignored as a cause. And the report encouraged aggressive measures to improve the living conditions and social well-being among immigrant communities in the city. Bishop McGucken wrote to Governor Warren following the committee's work to encourage such action.

Archdiocese of Los Angeles
714 West Olympic Boulevard
Los Angeles, California
June Twenty First 1943
His Excellency,
Governor Earl Warren,
State Capitol
Sacramento, California
My dear Governor Warren:

... [W]e would like to call your particular attention to the following facts and to additional action which we feel is needed if this situation is to be really solved. . . .

That no group should be allowed to take the law into its own hands and that prompt and effective law enforcement in the beginning could have prevented these so-called zootsuit riots.

None of the warring elements has clean hands. "Zoot suiters" have made vicious unprovoked assaults on citizens and on service men. Service men have been guilty of unprovoked assaults on not only "zoot-suiters" but innocent citizens, particularly those of minority groups.

There are many reported instances of police and sheriff indifference, neglect of duty, and discrimination against members of minority groups. There is no evidence to show that there was official sanction of such activities by either the Chief of Police or the Sheriff.

In order to assure the enforcement of law and order without discrimination, we urge the following action.

1. That you meet in Los Angeles with the members of the Committee, the Attorney General, Chief of Police, District Attorney, and Sheriff, and that the findings of the Committee be frankly discussed.

2. That the influence of your office and of the Attorney General be used with the press in order that such incidents may be properly reported and that no undue emphasis be placed on the part played in such disturbances by minority groups.
3. That with your backing and the assistance of the War Council, Attorney General, and Youth Authority, a statewide prevention program be organized.
4. That the Youth Authority establish facilities to which the local courts can commit leaders of these disturbances who have criminal records.
5. That you urge the Secretary of War and the Secretary of Navy to have shore patrols and military police units established in sufficient strength to adequately handle service personnel.
6. That the Chairman of this Committee be requested to organize an inter-racial committee composed of community leaders and have representatives from the Chamber of Commerce, A.F.L., C.I.O., Church, Social Agencies, and all minority groups. That this Committee be officially recognized by local government agencies, boards and officials, as a source of assistance in meeting problems as they arise. That to this Committee be referred such serious problems as the acute housing shortage, the present housing quota imposed upon minority groups, race discrimination in the use of public facilities, unfair publicity, and all other such problems which merely aggravate and inflame the groups concerned.

The members of this Committee feel that the situation on the East side, where Los Angeles has the largest concentration of persons of Mexican and Negro ancestry, is a potential powder keg, and the inter-racial committee, if quickly established, could do much to relieve this dangerous situation.

The draft of this letter has been seen and approved by the members of your Committee, who have directed me to forward it to you in their name.

I wish to take advantage of this opportunity to express to Your Excellency my appreciation of the honor which you have conferred upon me in asking me to assist you in the capacity of Chairman of this Committee.

Very Sincerely Yours,

Joseph T. McGucken

Auxiliary Bishop of Los Angeles

Source: California State Archives, Sacramento, California, Earl Warren Papers, F3640:2624, Admin. Files, DOJ Law Enforcement, 1943.

EXCERPTS FROM PAMPHLET *THE SLEEPY LAGOON CASE* PREPARED BY THE SLEEPY LAGOON DEFENSE COMMITTEE, 1943

In October 1942, the Sleepy Lagoon Defense Committee (first known as the Citizens' Committee for the Defense of Mexican-American Youth) was organized in response to the indictment of 22 young men for the murder of José Díaz. In early 1943, following the conviction in People v. Zammora *of 17 individuals, including 12 of them on either first-degree or second-degree murder charges, the committee prepared a pamphlet detailing the case and the onerous miscarriage of justice that it represented. Led by the work of influential journalist and progressive author Carey McWilliams, who became the committee's chairman and labor activist Alice Greenfield McGrath, who later became the committee's executive secretary, the committee carried on with much dedication and vigor its mission of rousing public opinion and laying the groundwork to overturn the convictions on appeal.*

THE SLEEPY LAGOON CASE Prepared by the Sleepy Lagoon Defense Committee (Formerly the Citizen's Committee for the Defense of Mexican-American Youth)
Los Angles, California, 1943

I

ON THE NIGHT of August 2nd, 1942, one Jose Diaz left a drinking party at the Sleepy Lagoon ranch near Los Angeles, and sometime in the course of that night he died. It seems clear that Diaz was drinking heavily and fell into a roadway and was run over by a car. Whether or not he was also in a brawl before he was run over is not clear.

On January 13th, fifteen American-born boys of Mexican descent and two boys born in Mexico stood up to hear the verdict of a Los Angeles court. Twelve of them were found guilty of having conspired to murder Diaz, five were convicted of assault. Their sentences ranged from a few months to life imprisonment.

The lawyers say there is good reason to believe the seventeen boys were innocent, and no evidence at all to show even that they were present at the time that Diaz was involved in a brawl, assuming that he actually was in a brawl, let alone that they "conspired" to murder Jose Diaz. Two other boys whose lawyers demanded a separate trial after the 17 had been convicted, were *acquitted* on the same *evidence*.

Seventeen for one! You don't have to be a lawyer to know that the Los Angeles District Attorney and the Los Angeles press were not "prosecuting" only 18-year-old Manuel Delgado or 19-year-old Henry Leyvas. Jose Ruiz, aged 17, was convicted "of murder in the first degree and of two counts of assault with a deadly weapon with intent to commit murder." You don't have to be a lawyer to know that Jose Ruiz did not stand alone at the bar of "justice."

It wasn't only seventeen boys who were on trial.

It was the whole Mexican people, and their children and their grandchildren. It was the whole of Latin America with its 130,000,000 people. It was the Good Neighbor Policy. It was the United Nations and all for which they fight.

It was that kind of trial.

It began to be that kind of a trial even before Jose Diaz met his death on August 2nd. The Los Angeles paper started it by building for a "crime wave" even before there was a crime. "MEXICAN GOON SQUADS." "ZOOT SUIT GANGS." "PACHUCO KILLERS." "JUVENILE GAND WAR LAID TO YOUTHS' DESIRE TO THRILL." Those were the curtain-raisers, the headlines building for August 3rd.

On August 3rd the death of Jose Diaz was scarehead news. And the stories were of Mexican boys "prowling in wolf-packs," armed with clubs and knives and automobile tools and tire irons, invading peaceful homes, beating and stabbing their victims to death.

On August 3rd every Mexican kid in Los Angeles was under suspicion as a "zoot-suit" killer. Cops lined up outside of dance halls, armed with pokers to which sharp razor blades were attached, and they ripped the peg-top trousers and "zoot-suits" of the boys as they came out.

Mexican boys were beaten, jailed. "Zoot-suits" and "Pachuco" hair cuts were crimes. It was a crime to be born in the U.S.A.—of a Spanish-speaking father or mother.

II

A LOT OF THINGS were happening in the world that summer of 1942, and they were not unrelated to what happened on Los Angeles in August.

Mexico declared war against the Axis in May. In June, Roosevelt, Churchill and Molotov reached an agreement on the urgent task of opening a second front. In August, the people of Brazil, outraged when the Nazis sank more of their ships, demanded war. Churchill went to Moscow in August.

All through that summer Vice President Wallace's historic May 8th speech was reaching deeper into the hearts of Latin American people, awakening in the common man of the hemisphere a new will to fight for the victory it foretold.

Americans, Englishmen, Russians, Chinese, Latins—men of different races but of the "same stamp"—were forging a global unity.

There was altogether too much unity in the air to suit the Axis book.

And something else happened in August, even more closely related to the events in Los Angeles.

The Inter-American Monthly, an authoritative journal published in Washington, D.C., reported:

Both the Mexican and U.S. governments are holding their breath as a ticklish experiment in racial relations is launched. To fill the need for agricultural workers in the U.S. West and Southwest, Mexican laborers are to be brought in on a temporary basis. A plan worked out between official agencies of the two countries specifies wage scales, conditions of work, immunity from military service; laborers will have their transport paid, and will return to Mexico when their work is done. In mid-August candidates for this mass migration were lining up a block deep outside the Ministry of Labor in Mexico City.

The trade unions in the U.S. conferred with the Confederation of Mexican Workers (CTM). Unions and governments worked together, in national and international unity. They were going to make sure that the Mexican labor battalions got a square deal. They were going to make sure that the wage scales and trade union rights of American workers were protected.

Unity was in the air, was growing.

And, while the Mexican and U.S. governments "held their breath," and the trade unions worked to make sure the "ticklish experiment in racial relations" worked—other forces got busy.

There were the old-time enemies of American labor. They wanted the new Mexican help to come cheap, and to keep it away from any fraternizing with American trade unionists. They wanted Mexican workers, but no fancy contracts to protect them.

The Falangists and Sinarchists and other Fifth Columnists in Mexico told the Mexican workers to stay home. They revived all the "negative memories," talked about "Yankee imperialism" and "gringo justice.". . .

In August, along with the first migration of Mexican war workers, Los Angeles had its newspaper "crime wave," its "zoot-suit" and "Pachuco" hysteria. Maybe that was an accident, but the timing was perfect.

And Sleepy Lagoon exploded like a well-placed time-bomb.

III

AFTER THE GRAND JURY had returned an indictment and before the trial itself began, Mr. Ed. Duran Ayres of the Foreign Relations Bureau of the Sheriff's Office, filed a statement.

That statement is the key to the Sleepy Lagoon case.

It isn't nice reading, but you will have to read a good chunk of it to understand why Sleepy Lagoon challenges every victory-minded person in the United States, Jews or Protestant or Catholic, Spanish-speaking or Mayflower descendant, immigrant or native-born.

"The biological basis," said Mr. Ayres, "is the main basis to work from."

How do you try a murder case on "the biological basis?" One that basis Hitler found every Jew in the world "guilty." Mr. Ayres took in even more territory:

Although a wild cat and a domestic cat are of the same family they have certain biological characteristics so different that while one may be domesticated the other would have to be caged to be kept in captivity; and there is practically as much difference between the races of man as so aptly recognized by Rudyard Kipling when he said when writing of the Oriental, "East is East and West is West, and never the twain shall meet," which gives us an insight into the present problem because the Indian, from Alaska to Patagonia, is evidently Oriental in background—at least he shows many of the Oriental characteristics, especially so in his utter disregard for the value of life.

[We pause for station identification. This is not Radio Berlin. It is the "Foreign Relations Department" of the Office of the Sheriff of Los Angeles speaking.]

Mr. Ayres continues:

When the Spaniards conquered Mexico they found an organized society composed of many tribes of Indians ruled over by the Aztecs who were given over to human sacrifice. Historians record that as many as 30,000 Indians were sacrificed on their heathen altars in one day, their bodies being opened by stone knives and their hearts torn out while still beating. This total disregard for human life has always been universal throughout the Americas among the Indian population, which of course is well known to everyone.

It was Juarez, the pure-blooded Indian who said, "Peace is respect for the right of others." Not blood-lust, but love and freedom led Juarez and the people of Mexico to take up arms against the foreign tyrant, Emperor Maximilian.

Proud Mexican children of Juarez, proud Indians and mestizos of Latin America, bound to us because you "hold the same truths to be worth fighting for and dying for!" Ed. Duran Ayres speaks for the Axis enemy.

President Roosevelt, saying "Hidalgo and Juarez were men of the same stamp as Washington and Jefferson," President Roosevelt speaks for us!

We stand with Vice President Wallace, who said that the Nazi "doctrine that one race or one class is by heredity superior and that all other races or classes are supposed to be slaves" is "the devil's own religion of darkness."

Seventeen Mexican boys were on trial, and Ed. Duran Ayres continued to argue their "biological" guilt. . . .

President Roosevelt said, in Monterrey:

In the shaping of a common victory our people are finding that they have common aspirations. They can work for a common objective. Let us never lose our hold upon that truth.

If Ed. Duran Ayres is right, then President Roosevelt lied, then the United Nations is a lie, and the people of Latin America are not our Allies but strangers and enemies, and unity, in the nation or in the hemisphere, cannot be.

IV

DIVIDE AND CONQUER. That is the Axis formula! That was the formula for trying the Sleepy Lagoon case. . . .

Fifteen American-born Mexican boys and two Mexican-born boys were punished for a single death. Mr. Ayres made it perfectly clear that this Nazi policy of "collective guilt," like his theory of "biological guilt" is to be accepted as the guiding principle for American courts. . . .

Divide and conquer. The harvest sown by Ed. Duran Ayres—and the Hearst press, and the California appeasers, and the labor-haters—that harvest was smugly reaped by the Axis which on January 13th got the verdict its agents had insured.

On January 13th the Axis radio beamed to Latin America carried the following message in Spanish:

In Los Angeles, California, the so-called "City of the Angels," twelve Mexican boys were found guilty today of a single murder and five others were convicted of assault growing out of the same case. The 360,000 Mexicans of Los Angeles are reported up in arms over this Yankee persecution. The concentration camps of Los Angeles are said to be overflowing with members of this persecuted minority. This is justice for you, as practiced by the "Good Neighbor," Uncle Sam, a justice that demands seventeen victims for one crime.

V

WE ARE AT WAR. We are at war not only with the armies of the Axis powers, but with the poison-gas of their doctrine, with the "biological basis" of Hitler and with his theories of race supremacy.

The unity of all races, creeds and colors has been sealed in blood, in the blood of our heroes of Bataan and Corregidor, Stalingrad, Tunis and Bizerte, in the vast expanses of China, in the African desert and the mountain passes of the Caucasus. Our coming victory on the continent of Europe will be won by "men of the same stamp" though different races, and it will be the victory of all—Indians, Malays, Chinese, Negroes, Russians, Slavs, French, English, Americans, yes, and of Germans, Italians and Japanese. The rivers of blood will wash away the fascist creed of "Aryan supremacy." And with it will go the last vestiges of discrimination in the United States, the Jim-Crow cars in the south, the signs in Los Angeles that still say "Mexicans and Negroes not allowed here."

That is not only the faith for which we fight, it is our armor and our sword, our weapon and our battle cry.

We are at war with the premise on which seventeen boys were tried and convicted in Los Angeles, sentenced to long prison terms on January 13th of this year. We are at war with the Nazi logic so clearly and unmistakably set forth by Mr. Ed. Duran Ayres, the logic which guided the judge and jury and dictated the verdict and the sentence.

And because this global war is everywhere a people's war, all of us are in it together, all of us together take up the challenge of Sleepy Lagoon.

VI

IN LOS ANGELES, a Citizens' Committee for the Defense of Mexican-American Youth has been organized. Its legal staff is studying the twelve volumes of the court record and will prepare an appeal. This appeal will set forth in detail the lack of evidence, the unreliability of prosecution witnesses, the lynch atmosphere created around the trial.

It will, for example, show how the boys were forbidden to get hair-cuts during the course of the trial, or to receive clean clothing from home. It will show how defense lawyer George Shibley charged that District Attorney Shoemaker "is purposely trying to have these boys look like mobsters, like disreputable persons, and is trying to exploit the fact that they are foreign in appearance."

And how District Attorney Shoemaker replied that "the appearance of the defendants is distinctive." The prosecution, he said, regarded as important evidence "their style of hair-cut, the thick heavy heads of hair, the duck-tail comb, the pachuco pants and things of that kind."

In the appellate court the defense will show that no eye-witness testimony in any way connected any of the boys with the death of Jose Diaz, that witnesses were intimidated, that the boys themselves were beaten and threatened, that defense attorneys were not permitted to consult their clients in the courtroom.

The defense lawyers have a case—a legal case—and they will try it in a lawyer-like way, in accordance with the laws of the state of California and the United States of America. The people of California and of the United States will back them up.

VII

AS WE TAKE the offensive against the Axis enemies everywhere in the world, we take the offensive against their agents and stooges and dupes in California.

Against Ed. Duran Ayres and his "biological basis."

Against Sheriff Eugene Biscailuz who complained, "I advocated months ago that we handle them like criminals, but it is hard to make society understand that children can be treated like that."

Against the Hearst press and its headline-made "crime waves."

Against the Sinarchists and the Falangists, and against every organized group, Mexican or American, that tries to disrupt our unity.

For this offensive we need an army, a big army and a united army. We need the united strength of the American trade unions with their more than eleven million members, fighting for the solidarity of labor at home and throughout the hemisphere.

We need the churchmen of all faiths, and their congregations to proclaim the unity of all races, creeds and colors, at home and throughout the hemisphere.

We need Americans of all strains and origins, Filipinos and Chinese, Poles and Czechs, Negroes and Jews and Puerto Ricans and Scandinavians and Irishmen to fight together against the attack on the Mexican minority as an attack against themselves.

And above all we need the Mexicans, all the Mexicans in the United States. Some of them came here long ago, to build our railroads and cultivate our fields. Some came in 1917, to help us win another war. And now thousands more are coming in answer to our call for help. We need them now to take the places of our boys gone to the fighting fronts. But we need them also to take up with us the challenge thrown down by Ed. Duran Ayres. We need all they bring us from their ancient culture, their long, proud, rich history. "Hidalgo and Juarez were men of the same stamp as Washington and Jefferson," President Roosevelt said. "It was therefore inevitable that our two countries should find themselves aligned together in the great struggle which is being fought today to determine whether this shall be a free world or a slave world." So too it is inevitable that all of us should fight together in the case of Sleepy Lagoon.

The seventeen kids believe in us. One of them recently wrote:

It makes me feel good to know that the people are trying to help us. I had gave up hope, but when I received your letter I said if the people are trying to help us well I got to have hope. I know that all of us here will try to make a good record. I know that the mothers are doing all they can for us.

Seventeen scared kids in San Quentin, trying to "make a good record."

We have pledged to do all we can for them.

WE, TOO, MUST "MAKE A GOOD RECORD."

ON THE GOOD RECORDS OF ALL OF US DEPENDS OUR COMMON VICTORY.

HERE IS HOW YOU CAN HELP THEM

Get every member of your organization and every friend to send letters to Governor Warren, Sacramento, California, asking for the release of the Sleepy Lagoon defendants. Send copies to us.

Order copies of this pamphlet for distribution among the members of your organization and your friends.

Contribute as much as you can and as quickly as you can. Thousands of dollars are needed at once to support the appeals for reversal of the convictions.

DO YOUR PART TO WIN THE WAR ON THE HOME FRONT!

YOU CAN HELP to crush the Axis Fifth Column in our midst by helping to free the 17 boys convicted in the Sleepy Lagoon Case * Much Axis propaganda has been made over these unjust convictions It is up to you to help show our minority groups that through our democratic institutions and the organized will of the people, such grave injustices are rectified. . . .

Source: Sleepy Lagoon Defense Committee, *The Sleepy Lagoon Case*. Hollywood: Mercury Printing Co., 1943.

EXCERPTS FROM SPECIAL OPERATION REPORT OF THE COORDINATOR OF INTER-AMERICAN AFFAIRS, JULY 9, 1943

For the administration of President Franklin D. Roosevelt, the riots in Los Angeles in 1943, occurring during World War II, were not only of domestic concern but also a diplomatic challenge. There was immediate concern that the attack against Mexican Americans in Los Angeles could have a damaging impact on relations between the United States and Mexico. The Office of the Coordinator of Inter-American Affairs (CIAA) was a federal agency promoting cooperation among American nations during the 1940s, especially in commercial and economic areas. It distributed films and produced radio broadcasts for Latin American countries in order to counter Italian and German propaganda that had tried to turn sympathies in the various countries against the United States. The CIAA became directly involved in helping to restore order in Los Angeles and to advise the state department of events as they unfolded. On July 9, the agency reported on the violence.

Special Operations Report-CIAA

The Los Angeles "Zoot Suit Riots."

The Facts

On Friday night, June 4, 1943, several hundred sailors stationed at the Los Angeles Naval Training Armory set out in organized groups bound for the Mexican district where they terrorized the inhabitants and beat up many youths in reprisal for numerous previous assaults during the past few months on soldiers and sailors by juvenile gangsters, one such assault having occurred on Thursday. At the first outbreak of violence, CIAA representative in Los Angeles J Churchill Murray, in charge of the "minorities" program in the Southern California region, contacted the CIAA Director of Inter-American Activities in the United States for directives and guidance in the situation.

According to the evidence submitted by CIAA representative and from previous field studies, the present situation seemed to be a juvenile delinquency problem rooted in community conditions and the primary concern of the local authorities. The CIAA representative was, therefore, to follow events closely but to remain in the background unless the emergence of a Mexican issue might require his direct participation. Nevertheless, he was authorized to operate anonymously when and where he could help in a constructive manner. Likewise the prestige, contacts, and resources of the Inter-American Center of Southern California was to be available.

The sailors were planning an even larger expedition on Saturday night but upon CIAA suggestion, the Armory authorities held the men confined to their posts under disciplinary instructions. However, a large number of sailors on shore leave from San Pedro, did march that night in mass formation through the Mexican district, assaulting Mexican youths and engaging in other disorderly acts. As a result "feeling was running very high, both in the Mexican community and among the sailors," and as a precautionary measure, following CIAA guidance in the matter, leaves of all sailors stationed at the Armory were cancelled on Monday, June 7. However, approximately 1000 sailors went on a rampage that night in the Mexican district, raiding theaters, bars, and dance halls, tearing zoot-suits off Mexican boys and assaulting those who resisted-50 servicemen against one Mexican. Later on the fighting spread to whites and negroes with civilian juveniles joining the soldiers and sailors. CIAA Los Angeles representative, touring the district with the Chief of Police, personally witnessed the entire disturbance and while the fighting was still in progress telephoned General Murray, Military Commander of Southern California, to inform him of the situation. General Murray promptly called out all reserves of military police and declared certain areas out of bounds for the army men that night. This was most helpful in eliminating the danger of a major riot situation as thousands of persons had congregated within a small down-town area with every restaurant, theater, and bar being invaded by rioters attacking Mexican boys. The police had already summoned out all their reserves but were unable to cope with the situation.

On Thursday, June 10, retaliation by Mexicans increased in severity—Mexican gangs attacked lone servicemen, an American girl was slashed with a razor; several street cars were stoned and gasoline flares tossed into a theater resulted in the shooting of one Mexican boy by police. Rowdyism of servicemen and Anglo-Saxon civilians greatly reduced in volume but became more violent.

CIAA Mitigates Violence

In order to insure protection to the Mexican population of Los Angeles and to reduce the possibility of fatalities which would breed resentment and mature latent antagonisms, the CIAA representative at the outset of the trouble, following directives issued by his chief in Washington, suggested the closing of Los Angeles to all enlisted naval personnel at a meeting with the military and civil authorities, where he emphasized the international aspects of the situation and the serious consequences which would result in discrimination in arrests. As a result this Office received assurances, which were carried out, that both Naval and Army personnel would be disciplined, while the Chief of Police and Sheriff promised that discrimination in arrests would not be practiced. After other conversations with Admiral Bagley, Commandant of the Eleventh Naval District and General Maxwell Murray, Los Angeles and its suburbs were declared closed areas for soldiers and sailors and an extremely critical situation was thereby avoided.

In addition, the CIAA representative also contacted leaders of the so-called pachuco boys who promised that their groups would try to stay off the streets and not engage in any provocative actions if the soldiers and sailors would do likewise. Police had heretofore been unable to control these Mexican juvenile gangs, feared by the entire Mexican community. In any objective evaluation of the situation the provocation and open hostility of Mexican boys toward men in uniform must be taken into consideration. The reasons for this are not clear; frequently, it is believed, the attacks have their origin in quarrels over Mexican girls, aggravated by the general tendency on the part of many Mexican delinquents to use knives and similar weapons in their personal quarrels, an advantage resented by their soldier and sailor opponents. The pachucos are also inclined to resolve their personal enmity by gang assaults on their individual victims.

CIAA Cooperates with Mexican Consulate

Since the beginning of the riots, CIAA Los Angeles representative, handling the Mexican angle according to his instructions, kept in almost continuous consultation with the Mexican Consulate, fully apprising it of the interest and actions taken by this Office. After taking immediate steps to avoid further bloodshed, our second objective was largely devoted to securing the statements which the Mexican Government felt to be necessary if a written protest to the Department of State was to be avoided. Mr. Calles and Mr. Aguilar, associate consuls for Los Angeles and Mr. Adolfo de la Huerta, Inspector General of Consuls in the United States and ex-President of Mexico, frankly discussed the requirements in this matter with the CIAA official.

The resentment on the part of the Mexican community, as well as of the Mexican Government during the rioting, was not against the arrest of pachucos but against those who took the law into their own hands and against the authorities who appeared to be condoning the attacks. This impression was created in large measure by the metropolitan dailies which were influenced not only by a desire for sensationalism but by a reluctance to present the actions of servicemen in an unfavorable light. Two serious consequences appeared likely to result: (1.) retaliatory attacks on Americans by Mexicans, increasing greatly the possibility of bloodshed. (Up until the time that statements secured by our Office were published, these retaliatory attacks were daily increasing in severity); (2.) serious international complications, because of the apparent refusal of military and civil authorities to condemn or apologize for the actions of lawless individuals. It therefore became extremely important that repudiation be made of this affair by the military and civil authorities, and the CIAA set out to secure such statements.

CIAA Secures Important Statements

The first such statement came from the Board of Supervisors. The Chief of Police also, complying with the request of the Inter-American Center, readily issued an even stronger statement which received wide publicity, promising prompt arrest of all violators of the law, even though in uniform. This was the first public statement by a law enforcement official that servicemen beating up Mexican boys would be arrested. In actual practice, however, they had already been arrested by the hundreds and turned over to the military police or shore patrol, but neither the Mexican nor the American communities were cognizant of this fact. A statement was also secured from the Sheriff assuring the Mexican community of impartial justice.

The Mayor, in the early stages of the rioting issued a statement which caused great offense to the Mexican community and to the Mexican Consulate. The statement expressed love for the Mexicans but warned them that they would be arrested whenever they violated the law, making no mention of the servicemen or Anglo-Saxon civilians who were then actually attacking Mexicans. Upon its publication the Mayor was immediately contacted and when the CIAA representative pointed out that his statement was inadequate from our point of view he readily sent a long letter to the Mexican Consulate, which met with their satisfaction and which was also published.

The delay of the military authorities in the early stages of the affair to make clear to civilians and servicemen alike that the Army and Navy would not tolerate vigilante action, threatened to become quite serious. With that in mind, CIAA representative conferred with Admiral Bagley, and upon being requested to do so, this Office suggested (1.) that he immediately reply to a telegram which the Mexican Consul had sent him several days before, and (2.) that he issue a statement to the press repudiating action of individual sailors who had violated both military and civil law. These suggestions were promptly carried out.

Next, General Maxwell Murray was visited and the CIAA official pointed out that the civil population did not seem to be sufficiently aware that the present vigilante action was strongly condemned by the Army officers and that the soldiers themselves did not seem to know it. After requesting our guidance in a proper course of conduct, it was suggested that inasmuch as it was undesirable for civilians to criticize soldiers in war time, the Army itself should clearly condemn individuals taking part in vigilante action, warning offending soldiers of military punishment. The following day a letter to that effect was sent to the Mexican Consulate and an extremely satisfactory statement from General Maxwell appeared in the press. When the statement from General Murray was received the Mexican Consulate wired his Embassy that full satisfaction had now been furnished by the military and civil authorities. Similar statements were forthcoming from the Governor, the Attorney General, the District Attorney of Los Angeles County, and other high officials. All of these statements received wide distribution and produced a perceptible relief in tension in both the American and Mexican Communities and met with the complete satisfaction of the Mexican Consul, who dispatched them to the Embassy in Washington. Sr. Padilla, Mexican Foreign Minister, in a telegram to the Inspector General of Consuls in the United States, made formal acknowledgment of appreciation for the assistance rendered by the Coordinator's Office in the situation. On June 27, a Mexican news broadcast also commented: "In regard to events in Los Angeles the Consul General of the United States telegraphed . . . that complete calm (now) reigns. . . . The Mexican Ambassador in Washington informed Lic. Padilla that the affair had been managed satisfactorily, with the cooperation of the Coordinator of Inter-American Affairs."

CIAA Contacts Local Press

The policy of local newspapers in not criticizing servicemen or photographing their arrest, headlining instead the arrest of zootsuiters was responsible for the impression among the Mexican population that only Mexicans were being punished and that military and civilian authorities condoned terrorism. The CIAA representative personally witnessed the arrest of hundreds of servicemen and Anglo-Saxons in addition to those Mexicans arrested. General Murray's Chief of Staff stated that 53 soldiers were being held in stockades as a result of one night's rioting and would be court martialed. Following discussions with attaches of the CIAA and the Inter-American Center, the local newspapers, after a few days of sensationalism, adopted a more constructive attitude, with the Los Angeles Daily News, on June 9, at the request of the Center, publishing a picture for the first time of Anglo-Saxons being arrested. Probably the most important service rendered by the CIAA sponsored Inter-American Council of Southern California was the secret meeting which it arranged, under the ostensible auspices of the Chamber of Commerce, bringing together in one room the Mexican Consul and all the law enforcement authorities involved in the situation, where all the problems were frankly discussed, and the Consul's viewpoint presented. This meeting did much to relieve increasing tension and prevent misunderstanding.

Other CIAA Activities

As an aftermath of the situation, investigations were commenced by the State Attorney General and the Los Angeles County Grand Jury. Both the American and Mexican communities seem to be ready to cooperate with the efforts of authorities to reach a permanent solution and carry out an effective program. The American Community in Southern California now recognizes the basic social character of the problem and appears to be sincerely determined to correct it. CIAA representative, on June 14, met with the Governor's committee and expressed the readiness of this Office to cooperate with the community as called upon and to extend the services of the Southern California Council in helping to carry out the program arranged by the Committee. The Coordinator's program of immediate amelioration meets with the support of practically all groups and will be accelerated rather than retarded by the recent crisis. From the long term point of view there is continued danger of similar incidents as long as the local powers remain unable to control pachuco gangs and until the social mal-adjustment causing these conditions are solved.

Mayor Bowron's Statements

On June 9, NAR telegrammed Fletcher Bowron, Mayor of Los Angeles, for his confidential estimate of the situation. The Mayor replied that the situation would not have any adverse international effect, laying the cause to bad "gangs of juveniles and older young men, most of whom are of Mexican blood but practically all of them American born."

In a statement to the press on June 9 the Mayor stated that he had informed the Department of State that the occurrences were not in any manner directed at Mexican citizens and that there was no question of racial discrimination involved, saying that the law was going to be enforced even though that required stern action on the part of the authorities.

In a radio address delivered that same evening the Mayor stated that in Los Angeles, as elsewhere throughout the United States, soldiers and sailors had been attacked by young gangsters, some of whom wore zoot-suits and "this probably led to the unfortunate attack upon Mexican and colored boys when young men from the armed forces, for all the world like college boys would act if some of their fellow students had been beaten up by students from a rival institution came piling into Los Angeles, looking for excitement and feeling that if there was going to be a fight anyway, they wanted to get in on it. The action of the servicemen was entirely understandable and largely excusable. It was unfortunate that Mexicans and negroes, whether they wear zoot-suits or not, happened along the street at the wrong time."

Telegrams from Pressure Groups

The following organizations sent telegrams to CIAA and other agencies in Washington requesting action in the situation:

Council for Pan American Democracy–(which was planning to bring a delegation to Washington to pressure various agencies for government intervention in Los Angeles)

Comite Patriotico Mexicani, Chicago

Los Angeles Industrial Union Council, CIO

New Jersey Metal Council, International Union, Newark

Mexican Civic Committee (West side) Chicago

Spanish American Section, International Workers Order

Axis and Mexican Radio Broadcasts

The Berlin radio was the first to comment on the situation in broadcast on July 11 wherein it stated that "instead of saving up their fighting enthusiasm for the front-line, United States soldiers are attacking harmless Mexicans" and there is "much disgust (in Mexico) over the behavior adopted by United States soldiers in Latin America toward their southern allies."

Rome radio on June 12 attributed the incidents to armed bandits composed of Mexicans, negroes, and adventurers.

Tokyo radio beamed to Latin America at first reported the incident rather objectively, but on a later broadcast sought to convey the impression that the soldiers and sailors were battling with American gangsters among whom were the few Mexicans.

On June 16 the Mexican domestic radio stated that the Secretary of Foreign Affairs had instructed the Mexican Ambassador in Washington to secure satisfaction and just indemnization.

Press Digest

The following paragraphs typify local press treatment and presents a running narrative of the proceedings:

Bellicose sailors cruised the East Side in taxi-cabs on Friday night, June 4, on the prowl in the zoot-suit belt where a number of their shipmates had recently been attacked by ruffians. Mexican youths were assaulted and four were treated for minor injuries.

On Saturday night, police reported soldiers, sailors, and marines were walking four abreast, increasing to a platoon of 30 or 40 after a few blocks, stopping wearers of zoot-suits on the way and summarily ordering them to remove their clothes. One squad of sailors barged into a dance hall causing a disturbance. Deputy Sheriffs arrested 9 sailors who were armed with rope ends but turned them over to the shore patrol without formal charges.

Twenty-seven zoot-suiters were arrested as they were assembling for a gang meeting, climaxing two days of seething friction between servicemen and wearers of zoot-suits. Some 250 extra police and scores of sheriff's deputies in the East Los Angeles, Firestone, and Vermont Avenue district have been cruising there as part of preparedness strategy.

Jail doors closed on 44 youthful gangsters while police cars continued to roam the zoot-suit section in search of other teen age thugs who have been attacking sailors, those arrested being only a small fraction of those police sought to apprehend as about 100 others escaped. According to the police the zooters admitted they planned to attack more sailors by jabbing broken bottlenecks in the faces of their victims, while beating sailors brains out with hammers and irons was also on the program.

The word went out to the zoot-suit gangs to stop all fighting among themselves and concentrate on the United States Navy. These groups have been forced to form a league by a turn of fortune that has left them both angry and fearful. Up until now they thought they were the toughest guys on earth but a few sailors have shown them otherwise. Those gamin dandies, the zoot-suiters, learned a great moral lesson from servicemen who took over their instruction.

Police records showed 110 persons hospitalized with serious injuries since the rioting began—92 civilians and 18 servicemen. Police estimated 100–150 more were hurt more or less seriously but went to private physicians to evade questioning. Bookings at Central Jail totaled 114—94 civilians and 20 servicemen. Another 400 had been arrested and held without charge until tension eased. Pictures of a cell full of arrested youths peering out from behind bars and at a police line-up were prominently displayed by most newspapers, as were wounded sailors.

On June 9, banner headlines proclaimed "Zoot Riots Linked to Hitler Agents."

Manchester Boddy wrote in his Daily News column, on June 8, "Los Angeles youth—by the hundreds—loosely organized in 'gangs', roaming the streets by night, armed with spikes, bits of pipe, broken bottle necks, and sharp knives-bent on destroying private property and terrorizing law-abiding citizens form a spectacle grim enough to warrant drastic measures. . . . Preliminary investigations completely exonerate Navy personnel from responsibility. . . . The situation is ugly enough, and no effort should be spared on the part of responsible officials to see that it is cleaned up completely and in the shortest possible time."

Mayor Fletcher Bowron was quoted as saying: "The city does not have adequate facilities for stopping such activities (juvenile delinquency and youthful gangsterism) because the police department has lost 27 percent of its personnel and all juvenile detention homes are filled to capacity."

Intervention of State Attorney Robert W. Kenney in the situation was asked at a meeting of nearly 100 representatives of various groups, presided over by Cary McWilliams, who also telegraphed the United states Attorney General's Office asking for an investigation of the situation.

On June 10 the Washington Daily News reported that field representatives of CIAA had begun an investigation. Governor Warren named a five-man committee to investigate and asked the State Attorney General to conduct a similar inquiry. At the District Attorney's request the County Grand Jury also undertook an investigation of the trouble. The California chapter of the National Lawyers Guild also demanded an investigation, with Martin Popper, Secretary, leading a delegation to Washington to confer with officers of the Department of Justice, the OWI, and other agencies. Included in this delegation was to be Mrs. Josephina Bright, a member of the Los Angeles Citizens Committee for the defense of Mexican-American youths.

Community leaders held meetings in an effort to get the city back to normal and to present evidence that the street battles represented a symptom not of racial discrimination but of an increasingly serious state-wide juvenile delinquency problem.

State senator Jack Tenney, head of a Committee which for two years has investigated subversive activities in California, continued to search for a possible connection between the activities of the juvenile gangsters and Axis agents, although the District Attorney, Fred N. Howser, of Los Angeles County is reported to have declared there was "absolutely no evidence to that effect", and said that this viewpoint was concurred in by the military.

Navy officers were said to be critical of the "collegiate" spirit of their young seamen as were Army leaders of soldiers getting out of hand. But they were also sharply critical of the police, alleging failure to protect individual sailors from dozens of attacks since January 1, while the city officials, off the record, stated that they felt the Navy had not exerted sufficient control over the drinking habits of their men. After visits to several bars, especially in less desirable sections of town, they are easy prey for young gangsters who beat and rob them in dark alleys after they have been enticed there ostensibly for other reasons by confederates. Another factor is the location of the Naval Reserve Armory adjacent to one of the Mexican colonies. Young seamen flirt with girls and their zoot-suit friends resent this.

Following a visit to Secretary Hull by the Mexican Ambassador who expressed his Government's concern over the disturbances, the Department of State announced that investigations so far had revealed no cases where Mexican citizens were involved, but would speed action on claims resulting from such cases, if there are any.

Mrs. Roosevelt commenting on the situation at her press conference stated that long-standing discrimination against Mexicans in Los Angeles, having roots in things that happened long before, was the reason for the recent conflict. . . .

Source: Of 4512 Coordinator of Inter-American Affairs: Los Angeles "Zoot Suit" Situation 1943, FDR-FDRPOF: President's Official Files, 1933–1945, Franklin D. Roosevelt Library, Hyde Park, New York.

WILLIAM BLOCKER, AMERICAN CONSUL GENERAL, CIUDAD JUAREZ, MEXICO TO SECRETARY OF STATE CORDELL HULL; CONCLUSIONS ON ZOOT SUIT DISTURBANCES, AUGUST 3, 1943

Worried about the international implications of the Zoot Suit Riots, U.S. secretary of state Cordell Hull on July 7 directed veteran diplomat William Blocker, American consul general in Ciudad Juarez, to travel to Los Angeles to confer with state and local officials and especially with Mexican consular officers. Blocker asked Consul Gerald Mokma of Tijuana, Mexico, to assist him in his investigation. In the course of their talks, they consulted with a number of Mexican diplomats, including Adolfo de la Huerta, inspector general of the Mexican Consulates in the U.S. and Alfredo Calles, Mexican consul at Los Angeles. Blocker's report to Secretary of State Hull took account of the many causes of the outbreak of violence. As many others had done, nevertheless, Blocker discounted racial hatred as one of those causes.

American Consulate
Ciudad Juarez, Mexico, August 3, 1943
Subject: Zoot Suit Disturbances at Los Angeles, California
. . . *Conclusions*
In summarizing the results of my investigations. . .

1) I am constrained to express the belief that race hatred had nothing to do with the zoot suit disturbances in Los Angeles.
2) It appears to be common knowledge that for a number of years trouble has been brewing in the slum districts of Los Angeles, because of the laxity of the police in controlling the restless, trouble-making, youthful element that has been permitted to gate crash dances, commit petty thievery, fight amongst themselves, and practically rule the social activities of the underprivileged people residing in those districts.
3) These gangs naturally resent any interference on the part of outsiders. With the coming of the war and the granting of shore leave to the large number of sailors in Los Angeles, many of them seeking entertainment sought out these localities and, naturally, the Mexican girls were attracted by the ready money most of them had in their pockets. The preference for the uniformed men by the girls irritated their local swains that resulted in an occasional fight wherein the sailors and soldiers were mishandled by the gangs of hoodlums. Typical of boys in the Navy, others came to their rescue, and the situation grew out of control.

4) The chief of police in Los Angeles more or less admitted that this condition existed, and that that due to the shortage on the police force of some 500 men, he was not able to effectively control it without a possible loss of life, which he was doing everything he could to prevent.

5) It being an off news week, the newspapers resorted to sensational journalism, and presented the picture in such a way, likely to increase sales, as to give the public the impression that the police were unable to cope with the situation, and that they were in need of assistance from the armed forces in breaking up the gang of zoot suiters. This statement appears to be borne out by Mr. Eduardo M. Quevedo, President of the Latin-American Coordinator's Council for Youths in the Mexican colony. Mr. Quevado has publicly expressed the opinion that these situations were brought on in retaliation, which was urged by the local press who virtually dared soldiers and sailors to mete out punishment to zoot suiters.

6) Mr. Quevedo admits that the Mexican community was at fault for permitting the zoot suit element to exist in its midst, and blames the police, because they took no steps to prevent the disorders to protect law-abiding Mexicans and, therefore, hints that there is some discrimination in the city, which has been allowed over a long period of time. I understand that he has pointed out on several occasions that although the Mexican community in Los Angeles numbers about 350,000 people, the Los Angeles police for includes no representative group of Spanish-speaking officers, and as a result the police department does not have representation familiar with the Mexican people.

7) Obviously, the disturbances resulted from service men frequenting the slum districts, crashing Mexican-American parties, and paying too much attention to Mexican-American girls.

8) Considerable blame may be given to the Los Angeles newspapers for the unfortunate publicity which the incident achieved. This publicity obviously aroused sailors and soldiers and the civilian population who participated in further incidents. The newspapers may also be blamed for the international concern given the situation by Mexico.

9) The background to this trouble may be attributed to the result of slum conditions existing in the city of Los Angeles, for which corrective measures had not previously been taken.

10) There is nothing to indicate that the Axis powers were involved in any way, but there is a strong possibility that some of the undesirable

publicity given the affair, the dissemination of some propaganda among the hoodlum element and their parents may have emanated from the Communist party group headed by one Josephine Bright and a Mr. Connally. They appear to have attempted to introduce the racial angle in these riots, and to have attempted to make heroes out of the hoodlums by demanding connection with this angle of the case. . . .

11) It seems to be generally believed by those who have made a study of the zoot suit problem in Los Angeles that sociologically it can be attributed to the local economic, social, and political conditions brought on by neglect of state, county and city governments to take proper community action free from politics in introducing a remedy to solve these conditions, which have been wisely pointed out as follows: Establishment of recreational and trade school facilities, increase in facilities for juvenile detention and correction, urging of religious and charitable institutions to give more attention to the improvement of the slum conditions, and of selecting and finding middle class leadership among Mexican-Americans in the community, which now appears to not exist. If it does, they are saturated with political ambitions.

12) It appears to be the unanimous opinion of all the investigative agencies and law enforcement officers I interviewed that Mexican Consul Aguilar, of the Mexican Consulate at Los Angeles, did not show any disposition to cooperate with the authorities, but to the contrary was prone to seize the slightest pretext as a basis of complaint charging racial discrimination. When called upon practically daily by the police department and the sheriff's office to furnish them with a list of any Mexicans involved in the zoot suit disturbances, he was unable to do so, but appears to have attempted on several occasions to assume the role of the protector of people of Latin extraction, and to have made reports to his government intimating racial hatred and racial discrimination by the police department and apathy in granting the proper protection by law-abiding Mexican citizens. The Mexican Consulate, working in connection with the Mexican colony, appears to have taken the view that the Los Angeles police knew that the riots of June 7, 1943 were on the way, but took no steps to prevent them, or to protect law-abiding Mexicans, thus alleging that doubtlessly the primary phase of the affair was discrimination, which the City of Los Angeles has over long allowed. The Mexican Consul also is said to have reported to the Mexican Foreign Office that Axis subversive

influence existed and was inspired by sensational newspaper reports on the disturbances. From the best I can understand, after talking with Consul General de la Huerta, no reports were made to the Foreign Office indicating Communistic agitators, although our investigators feel that there was some activity of this kind shortly after the disturbances. I am constrained to express the belief that the Mexican Consular Service has not only in this case, but in many cases along the border and adjacent to the border, been too overzealous in alleging racial discrimination against American citizens of Latin extraction who had no claim to call for consular intervention. I am also inclined to believe that Mexican consular officers have on frequent occasions resorted to too much publicity when presenting cases to the authorities alleging racial discrimination when they were pure and simple cases of class distinction liable to be found in any country, and particularly in Mexico where class distinction exists. I feel that if the truth were known, persons of the "peon" type have been used as test cases by Mexican societies acting in connection with the Consulate to prove racial discrimination; in other words, they have stepped down in the lower strata of their people who are themselves underprivileged in Mexico as far as class distinction is concerned in attempting to force acceptance of these people upon the higher intellectual element in communities in the United States.

13) I am confident that there is no basis for the Mexican Government to file indemnity claims, although it is clearly stated in the telegram of Mexican Consul General de la Huerta that he was looking into this phase of the situation. . . .

Source: William Blocker to Secretary of State, August 3, 1943, Dispatch # 1855, Zoot Suit Disturbances at Los Angeles, California, National Archives and Records Administration, RG 59 General Records of the Department of State, Decimal File, #811.4016/651.

■■■■■■

ORSON WELLES TO CALIFORNIA PAROLE BOARD, SAN QUENTIN, CALIFORNIA, MARCH 1, 1944

Orson Welles, acclaimed actor, director, writer, and producer in theater, radio, and film, often lent his voice to progressive political causes. In November 1942, he chaired an invitational forum of individuals in the Hollywood motion picture industry to raise funds for the defense of the 22 Mexican-American defendants in the Sleepy Lagoon murder case.

Long after the conviction and imprisonment of 17 of the individuals, Welles continued to fight for their release. He worked with the Sleepy Lagoon Defense Committee and in early 1944 sent a letter of support to the parole board at San Quentin. In October, the Second District Court of Appeals overturned the verdicts.

March 1, 1944
Parole Board San Quentin California
Gentlemen:

After a very careful examination of the records and facts of the trial, I am convinced that the boys in the Sleepy Lagoon case were not given a fair trial, and that their conviction could only have been influenced by anti-Mexican prejudice. I am convinced, also, that the causes leading up to this case, as well as its outcome, are of great importance to the Mexican minority in this community. That is to say, the case has importance aside from the boys incriminated—the whole community is undermined. Any attempt at good relations is impaired—as is the importance of unity in the furtherance of the war effort. To allow an injustice like this to stand is to impede the progress of unity.

I have heard of the splendid record the boys have made in San Quentin— each having made a fine showing for himself in behavior, cooperation, etc.

Because this case is a very special one for the above reasons, I am of the opinion that it merits special attention on the part of the Board Members. Many people in the film colony have expressed great interest in it, and I feel I am speaking for them, too, in making this plea.

Sincerely,
Orson Welles

Source: "Zoot Suit Riots," 2002, American Experience, PBS. Available at http://www.pbs.org/wgbh/amex/zoot/eng_filmmore/ps_welles.html.

EXCERPTS OF APPELLATE DECISION IN
PEOPLE v. ZAMMORA, 1944

In October 1944, the judicial fiasco of People v. Zammora *that had resulted in the conviction and imprisonment of multiple defendants in the Sleepy Lagoon murder was finally reversed. In May, the Second District Court of Appeals began hearing the appellate case argued by attorney Ben*

Margolis. Five months later, Associate Justice Thomas P. White, with the concurrence of Presiding Justice John York and Justice William Doran, held that the evidence presented in the earlier trial was insufficient to establish guilt. The appellate decision affirmed that the constitutional rights of the defendants had been violated, that the actions of the trial judge, Charles W. Fricke, had been biased, and that there was essentially no evidence that tied the convicted young men to the crime. Based on the appellate decision, Judge Clement D. Nye, of the Superior Court of Los Angeles, dismissed the case on October 28. The Sleepy Lagoon defendants were free.

People v. Zammora (1944) 66 CA2d 166
THE PEOPLE, Respondent, v. GUS ZAMMORA et al., Appellants.
COUNSEL
Robert W. Kenny, Attorney General, Eugene M. Elson, Deputy Attorney General, Fred N. Howser, District Attorney, and John Barnes, Deputy District Attorney, for Respondent.
Katz, Gallagher & Margolis, Ben Margolis, George E. Shibley and Selma Mikels Bachelia for Appellants.
OPINION
WHITE, J.

In an indictment returned by the Grand Jury of Los Angeles County, 22 defendants were jointly charged, in count I, with the crime of murder and, in counts II and III, with the crime of assault with a deadly weapon with intent to commit murder. After the entry of "not guilty" pleas as to all counts of the indictment, trial was had before a jury, resulting in the acquittal of five defendants on all three counts. Of the remaining defendants, five were acquitted of the murder charge, but were convicted of minor offenses necessarily included in the remaining two counts. The other 12 defendants were convicted on all three counts; three being found guilty of murder in the first degree and nine of murder in the second degree. This appeal . . . is prosecuted by the last mentioned 12 defendants, against whom verdicts of "guilty" were returned, as follows:

Epitomizing the factual background which gave rise to this prosecution, it appears from the record that, on the evening of August 1, 1942, a birthday party was in progress honoring Mrs. Amelia Delgadillo. The party was held at her home and was attended by her husband, other members of her family and some twenty or thirty other invited guests. The record discloses that some eight or eleven uninvited persons were also in attendance.

The Delgadillo home is located on what is known as the "Williams Ranch," situate in the vicinity of Slauson and Atlantic Boulevards in the county of Los Angeles.

At the birthday party, on the evening in question, the guests indulged in dancing out in the patio to the music of an orchestra, which played from 9 P.M. until 1 A.M. After the departure of the musicians, a radio was placed in the back yard and members of the family with a few remaining guests continued dancing until approximately 1:45 on the morning of August 2nd.

Sometime before midnight, several of the defendants in this case had gone to a small pond or reservoir also located on the Williams Ranch about a half mile west of the Delgadillo home, and designated by the boys and girls who, from time to time, congregated there, as "Sleepy Lagoon." While the aforesaid group, consisting of some of the boys who later became defendants in this case and their girl companions were at "Sleepy Lagoon," they were set upon and beaten by another crowd of boys identified only as "boys from Downey."

The record also discloses that some eight or ten of these so-called "Downey boys" were among the uninvited guests at the Delgadillo party, and, earlier that evening, two of them became involved in an argument with their host and his son-in-law, because their host told them there was no more beer. One of those boys "grabbed" a chair in a threatening manner, but the other "grabbed" him with both hands on his shoulders, turned him around, and pulled him back outside of the patio gate. The witness, Eleanor Delgadillo Coronado was sitting in the patio across from the gate. She testified: "When I seen him, and I got up and then went to the kitchen door . . . because . . . when I seen these two boys come up, I thought they were going to start trouble or something."

Following the aforesaid attack upon some of these defendants by the so-called "Downey boys" at "Sleepy Lagoon," the former left the scene of the altercation and repaired to the vicinity of Vernon and Long Beach Avenues, some five miles distant from "Sleepy Lagoon." This last named location, it appears, was a place at which a group of young people from the 38th Street neighborhood congregated. We think it is a fair statement to say that the defendants who had been beaten up at "Sleepy Lagoon," smarting under the effects of the beating administered to them, returned to the vicinity of Vernon and Long Beach Boulevards for the purpose of enlisting the aid of their friends and going again to "Sleepy Lagoon" for the avowed purpose of "fighting it out" with the boys from Downey. Thus reinforced, a number of boys and girls, including the defendants, ranging in age from 14 to 22 years, went out towards "Sleepy Lagoon" in several automobiles, variously testified to as being from five to ten in number. There is evidence that, prior to embarking upon the last mentioned trip, one of the defendants, Angel Padillo, who accompanied the caravan, obtained a box of shells for his 22 rifle, which he took with him. The evidence on this point is in conflict, but, in any event, it is conceded the rifle was not utilized in the commission of the alleged homicide or either of the two assaults charged against the defendants. Upon arrival at "Sleepy Lagoon," it was discovered that the boys from Downey had departed. Thereupon, some of the party disembarked from their automobiles and proceeded on foot to the Delgadillo home, where the aforesaid party was in progress, while others proceeded thereto in their automobiles, where most of them alighted from their vehicles.

What transpired thereafter will be discussed presently, but we pause here to give consideration to respondent's claim that, in returning to "Sleepy Lagoon," the defendants had entered into an unlawful combination or conspiracy, the object of which, as the result of their malignant hearts, was to commit murder in satisfaction of their lust for revenge.

We have painstakingly read the reporter's transcript in this case, containing, as it does, more than 6,000 pages. We have studiously read and considered the briefs filed herein, which total some 1,400 pages, and from a reading thereof we are persuaded that there is no substantial evidence to support the claim that when the defendants left the vicinity of Vernon and Long Beach Avenues they had "murder in their hearts" or even that they had then formed any intent to go to the Delgadillo home. As we view the evidence, it strongly supports the theory that some of the defendants were intent upon meeting the "Downey boys" and engaging in a fist fight with them in retaliation for the attack made upon some of the defendants earlier that night as "Sleepy Lagoon." It was only when these defendants discovered that the objects of their search had departed from "Sleepy Lagoon" that they determined upon going to the Delgadillo home. As to what prompted this decision upon their part the evidence is in extreme conflict. At all events, it can be said that the evidence does not reflect any unanimity of purpose. There is some testimony that one of the defendants, who had previously been at the party and had danced with one of the Delgadillo girls, stated that it was a "good party" and suggested that the group go there. There is other evidence that, when defendant Leyvas and some of his codefendants entered upon the Delgadillo premises, they demanded to know the whereabouts of the "men who had beaten them up." Some of the defendants had no knowledge of the party and no longer expected to find the "Downey boys," but just followed the others. But it belies the record to assert that what happened subsequently at the Delgadillo party was the result of a collective intent upon the part of the defendants to commit murder, and that the conduct, behavior and actions upon the part of the defendants at the party manifested a conspiracy to commit murder or assaults with intent to commit murder. The most that the record reflects in this regard is that until their arrival at "Sleepy Lagoon" and their failure to find the "Downey boys" there, defendants had a common intent to encounter the "Downey boys," and thereupon engage in a course of disorderly conduct, breach of the peace, or battery. As we shall hereafter in this opinion point out, the jury, by their verdicts, rejected the theory of the prosecution that the defendants had engaged in a conspiracy; and we think rightly so in the light of the evidence presented to which we subsequently shall refer.

Following the entry of some of the defendants into the Delgadillo premises, a general "free for all" fight ensued. After this controversy and the exit of the defendants from the Delgadillo premises, one Jose Diaz was found lying unconscious in the dirt outside the fence south of the Delgadillo premises, and later died. There is no evidence as to his whereabouts or actions during the "free for all" fight involving the defendants. People's witnesses testified that he was seen leaving the Delgadillo premises, accompanied by two other guests who were not produced as witnesses, several minutes before the arrival of any of the defendants.

In describing the injuries upon the body of the deceased, the autopsy surgeon testified:

"Further examination showed the backs of both hands to be contused and somewhat swollen with abrasion of the knuckles of the little and ring finger on the left hand, and the second finger of the right hand. The facial features were swollen and there was contusion over the left side of the lower lip and also the upper lip; there was contusion over the prominence of both cheeks and abrasions over the outer angle, the right angle of the mouth. The left ear was quite markedly contused, and there was extensive ecchymosis of the scalp over the left side of the head. Upon opening the skull the brain was found to be contused and there was a profuse subdural hemorrhage. The base of the skull was fractured, the fracture line running along the lesser wing of the sphenoid bone on the left side."

The autopsy surgeon also testified that the chemical analysis of the blood of the deceased, made at 7:30 A.M. on August 2, showed 0.12 per cent alcohol, and testified that the margin of intoxication is generally accepted as 0.15 per cent. This physician also testified that, from the time one stops drinking, the alcoholic content of the blood of a living person recedes, so that it would be impossible for him to say whether or not Jose Diaz was intoxicated a few hours before his death. This witness said the swelling of Jose Diaz' hands was similar to that caused by delivering blows with fists, and that

"[t]he appearance on the left side of the head of the ecchymosis of the scalp and the crushing effect on the left ear indicated to me that some other instrument than a fist had been used to bring that injury about."

He later said, with respect to the cause of this injury, "If this decedent had fallen to the ground . . . the head could have hit a protruding rock or something else other than a smooth surface."

As a result of these injuries and primarily because of the profuse hemorrhage and skull fracture, Jose Diaz died about four o'clock the same morning in the hospital to which he was taken.

One Jose Manfredi, who is the victim mentioned in count II, received a stab wound three or four inches long and about three-quarters of an inch deep, on his chest just below the heart. He also had a fracture of the frontal wall of the sinus, a basal skull fracture, concussion of the brain, and a broken left hand. He was taken to the general hospital and did not fully recover consciousness until about two o'clock on the following afternoon, August 2nd.

Cruz Reyes, named as the victim in count III of the indictment, received a stab wound in the abdomen and suffered contusions about his body.

The victims of the assaults alleged in counts II and III of the indictment claim to have been stabbed early in the fight while they and some of the defendants were in the Delgadillo patio, and later to have received severe beatings with steel instruments wielded by numerous boys on the east side of the Delgadillo premises. . . .

Upon reading the voluminous transcript of the testimony adduced at the trial, one is immediately impressed that there is a great volume of evidence establishing the fact that a majority of the defendants committed one or more assaults and that in some instances weapons which could be classified as deadly weapons were used. However, such incriminatory evidence is contained in the many written statements taken from defendants after their arrest and in which they made accusatory declarations against codefendants, and which accusations were, as held by the trial court, inadmissible against such codefendants. When the admissible evidence is separated from the inadmissible, as we have done in the foregoing narrative of the factual background surrounding this prosecution, it becomes apparent that, except as to the defendant Parra, tangible and substantial evidence is woefully lacking to identify any of these appellants as having committed an assault with any deadly weapon upon either of the victims named in counts

II or III, and as to all the appellants the record is devoid of any evidence directly showing that any of them committed an assault upon the decedent, Jose Diaz. It is not surprising, however, that the jurors, lacking legal training and experience, found it extremely difficult to keep before them the admissible, as distinguished from the inadmissible evidence in a trial which lasted for 13 weeks, involved 22 defendants and 66 separate charges. From the testimony herein, it appears that, as to six of these appellants, there is an utter lack of evidence that they directly committed any assault. As to the others the evidence shows three of the appellants committed an assault or assaults with their fists, while, of the remaining three, the evidence indicates that an assault was committed by one with the use of his fists and by kicking; another was guilty of an assault with a stick; and the remaining appellant Parra committed an assault with a knife, if the evidence of and concerning appellant Parra to which we have hereinbefore referred be considered as satisfactory and sufficient to establish guilt beyond a reasonable doubt. . . .

While jurors are the sole and exclusive judges of the value and effect of evidence, their discretion and power in that regard is not absolute. Just verdicts cannot be founded upon unreasonable inferences, speculation or suspicion, but must be grounded upon satisfactory evidence and reasonable inferences predicated thereon. . . .

In the instant case, it is true that appellants had opportunity for the commission of the crimes charged in the indictment. But others had the same opportunity. The sufficiency of the jury's verdict must be tested in the light of whether the evidence upon which the verdict is framed was of such a character that it can be said therefrom that no reasonable doubt of the defendants' guilt existed.

It was the contention of the prosecution that appellants had conspired together to commit murder, assaults with intent to commit murder, assaults with a deadly weapon and assaults by means of force likely to produce great bodily injury; that the objective and common design of such conspiracy was to wreak vengeance upon and against the so-called "Downey boys" who had allegedly assaulted some of the appellants earlier on the night in question; and that, in furtherance of such common design of revenge, and, as a natural and probable consequence of such common design and conspiracy, one or more members of such unlawful combination committed all of the crimes charged in the indictment. However, our examination of the record in this case convinces us that there is a complete lack of material and relevant evidence from which the jury could properly find or infer that appellants formed a conspiracy of the kind and type, or for the purposes, claimed by the prosecution. The most shown by the evidence is that appellants banded themselves together to "have it out . . . with their fists" with the "Downey boys" in retaliation for the fistic encounter that had taken place earlier that night. But, to say that they combined together with the avowed purpose of committing murder does violence to the factual situation presented by the record herein. There is also a total lack of evidence to show that any of the appellants murdered Diaz. . . .

Because a number of defendants are principals, in an offense of assault, battery, disturbance of the peace, riot, rout or unlawful assembly, it does not necessarily follow that all would be principals in an offense of murder or felonious assault that might occur during such a disturbance. . . .

We come now to a consideration of appellants' claim that the trial judge made numerous prejudicial remarks of and concerning defense counsel, thereby being guilty of misconduct during the trial.

The record herein discloses that throughout the protracted trial, because of the number of defense counsel and the seating arrangements in the courtroom, counsel, and at times the court, experienced difficulty both in hearing and seeing what was transpiring. Instead of being "guilty of serious misconduct" as charged by the court, counsel was, in apparent good faith, attempting to protect the rights of the defendants. This was not only his privilege, but his sworn duty. The reprimand and severe castigation administered by the court was as undeserved as it was unwarranted. . . .

We are satisfied that the trial judge injured materially the defense of appellants by the character of rebukes he administered in the presence of the jury when, in most instances, not even a mild rebuke was deserved. Defense counsel was held up to the jury as one who, in an endeavor to present a defense, would resort to unethical and even iniquitous practices. Imputations upon the good faith of counsel made in the presence of the jury, can unjustly injure the cause of a defendant and thereby deprive him of that fair and impartial trial to which everyone is entitled. We do not wish to be understood as holding that the judge of the trial court is without power to direct the course of the trial, or that he is to act merely as an umpire between two contestants, but it should be remembered as an indisputable fact that every remark made by the trial court tending to disparage either party to a cause or counsel has more or less effect upon the jury, unskilled as a rule in court proceedings and, we think it may fairly be said, ever ready to accept any intimation from the court as to what their verdict should be. . . .

While it is true that, in his instructions to the jury, the trial judge admonished them to "entirely disregard and not to consider for any purpose any remarks between court and counsel during the course of the trial," it would have been better judicial practice not to indulge in such comments, for as heretofore pointed out, jurors watch courts closely, and place great reliance on what a trial judge says and does. They are quick to perceive a leaning of the court. Every remark dropped by the judge, every act done by him during the progress of the trial is the subject of comment and conclusion by the jurors, and invariably they will arrive at a conclusion based thereon as to what the court thinks about the case. Hence it is that judges presiding at trials should be exceedingly discreet in what they say and do in the presence of a jury lest they seem to lean toward or lend their influence to one side or the other. However impatient a trial judge may be with a defense, he should be careful not to indicate such impatience by remarks or comments made during the course of a trial which will prejudice a defendant. . . .

During the examination of some of the appellants, an attempt was made to show that statements allegedly made by such appellants were not free and voluntary, but were obtained as a result of the use of force, threats, intimidation and fear. Objection to this line of testimony was sustained. These rulings were erroneous. While respondent contends that the statements were not offered as confessions and that it was unnecessary to lay the foundation required by law for the admission of a confession, nevertheless the defense should have been permitted to show all of the facts and circumstances surrounding the making of the alleged admissions from the time defendants were arrested. Such testimony was clearly material to aid the jury in determining the weight to be given any such statements or admissions. In other words, the manner in which such statements were obtained and the circumstances surrounding the making of the claimed admissions were facts to be considered by the jury in determining the weight to be given thereto. . . .

Appellants' final assault upon the judgment of conviction is grounded on the claim that prejudicial error was committed by the court, which deprived appellants of their rights guaranteed by the due process clause of the Fourteenth Amendment to the Constitution of the United States, and article 1, section 13, of the Constitution of the State of California, in that the right of appellants to defend in person and with counsel was unduly restricted by the seating arrangement of the appellants in the courtroom, which, together with certain rulings of the court, prevented the defendants from consulting with their counsel during the course of the trial or during recess periods. . . .

[I]t is obvious that, under the court's rulings, it was impossible for counsel to leave their table, consult with their clients in another part of the courtroom, and at the same time protect the record and listen to the testimony being given. Likewise, it was not possible for the defendants to call matters to the attention of their counsel while witnesses were testifying, or call attention to claimed inaccuracies in the testimony or to suggest to counsel questions for cross-examination.

To us it seems extremely important that, during the progress of a trial, defendants shall have the opportunity of conveying information to their attorneys during the course of the examination of witnesses. The right to be represented by counsel at all stages of the proceedings, guaranteed by both the federal and state Constitutions, includes the right of conference with the attorney, and such right to confer is at no time more important than during the progress of the trial. A defendant in a criminal case is not required to leave his defense in the hands of his counsel, because the Constitution guarantees him the right "to appear and defend in person and with counsel." This quoted phrase from our state Constitution does not limit the right to defend in person "or" with counsel, but explicitly says "and" with counsel. A basic part of a defendant's right to counsel is that of consultation whenever necessary. To afford to the defendant the benefits of the foregoing clause of the Constitution, it is essential that he should be allowed to consult with his counsel not only prior to the commencement of his trial, but during the actual progress thereof. The framers of the Constitution and the People, in adopting it, deemed it essential to the protection of one whose life and liberty is involved in a prosecution for crime that he shall have the right to "appear and defend in person and with counsel." If he be deprived of his life or liberty without such right to appear and defend, such deprivation would be without that due process of law required by the Constitution. The Constitution primarily guarantees a defendant the right to present his case with the aid of counsel. That does not simply mean the right to have counsel present at the trial, but means that a defendant shall not be hindered or obstructed in having free consultation with his counsel, especially at the critical moment when his alleged guilt is being made the subject of inquiry by a jury sworn to pass thereon.] At such time, in order that he may have absolute freedom to assist by suggestion and information in his own defense, the accused has the right to sit with his counsel, or at least to be so situated that he can freely and uninterruptedly communicate and consult with his attorney. It is the court's duty to provide adequate quarters and facilities, which the court has the power to do without limitation. . . .

The difficulties which presented themselves to the court by reason of the large number of defendants and counsel, together with the limited courtroom space, is the result of the failure of the court to act in this regard. Under such circumstances, it is not the Constitution or the rights guaranteed by it that must yield. That a joint trial of numerous defendants speeds the wheels of justice and provides not only an expeditious but a less burdensome method for disposing of criminal cases furnishes no valid argument for depriving a defendant charged with crime of his right to the effective and substantial aid of counsel at all stages of the proceeding. To do that, as was said in Powell v. Alabama, 287 U.S. 45 [53 S.Ct. 55, 77 L.Ed. 158, 84 A.L.R. 527], "is not to proceed promptly in the calm spirit of regulated justice, but to go forward with the haste of the mob."

Respondent directs our attention to but one case upon which he relies, that of United States v. Gilbert, 2 Sumn. 19, Federal Case No. 15204 (1834), wherein the opinion was written by Mr. Justice Story, and in which case the conviction was attacked on the ground that the defendants "were not allowed to be placed near to the counsel, for the purpose of instructing counsel in their defense, as they deemed necessary." The cited case does not aid respondent because the court therein stated that the defendants were placed within a reasonable distance from their counsel who could constantly have the freest access to them, and the trial court stated that "every delay of time for this purpose would be cheerfully given; and it was accordingly given." Also, the record in United States v. Gilbert, supra, reveals that the defendants "might communicate with their counsel freely and as often as they wished. And this was accordingly done." No such freedom of communication and consultation between the defendants and their counsel prevailed in the case at bar. As an assurance against ancient evils of tyrannical governments, our country, in order to preserve "the blessings of liberty", wrote into its basic law the requirement, among others, that the forfeiture of the lives, liberties or property of people accused of crime can only follow if procedural safeguards of due process have been obeyed. To hold under the circumstances here present that the defendants were accorded their constitutional right to "appear and defend in person and with counsel" would simply be to ignore actualities.

No other assignments of error or claimed grounds for reversal require consideration.

We are not unmindful of the flagrancy of the offenses charged. Nor are we insensible to the need and importance of strictly enforcing the law for the prevention of such crimes. It is greatly to be desired for the safety of the public that the guilty be apprehended and punished for their crimes. But, as a stabilizing influence looking toward the permanence of our institutions, it is of equal or greater importance that the guaranty of a fair trial in accordance with the meaning and intent of the Constitution and statutes should be assured and that such a trial be made a certainty so far as possible within the bounds of average human ability, attended by its unavoidable imperfections and frailties.

In appellants' briefs filed herein, we note the charge that the prosecution of these defendants is the result of racial prejudice. This claim is without foundation and finds no support in the record. While it is true that practically all of the defendants are of Mexican birth or ancestry, it should be remembered that the victims named in the indictment are also of Mexican lineage. Jose Diaz, with whose murder the defendants were charged, had the right to live. The two victims named in counts II and III of the indictment possessed a natural right to freedom from illegal and unlawful attack and injury. The picture presented by the record in the case is one wherein the Delgadillo family, also of Mexican extraction, were holding a social gathering in honor of the birthday of the mother of that family. In so doing they were entitled, as is every other family under our form of government, to be protected against the invasion of their home and homelike activities by a band of hoodlums. It would be a sad commentary upon our vaunted protection of the right to "life, liberty and the pursuit of happiness" if law enforcement agencies did nothing to vindicate the rights of this family to be free from such an attack as was allegedly made upon them and their guests. However, there is no ground revealed by the record upon which it can be said that this prosecution was conceived in, born, or nurtured by the seeds of racial prejudice. It was instituted to protect Mexican people in the enjoyment of rights and privileges which are inherent in every one, whatever may be their race or creed, and regardless of whether their status in life be that of the rich and influential or the more lowly and poor.

The judgments and orders denying motions for a new trial, from which this appeal was taken, are, and each of them is, reversed, and the cause remanded.

York, P.J., and Doran, J., concurred

Source: *People v. Zammora.* 66 Cal. App. 2d 166 [Crim. 3719, Second Dist, Div One, Oct., 4, 1944], http://online.ceb.com/calcases/CA2/66CA2d166.htm.

Glossary

Axis powers: Countries who joined as a force against the Allies in World War II. The three major Axis powers were Germany, Italy, and Japan.

Ayres Report: During the grand jury proceedings at the time of the Sleepy Lagoon murder in 1942, Edward Ayres of the Los Angeles Sheriff's Department presented a report that described people of Mexican heritage as biologically inclined toward violence. The overt race theory in the report fed into the cultural prejudice and hostility against Mexican Americans in wartime Los Angeles.

"Battle of Los Angeles": On the night of February 24, 1942, a report circulated about an unidentified aircraft approaching the city. Wartime hysteria soon ensued. Shortly after 3 A.M., on February 25, anti-aircraft units of the 37th Coast Artillery Brigade began firing tracer bullets and ordnance into the sky. Yellow searchlights swept the area and sirens wailed. Later investigations suggested the unidentified objects in the sky may have been weather balloons.

Caló: A dialect with roots in zincaló (a Spanish gypsy dialect) and argot of the Mexican urban underworld. Much of so-called Pachuco slang was derived from Caló.

Chicano/Chicana: Term reclaimed and redefined by a new generation of bilingual and bicultural Americans of Mexican descent during a 1960s grassroots political mobilization known as the Chicano Movement. Prior to this, Chicano was a derogatory term used in reference to recently immigrated Mexicans in the United States. Before the 1960s, the names Mexican, Mexican American, and Hispanic were used interchangeably.

Citizens' Committee for the Defense of Mexican-American Youth (CCDMAY): Founded in 1942 by labor organizer LaRue McCormick, the CCDMAY was a group dedicated to fighting racism and discrimination against Mexican-American adolescents.

Citizens' Committee for Latin American Youth (CCLAY):   Formed under the auspices of city officials of Los Angeles in 1943, the CCLAY, composed of prominent professionals such as Mexican-American lawyer Edwardo Quevedo, examined the discrimination, negative press, juvenile delinquency, and other matters affected by racial and cultural barriers.

Congress of Industrial Organizations (CIO):   A federation of unions that organized workers in industrial unions in the United States and Canada from 1935 to 1955. Members of the CIO took an active role in assisting in the appeal of Sleepy Lagoon murder trial.

Coordinator of Inter-American Affairs: A U.S. agency with the executive office of the president promoting inter-American cooperation during the 1940s, especially in commercial and economic areas.

El Teatro Campesino: A theater company located in San Juan Bautista, California. This troupe is dedicated to addressing vital issues in the Latino community by using theater as a form of political resistance and to celebrate Chicano culture.

"Good Neighbor Policy":   A stated policy of the administration of President Franklin Roosevelt, first described in his inaugural address in 1933, that expressed non-interference and non-intervention in the domestic affairs of Latin America. The policy sought to rid the U.S. government of any base prejudices and cultural bias about Anglo-Saxon superiority in its dealings with Latin American countries. In following through on the policy, the administration began supporting cultural exchanges and outreach programs.

Jingoism: Extreme nationalism that shapes forceful and aggressive foreign policy.

Latino: Term used to describe all people of Mexican and Latin American descent living both inside and outside of the United States.

McGucken Committee: Formally called the California Citizen's Committee on Civil Disturbances in Los Angeles, the group was formed in 1943 following the riots in Los Angeles by Governor Earl Warren and was chaired by Catholic Bishop Joseph T. McGucken. Its report called for ameliorative measures to help the poor immigrant Mexican-American youth in the city and cited racism as a likely factor for the outbreak of violence.

Mexican American: Spanish-speaking people of the southwest.

Nativism: An opposition to the presence of immigrants and immigrant flows into one's country.

Office of War Information: A U.S. agency created in June 1942 to disseminate information favorable to the United States and to inspire patriotic fervor in the American public during World War II.

Pachuco/Pachuca: In the United States, a term of mixed origins used to define young Mexican Americans of low social status belonging to adolescent gangs and usually wearing distinctive "Zoot suit" type clothes and using degrees of Caló dialect.

People v. Zammora: The case popularly known as the "Sleepy Lagoon Murder Trial" in which 22 Mexican-American defendants were charged with the murder of José Díaz in 1942. The convictions of 17 young men, later overturned on appeal, is considered one of the most injudicious miscarriages of justice in the history of California.

"Sleepy Lagoon":   A reservoir near the point at which Atlantic Boulevard crosses the Los Angeles River that was used by Mexican-American youths as a swimming hole and gathering spot.

Sleepy Lagoon Defense Committee: A grassroots defense committee, formed by Carey McWilliams and other progressive activists and comprised primarily of Mexican-American community members and high-profile actors such as Anthony Quinn, established in 1943 to defend those convicted in the Sleepy Lagoon murder case.

Tenney Committee: The Fact-Finding Committee on Un-American Activities of the California Senate, chaired by Senator Jack Tenney. For a decade beginning in 1941, the committee investigated activities of groups and individuals suspected of subversive activities.

Xenophobia: Fear and hatred of foreigners and strangers.

Yellow journalism: Sensationalist news reports used to boost sales and frame public opinion.

Zoot suit: Clothing style characterized by oversized pants and jackets, broad-brimmed hats, and hanging watch chains, worn by African-American and Mexican-American youth as a cultural symbol of urban identity, rebellion, and style, often linked to African-Cuban jazz music and jitterbug dance. Clothes sometimes referred to as "drapes."

Annotated Bibliography

Acuna, Rodolfo F. *Occupied America: A History of Chicanos*. 7th ed. New York: Prentice Hall, 2010.

Authored by one of the most influential scholars of Chicano studies, this book serves as a foundation for understanding recent Mexican history and the forces facing immigrants in the United States. Its exploration of various aspects of race, ethnicity, and class is especially revealing for an understanding of the explosive forces underlying the violence and chaos that broke out on the streets in wartime Los Angeles.

Alvarez, Luis. *The Power of the Zoot: Youth Culture and Resistance during World War II*. Berkeley: University of California Press, 2009.

Alvarez's work is enormously valuable in establishing the nature of cultural forces behind those who donned Zoot suits not only in Los Angeles but also in cities across the country. Through an impressive use of oral histories and previous studies, this examination explores the isolation felt by racial minorities during wartime mobilization and the reaction and rebellion by young people against their marginalization through clothes, music, dance, and rebellion.

Barrett, Edward. *The Tenney Committee: Legislative Investigation of Subversive Activities in California*. Ithaca, NY: Cornell University Press, 1951.

A staunch anti-Communist crusader, Jack Tenney was chair of the California State Senate's Committee on Un-American Activities from 1941 to 1949. This volume, published only two years after Tenney was no longer head of the Committee, is still a valuable source in assessing the operations, methods, and assumptions that the committee brought in investigating the Sleepy Lagoon murder and the Zoot Suit Riots, both of which Tenney and others on the committee were convinced had been exploited by the international communist movement.

Escobar, Edward. *Race, Police, and the Making of a Political Identity: Mexican Americans and the Los Angeles Police Department.* **Berkeley: University of California Press, 1999.**

The reactions of the Los Angeles Police Department to the violence that broke out on city streets in June 1943 shed much light on the testy relationship between the immigrant Mexican-American community and the force. Escobar's work examines the history of that relationship from the turn of the century to the era of the riots.

Griswold del Castillo, Richard. *World War II and Mexican American Civil Rights.* **Austin: University of Texas Press, 2008.**

A compilation of scholarly essays and primary source documents, this is an important work that demonstrates the groundwork battles for Latino rights established just before and during World War II that led to later victories in the Chicano movement. Griswold del Castillo and others carefully researched federal government documents and other archival collections heretofore unused by other writers.

Jones, Solomon. *The Government Riots of Los Angeles 1943.* **Thesis. University of California, Los Angeles, 1969. Reprinted by R and E Research Associates, San Francisco, 1973.**

Linking the oppression of the Mexican-American population to other minority populations from African Americans to Asians, this thesis, completed a quarter century after the Zoot Suit Riots, is harshly critical of government at all levels in dealing with emerging movements to overcome social and economic deprivation. The work is especially valuable in using an array of newspaper and local government document resources.

Leonard, Kevin. *The Battle for Los Angeles: Racial Ideology and World War II.* **Albuquerque: University of New Mexico Press, 2006.**

In the early 1940s, Los Angeles was home to the nation's largest Japanese-American and Mexican-American communities as well as a growing African-American population. *The Battle for Los Angeles* examines the stereotypes and racial caricatures accepted by the predominately Anglo citizenry, especially as exemplified in the media. The book is valuable in offering context to understand racial and cultural attitudes surrounding the riots in 1943.

López, Ian Haney. *Racism on Trial: The Chicano Fight for Justice*. **Cambridge, MA: Belknap Press of Harvard University Press, 2004.**

Although the book focuses on events and criminal trials over two decades after the Zoot Suit Riots, its story of the rise of the Chicano movement provides extraordinary insight into race consciousness and prejudice facing Mexican Americans. The issues of judicial and police discrimination so apparent in Los Angeles in the early 1940s and the events surrounding the Zoot Suit Riots come into sharp focus decades later as Chicano militancy challenges the dominant power structure.

Mazón, Mauricio. *The Zoot-Suit Riots: The Psychology of Symbolic Annihilation*. **Austin: University of Texas Press, 1984.**

Mazón's study, the first to use extensive FBI and military records relating to the Los Angeles riots of 1943, provides a penetrating analysis of the emotional and psychological underpinnings of race and ethnicity surrounding the explosive tensions in the city. The book is especially revealing in tracing the cultural and linguistic traditions that formed the character of the pachuco movement and the resistance and hostility it faced.

McWilliams, Carey. *North from Mexico: The Spanish-Speaking People of the United States*. **New York: Praeger, 1990.**

Progressive writer, lawyer, and journalist Carey McWilliams not only chaired the Sleepy Lagoon Defense Committee but also immersed himself in the investigation of the Zoot Suit Riots. In 1949, he published *North from Mexico*, a penetrating and deeply sympathetic account of Chicano history that continues to have a major influence in classrooms and scholarly research many years after its publication. Chapter 13, titled "Blood on the Pavements," is a riveting account of Los Angeles's week of violence in June 1943.

Pagán, Edwardo Obregón. *Murder at the Sleepy Lagoon: Zoot Suits, Race, and Riot in Wartime L.A.* **Chapel Hill: The University of North Carolina Press, 2003.**

Reflecting research in an impressive array of available primary and secondary sources, including oral histories with a number of individuals who provided firsthand testimony, Pagán's work is a masterful scholarly study. Behind the Sleepy Lagoon murder and its aftermath and also behind the riots in June 1943, the author asserts, were a variety of explosive tensions and complex forces at work, including demographical changes, race, youth culture, and the pressures of wartime mobilization.

Peiss, Kathy. *Zoot Suit: The Enigmatic Career of an Extreme Style*. Philadelphia: University of Pennsylvania Press, 2011.

In understanding the history of the Zoot Suit Riots, Peiss's examination of the history of the "drape shape," of the suit itself, is a welcome addition to the literature bearing on the wartime events in Los Angeles. Peiss traces the beginnings of the fashion in the African-American community decades earlier, its embrace by Mexican-American pachucos, its symbol, on the one hand, as resistance to oppression and, on the other, as social dysfunction and a trigger for disorder and violence.

Ramirez, Catherine. *The Woman in the Zoot Suit: Gender, Nationalism, and the Cultural Politics of Memory*. Durham: Duke University Press, 2009.

In exploring the female element of the Mexican-American Zoot suiter, *la pachuca*, this book is a valuable addition to historical studies that have largely focused on the male hipsters who inflamed passions among Anglos in Los Angeles. Instead, Ramirez looks at the young women who joined their male counterparts among youth gangs and whose identity was also shaped by cultural forces on the immigrant community and whose participation was also an expression of rebellion and Chicano nationalism.

Sanchez, George. *Becoming Mexican American: Ethnicity, Culture, and Identity in Chicano Los Angeles, 1900–1945*. New York: Oxford University Press, 1995.

This illuminating book describes the acculturation of Mexican immigrants in Los Angeles from 1900 to 1945. Examining formal organizations that worked to help newcomers from Mexico to family networks, religious institutions, work patterns, language, and cultural practices, this is a formidable research work of great value in understanding the obstacles facing Mexican Americans as they adjusted to life in Los Angeles.

Valdez, Luis. *Zoot Suit and Other Plays*. Houston, TX: Arte Publico Press, 1992.

Two decades after the Zoot Suit Riots, a young playwright named Luis Valdez joined Cesar Chavez's farmworker movement in 1965 and created "El Teatro Campesino" ("the Farmworkers' Theater"). Valdez's monumental influence in launching Chicano theater productions included, in 1978, the play *Zoot Suit*, whose appearance in New York made Valdez the first Chicano director to have a play produced on Broadway. This book includes not only *Zoot Suit* but also other of his plays that, through artistic expression, tackled issues facing Latinos and made forceful calls for social change.

Weitz, Mark. *The Sleepy Lagoon Murder Case: Race Discrimination and Mexican-American Rights*. Lawrence: University Press of Kansas, 2010.

Weitz's work is the best treatment of the Sleepy Lagoon trial in contributing to an understanding of the legal aspects of the case as well as the courtroom dynamics at play. Countering the unrelenting judicial misconduct in the original trial was the work of crusading journalists and activists, Mexican-American organizations, and even Hollywood celebrities. Although the boys convicted in the hostile courtroom could never recover their long time in jail, the appeals process worked, reinforcing the critical issues of defendant's rights to counsel and judicial impartiality.

"Zoot Suit Riots." 2002 PBS American Experience. http://www.pbs .org/wgbh/amex/zoot/eng peopleevents/e_murder.html.

In 2002, PBS American Experience produced a documentary on the Zoot Suit Riots, directed by Joseph Tovares; the show was rich in first-person recollections that are made available at the preceding website. This rich resource trove also includes timelines, images, maps, and narrative accounts.

Index

Note: The annotation of an italicized "f" indicates a reference to a figure on the specified page.

About the Author

ROGER BRUNS is a historian and former deputy executive director of the National Historical Publications and Records Commission at the National Archives in Washington, DC. He is the author of many books, including *Encyclopedia of Cesar Chavez: The Farm Workers' Fight for Rights and Justice*; *Negro Leagues Baseball*; *Icons of Latino America: Latino Contributions to American Culture*; *Preacher: Billy Sunday and Big-Time American Evangelism*; and *Almost History: Close Calls, Plan B's, and Twists of Fate in America's Past*. He has written several biographies for young readers on such figures as Cesar Chavez and Martin Luther King, Jr.